Integrating Hypnosis
with Psychotherapy

# Integrating Hypnosis with Psychotherapy

*The Legacy of Buddhism and Neuroscience*

DANIEL L. ARAOZ

McFarland & Company, Inc., Publishers
*Jefferson, North Carolina, and London*

LIBRARY OF CONGRESS CATALOGUING-IN-PUBLICATION DATA

Araoz, Daniel L., 1930–
    Integrating hypnosis with psychotherapy : the legacy of Buddhism and neuroscience / Daniel L. Araoz.
    p.    cm.
    Includes bibliographical references and index.

    ISBN 978-0-7864-7038-9
    softcover : acid free paper ∞

    1. Hypnotism — Therapeutic use.   2. Psychotherapy.
I. Title.
RC495.A728  2012
616.89'16512—dc23                                   2012010653

BRITISH LIBRARY CATALOGUING DATA ARE AVAILABLE

© 2012 Daniel L. Araoz. All rights reserved

*No part of this book may be reproduced or transmitted in any form or by any means, electronic or mechanical, including photocopying or recording, or by any information storage and retrieval system, without permission in writing from the publisher.*

Front cover images © 2012 Shutterstock

Manufactured in the United States of America

*McFarland & Company, Inc., Publishers*
  *Box 611, Jefferson, North Carolina 28640*
    *www.mcfarlandpub.com*

To all the people who have enriched my life.

In retrospect, I realize that every single person who shared
my world, even for minutes, young or old, kind or nasty,
friend or enemy, close to or distant from me,
has influenced my life toward wisdom and goodness.
To each one I sincerely say with this book
Thank you.

# Table of Contents

*Acknowledgments* ix
*Preface* 1
*Introduction* 3

1. Hypnosis in Psychoanalysis and Psychotherapy 11
2. Therapeutic Hypnosis 17
3. Development of Understanding of Hypnosis 36
4. Fantasy in Human Sexuality and Thinking 48
5. Dreaming, Fantasy and Auto-hypnosis 62
6. Auto-hypnosis as Therapeutic Regression 75
7. The PDM Personality Types in Hypnoanalysis 84
8. Principles of Hypnoanalysis 114
9. Mind Training/New Hypnosis as Experiential Learning 125
10. Unconscious Resources Activated with Mind Training 136
11. Hypnoanalysis as Holistic Psychoanalysis 148
12. Practical Hypnoanalysis 161

*Conclusions and Recommendations* 171
*Appendix: A Case of Gender Confusion* 179
*References* 201
*Index* 209

# Acknowledgments

I would like to thank several important groups of people who have made this book possible. First, the many patients who for the last forty years have helped me consolidate these ideas and validate the method of hypnoanalysis. They were the natural "subjects" to test that method. Second, the psychoanalysts-in-training whom I supervised and taught at the American Institute for Psychotherapy and Psychoanalysis (AIPP) where, from the mid–1970s to the mid–1980s, with the strong support of Dr. Ross Thalheimer, its founder and director, I taught a course on Hypnosis and Psychotherapy. In this group I include the many who chose me as supervisor of their private practice or as their analyst. Third, my own analysts and instructors, for their caring and sharing of their wisdom, especially Dr. Heinrich Racker in Buenos Aires and Dr. Harold Greenwald in New York. Many more deserve special mention, and I could have selected several psychoanalysts who were most influential in my professional development related to this book, but my mental list became too long. I began to fear that I was forgetting significant people from the many years since I started in this field. To avoid mistakes I decided not to name anyone else.

Another group of important people are my colleagues at LIU Post, a campus of Long Island University who, since 1973, have supported my efforts, encouraged me, and acclaimed me. I also mention with gratitude my many current professional colleagues and friends. I always felt welcome and they always showed interest in my work. My wife, Marie, also a psychologist and psychoanalyst, my brother Fernando and my sister Mechy, with the many relatives around each of these people, deserve many thanks for their understanding, unremitting love, and support. Finally, my gratitude goes to my son, Lee, and my daughter, Nadine, with their spouses and my seven grandchildren.

# Preface

The type of hypnosis I discuss in this book is substantially different from traditional hypnosis. As a matter of fact, I believe that the noun used for this experience is a misnomer: *hypnos*, referring to sleep in Greek, does not describe what this experience is all about. However, the mistake is quite universal. I insist on hypnosis as being a *mind exercise* of the subject practicing it, the results of which come not from the activity of the "operator" or hypnotist. Thus, hypnosis, the practice *to train our mind*, is dependent on two truths: first, what neuroscience has recently taught us about the brain and thinking since it discovered the plasticity of the brain as a scientific fact; and second, what Buddhism has taught for twenty-five hundred years, namely the mind activities that are essential for hypnosis: sharp mental focusing and detailed visualization, the basic practices of Buddhist meditation. Zen Buddhism, in this book, refers specifically to the practice of meditation.

Consequently, the open-minded reader will discover a different hypnosis than what most people understand it to be. This book's is an effective method of mind training, as just stated, in tandem with Buddhism's tradition to obtain better control of our thinking and thus of our feeling and our entire world because we are what our thoughts make us, according to the evidence provided by modern neuroscience. Also the concept of psychodynamic therapy (PDT) is presented in unfamiliar fashion for many readers. I consider *psycho*therapy to be basically psychodynamic, that is an interpersonal communication where the patient is at the center and the psychotherapist helps in the voyage of introspection, self-analysis and self-discovery. The symptom is not the whole story and to end therapy when the symptom is under control, with no investigation of its causes and purpose, is to do an incomplete job. Insight, an intellectual activity, is necessary to change. The practitioner helps the patient to tighten, adjust and modify the areas of change in one's life that were discovered in the previous stage of analysis or introspection. Therefore, although originally psychoanalytical, PDT is *practical analysis* in Renik's (2006) view, centered on *catharsis*, Breuer's (Breuer and Freud, 1893/2000) therapeutic technique (the talking cure) which Freud appropriated without giving Breuer, his mentor, any credit for it (see Breger, 2009).

The monumental research of Shedler (2010) on the efficacy of PDT, comprising 751 studies and 41 meta-analyses, is based on seven identified PDT characteristics. These, he found, are what make any form of mental therapy effective. The interaction of the patient and therapist makes these characteristics possible. If a therapist who practices any type of therapy (behavioral, systemic, group, cognitive or any other) includes catharsis in any of its seven characteristics, all these therapies will be effective. I insist on the cathartic method, though in practice I bypass many of the traditional forms of applying it. In addition, because human thinking is largely imaginative or dependent on fantasy, hypnotic techniques enrich and expand the effect of PDT, as the book will show in different ways and by means of clinical cases. In sum, to obtain the benefits of PDT, we must practice within the characteristics of the cathartic style discovered by Shedler. And hypnosis activates all the feelings and thoughts that PDT works on. Lastly, because much of our thinking is mingled with feelings, as neuroplasticity has shown, we take advantage of Buddhism's long experience to make hypnosis therapeutically effective.

To conclude, the book celebrates the unique moment in history in which we are lucky to be: psychotherapy is scientifically proven valid as well as definitely efficacious and hypnosis is justified by neuroscience as a convenient method to train our mind in order to change our brain.

Note: I use feminine and masculine pronouns interchangeably both for patients and for clinicians in an attempt to remain as nonsexist as possible in my writing. The nouns *patient* and *client* have the same meaning in this book. I also use the following terms to indicate *psychodynamic psychotherapy*: analysis, psychoanalysis, hypnoanalysis, psychotherapy, therapy. To refer to the providers I take advantage of the corresponding nouns, not making a sharp distinction among the different nuances of those offering psychodynamic therapy.

# Introduction

Clinical hypnosis in psychodynamic therapy, in psychoanalysis, or in hypnoanalysis, is the central theme of this book. But because the ultimate goal of analysis is to live a better life, I offer this book to any person who wants seriously to improve and enrich his or her life and apply the hypnotic methods and techniques to daily living. Everything about hypnosis in this book can be used by people who want to learn how to change their thoughts for their benefit. For that reason, some chapters end with suggestions for using hypnosis in daily living. However, the word *hypnosis* itself is the source of much misunderstanding. Moreover, I distinguish *auto-hypnosis* from *self-hypnosis*, the former for therapeutic and positive, Creative Imagination work, the latter for the many practical reasons to use it, be it learning, entertainment, police investigation, and so on, as well as for negative self-hypnosis (NSH), which is self-defeating and mostly unconscious. Also, in this book I use *fantasy* and *imagination* for both unconscious and conscious mental imagery, and combine Creative Imagination (CI) with New Hypnosis, which is different from traditional hypnosis. Both fantasy and imagination refer to the same mental activity on which hypnoanalysis depends. This mental activity is all-important for understanding hypnosis in general, no matter what we call it, and it is currently much researched. We deal with the mind-body issue, the influence of thought on the functioning of the body, of mind on brain. New as this area of neurological study might seem to many, it has been growing since the acceptance of the *placebo effect* and of *lie detectors* in the early 1930s, and flourished in the late 1980s and early 1990s with the great advances in neuroscience, thanks to MRIs and other super-sophisticated machines that have helped brain research ever since. The influence of Buddhism and neuroscience will be explained later.

This book does not deal with hypnosis as it is understood by most, even professionals in our society, where one person is under the control of another. It deals with the *activation of the patient's fantasy* in order to create a *new inner reality of the self,* so that this reality can *take the place of the old one* for the personal enrichment of the individual. Thus, the mental work we study is *creative imagination, mind control, mind training,* or *mental reprogramming.* What happens when Creative Imagination activity is proposed by the therapist and the patient really gets engaged is that she, trusting her unconscious, experiences herself very differently than when she is in the ordinary mode of thinking. In this activity she is using *auto-hypnosis,* reprogramming her mind and thus physically changing her brain. Here neuroscience comes into play. This method puts a much greater emphasis on the patient than traditional hypnosis, which gives the power to the voice of the hypnotist. This is one of the most important aspects of New Hypnosis. Because the greater emphasis is on the patient, we realize that *all effective hypnosis is auto-hypnosis* and the clinician takes the role of guide.

Even though I deal with New Hypnosis or, perhaps more accurately, with hypnotic activities and phenomena, my method of New Hypnosis is very specific. There is no hypnosis until the patient takes over, as it were, from the clinician, accepting the passive activity of *allowing his fantasy to take him into the inner world on which he is focusing in his mind.* Passive activity or active passivity are foreign concepts in our culture but commonly used in Buddhism, where the person can be unconsciously active in his conscious passivity. The essence of Buddhism is that I cannot rely only on my intelligent mind in order to know myself and, through this, the entire universe. I have to learn to "let go" into the experiential learning, with which we shall deal again and again. The three classical Asian teachings, Confucianism, Buddhism, and Taoism, though different, have much in common. When I use the phrase Zen Buddhism, quite familiar now in our culture, I include aspects of the three classical Asian teachings because Zen Buddhism integrates them in its essence, and is perhaps their purest form. Zen refers simply to the sitting position adopted for meditation. Fantasy becomes reality for the time the person is in hypnosis, very much like the experience of meditation in Buddhism. Milton H. Erickson, MD, who was, like all respected mental health practitioners in his time, trained psychoanalytically (Rossi, 1980), referred in different ways to this unique experience of giving up conscious mental control and allowing oneself *to be taken by one's fan-*

*Introduction*

*tasies and what they represent*. Indeed, this process is hypnotic, especially for Jung's followers—a special manner of using one's mind, experiencing the vivid reality of one's fantasy. This is also very Buddhist: you must let go of your *ego* or "self" and connect with your "nature." The goal always is to get the patient to do it without the guidance of the therapist. In New Hypnosis, the therapist does not "hypnotize" the patient, but is merely a guide who steps aside as soon as the patient begins to accept his inner world of self-knowledge, healing, and change. An analogy is the parent teaching the child to ride the bicycle. The moment the child starts balancing and controlling the bike, even though waving and insecure, the parent lets her go, and soon the young child will be completely on her own.

The New Hypnosis is of the same nature as auto-hypnosis, and both provide the patient similar types of experience. However, in most cases, a person cannot get into auto-hypnosis without the help and teaching of a guide or *master*, as the Buddhists call him. The distinction between the two is simple: with the help of the clinician it is hypnosis, but when the patient enters this experience by himself, it is auto-hypnosis.

The other element connected with human fantasy is sexuality (see Chapter Four), which cannot be understood without the role of imagination, to the point that there is no sexual activity without fantasy, and most human sexual "activity" is in the mind. Because of this, we can refer symbolically to hypnoanalysis as a psychoanalytic kaleidoscope involving hypnosis, fantasy, and sexuality. I hope this book will make the reader aware of the many psychodynamic riches hypnosis or Creative Imagination offers, and I hope clients will reap the multiple benefits from learning and practicing auto-hypnosis, so that they will be able to continue introspection (self-analysis) for the reminder of their lives.

My book *The Symptom Is Not the Whole Story* (2006a) addressed itself to non-analytic colleagues interested in psychoanalysis. This one is directed first to psychoanalysts and other mental health practitioners who have in-depth or at least systematic psychodynamic training but with, unfortunately, antiquated ideas about hypnosis. The second important audience for this book is all those seriously interested in their own personal growth and enrichment. However, what I am dealing with is very far from the traditional and popular view of hypnosis. Indeed, it is closer to mental imagery or fantasy work and to Buddhist meditation. My hope is to provide practitioners with solid information and professional tips to integrate hypnosis or Creative Imagination in their psychodynamic work with patients and to bring to others practical techniques to improve the content of their thinking. This book could be called *Practical Hypnoanalysis,* following Renik's (2006) example, embracing all and every psychodynamic therapy, including psychoanalysis in its traditional version. Real therapy for humans, in my view, always has to be "analytical," that is, with acceptance of and work with unconscious dynamics. Less than this is not psychotherapy but "pedagogic therapy" or behavioral training.

One of the reasons for my interest in discussing and promoting this view of hypnosis in psychodynamic therapy and psychoanalysis is that we are in a unique period in the history of psychotherapy, as well as of hypnosis. For the first time in human history, we know with scientific certainty many of the neurological mechanisms of human change, and not only *what* is Creative Imagination or hypnosis but *how* it works in our brains. Neuroscience found out, through studies conducted with the new machines of the last thirty years, that whatever we are, or do, is closely related to the neural circuits we have established unconsciously in our brain. To use a comparison, these circuits are a track of neurons in the brain, similar to those paths in a rural field made by people's taking a shortcut walking on the grass. The very good news is that we can change the neural pathways in our brains by training our minds— our minds can change our brains. This idea is deeply ingrained in Buddhist thought. Their holy book, the Dhammapada, starts with a sentence that indicates just that: *we have become what our thoughts have made us.* This is what hypnosis or Creative Imagination is and does: training our mind to change our brain by a method that uses focused attention and imagination, similar to the way physical exercise changes our bodies. Moreover, neuroscience helps us understand the ancient practice of meditation so central to Buddhism. Actually, the Dalai Lama has given the scientific study of neuroscience great impetus with his now-discontinued yearly meetings in exile, attended by the top neuroscientists in the world, clearly described by Begley (2007) in detail. In the last chapter of this book I try to outline and explain the great truths of both psychoanalysis and Buddhism, as they create a practical parallel for us and for our patients to learn how to live fully, productively, caringly, and joyously. For example, Freud discovered the value of free association, in which the logical mind is abandoned; Zen Buddhism teaches that the only way to reach enlightenment is not through reason but through inner experience.

Because of these arguments, it may serve well not to use the term hypnosis and to think more of mental concentration and training in meditation, of visualization or dynamic imagery or any similar expression, which I have summarized in several chapters, especially chapters 1 and 2. Whatever we call the method — mind training, dynamic imagery, visualization, or any similar expression — I try to summarize it in the phrase Creative Imagination, by which I mean New Hypnosis. Whatever we call the method, the central truth discovered by neuroscientists is that *we can train our minds in order to change our brains*, as Begley titled one of her books (2007), a version of the basic Buddhist principle that *"we are what our thoughts have made us."* This process is discussed by Doidge (2007), a psychiatrist, researcher, and psychoanalyst who explains clearly how psychoanalysis is a neuroplastic therapy, and by medical scientist Jeffrey Schwartz (Schwartz & Begley, 2002), who emphasizes the elements of hypnosis and Buddhist meditation in the training of the mind to change the brain. What was not generally known in the 1960s is that training the mind produces physical changes in the adult brain as much as in the young brain. New Hypnosis or Creative Imagination, being one validated method of training the mind, is therefore the first step in the process of self-transformation. Any habit, value, attitude, belief, reaction, bias, fear, or desire that we think is "part of ourselves" has established a specific neuronal circuit in our physical brain, which becomes stronger every time we activate it by behavioral, emotional, or cognitive use. The famous Shakespearean statement of Hamlet, that "thinking makes it so," is scientifically true. On the other hand, the neural pathway not activated by repetition disappears over time through lack of use.

Psychoanalysis is an effective and proven method to help people change by discovering the effect of previous experiences on the formation of personality. Kandel (2006), a 2002 Nobel Prize winner, explains that learning takes place as our individual neurons modify themselves and solidify their synaptic connections with each other. Thus, in successful analysis and psychodynamic therapy, the patient makes needed changes in the neural connections without realizing that this is happening. Now we have scientific evidence of this neurological process (Rossi, 2002) and its importance in psychotherapy: the neural structure of the brain changes with the activation of the right genes (Rossi, 2002). Creative Imagination or its result, hypnosis, accomplishes all this smoothly and directly. Now we need another wave of researchers, following Rossi (2002), to delve into his discovery that, ultimately, the personality changes produced in the long analytical process are definitely related to neural pathway changes. Moreover, hypnoanalysis, as Wolberg (1945), Erika Fromm (1972, 1992), or Watkins and Barabasz (2008) claim, is the type of hypnosis I identify as Creative Imagination, which can shorten the analytic work. The early authors made this assertion based on their clinical experience, but without knowing what we know now about hypnosis and neuroplasticity.

The unresolved difficulty for those who work with applied neuroscience is that, even though the sought-for change or therapeutic goal can be produced quickly, in order to succeed the patient has to learn to concentrate intensely in his mind activity (Begley, 2007; Doidge, 2007). According to Schwartz's (Schwartz & Begley, 2002) careful and prolonged research, the obsessive-compulsive patient has to spend two half-hour sessions a day for about two months in order to attain the desired goals. Hopefully, his research will be expanded to the use of hypnosis to find out if the two months can be significantly shortened. On the other hand, Buddhist monks give even more time to this mind training. Unfortunately for our overscheduled citizenry, the reduced daily schedule of two intense 30 minutes of concentration is very seldom possible. Here is where Creative Imagination comes in, evolving from what I have previously called New Hypnosis (Araoz, 1985a). In the mental state of hypnosis, concentration is easier, as is time distortion. Often spontaneously, the patient who returns to the ordinary manner of thinking cannot believe that he spent only a few minutes in hypnosis. In similar ways, the patient learns to use his or her fantasy in such a way that a few minutes are experienced as hours or even days. Instead of trying to concentrate without distractions, the patient enters into Creative Imagination activity or hypnosis, and in it experiences intense concentration until he or she obtains the intended goals. But we still do not have the formal research on this point.

Creative Imagination, developing from hypnosis, is the method to use a neurological mechanism that naturally changes what we want to change in our life. In "psycho-hypno-therapy" this work can reconstruct beliefs, expectations, ways of explaining experiences, and much more.

## Introduction

Compared to our predecessors, we are lucky to understand what happens from a physiological perspective using hypnosis. This book keeps in mind the reality of brain plasticity in the clinical use of Creative Imagination.

Last but not least, the reader will notice that I use many cognitive behavior therapy (CBT) techniques and methods. My integrative philosophy and clinical practice lead me to take advantage of the CBT richness, because I am a psychoanalyst and thus I must move past the symptom to truly help the patient. I consider the job half done if I stop therapy before the mystery behind the symptom is resolved. One of my books has CBT in its title (Araoz, 1992). However, I view CBT as *part* of my therapeutic work. Once the symptom is under control, thanks to the cognitive-behavioral methods, I move on to the unconscious and help the patient analyze her or his inner dynamics that either created the symptom or kept it longer than needed. My motto, *The symptom is not the whole story* (Araoz, 2006), reveals and summarizes the integration of CBT and psychoanalysis that is my professional trademark.

Finally, it is obvious that any serious individual can practice and learn this method. Without the help of psychotherapy, the person realizes that there are good results from practicing Creative Imagination. What this book presents is not limited to psychodynamic therapy but extends to all aspects of daily living.

CHAPTER 1

# Hypnosis in Psychoanalysis and Psychotherapy

Hypnoanalysis is not popular among American psychoanalysts. This negative attitude, which I have explained elsewhere (Araoz, 2006b), has to do with two pivotal misunderstandings on the part of modern practitioners. One is the lack of knowledge about hypnotherapy since Milton H. Erickson (Rossi, 1980), not recognizing that this New Hypnosis is very different from traditional hypnosis. (For a comparison of the two, see Araoz, 1985a.) The second misunderstanding is about Freud's "rejection" of hypnosis that many believe was absolute and definitive, but that Gravitz and Gerton (1981), in the research conducted by the former on the history of psychoanalysis, found to be completely different, as Chapter 3 shows (see also Araoz, 2006a).

## Hypnoanalysis

In the past, a few eminent authors wrote about hypnoanalysis. The best known was New York psychiatrist Lewis Wolberg (1945), who was one of the first to use the term combining hypnosis and psychoanalysis. Following him ideologically comes Chicago psychoanalyst Erika Fromm, who first with Daniel Brown (Brown & Fromm, 1986) and later with Michael Nash (Fromm & Nash, 1997), explained clearly and without complications the nature, use, and benefits of hypnoanalysis. Others followed in the next four decades, one of the most recent contributions being that of Watkins and Barabasz (2008). With this wealth of theoretical and practical information for the clinician, one must ask, Why yet another book on hypnoanalysis? My response is that the great names just mentioned emphasized hypnosis or Creative Imagination techniques, to be used in psychodynamic work by the power of the therapist. Many psychoanalysts, misled by the misconception of telling patients what to do and how to behave, seem to consider reading about hypnosis, even for therapeutic goals, a waste of time. Because of this, my intention in this volume is to emphasize psychoanalysis in its essence and the potential use of hypnosis according to the enriched information we have since neuroscience discovered brain plasticity, and definitely after Wolberg, Erika Fromm, and even Watkins and Barabasz's magnificent book. With this goal in mind, I review the essentially psychodynamic nature of hypnosis, its development from Freud's time to the current Ericksonian New Hypnosis or Creative Imagination, and its clinical application in today's psychoanalysis, emphasizing relational theory. But even more differently than other authors, I introduce the ideas of the growing concept of neuroplasticity, as explained by the serious research, already mentioned, of Schwartz (Schwartz & Begley, 2002), and as presented by Doidge (2007) and many more. Even though the connection of psychoanalysis and neuroplasticity is the scientific basis of the book, it is imperative to emphasize some of the important realities necessary to understand Creative Imagination or New Hypnosis, including the relationship of New Hypnosis with Buddhism. I am also referring to fantasy, without which there is no true hypnosis, as well as to sexuality, or rather gender, as a very important aspect of personality, much of which is manifested in hypnotic fantasy, although unconsciously. Last, I am referring to New Hypnosis (Araoz, 1982), developed by me from Erickson (Rossi, 1980), as it appears in the daily mental life of humans as fantasy and sexuality. These three (fantasy, sexuality, hypnosis) are so intertwined that they overlap considerably. Hence my metaphor of the way a kaleidoscope functions. We cannot focus on one element without involving the other two. The metaphor of the kaleidoscope also connects with the brain changes studied by neuroscience.

## Hypnosis Centered on the Patient as an Individual

The book intends to reveal the advantages of using Creative Imagination or New Hypnosis in psychoanalysis and psychoanalytic psychotherapy, thus combining hypnotic and psychoanalytic methods. It also intends to teach practitioners how to use hypnoanalysis naturalistically, by emphasizing and encouraging fantasy elements of the patient at every step of the analytic process. Oversimplifying things, we can say that in hypnoanalysis fantasy, when it appears in any form, is used more directly than in regular psychoanalysis, and is encouraged whenever something happens that can be "translated" into a fantasy. Here I must emphasize that this use of hypnosis becomes a spontaneous and natural occurrence, while traditional hypnosis is almost "forced" on the patient. The former is recognized by the trained clinician, even if the patient is not aware of it, when he is more vividly involved in his creative imagination, as if he were now part of the scene that he is reliving or rehearsing in his mind. Traditional hypnosis, unlike this, is the result of therapist-directed *inductions* that are almost "imposed" on the patient.

To illustrate this, I use a simple clinical vignette. But before introducing it I want to remind the reader that a very large amount of what we know about both psychoanalysis and clinical hypnosis comes from what clinicians have learned, at least in recent years, from patients' experiences, reactions, and results in clinical work. These become our data. These constitute our scientific evidence. Much information on hypnosis as such comes from laboratory experiments. But it would be unwise to limit ourselves to that evidence, ignoring what we obtain in our daily clinical work from our patients. Because of this important reason, especially in this age when it has become imperative to use methods that have been scientifically validated, I will present many brief clinical cases and vignettes.

> Ellie had been in analysis for three years. She frequently started the session by saying, "I have nothing to say." The clinician who does not use hypnosis may respond in various non-direct fantasy ways, for instance, by remaining silent for a few seconds, by asking a transference question like, "How do you think I feel when you say that you have nothing to say?" A non-transference question could be, among many others, "What were you thinking in the last half hour when you were getting ready to come here, and when you were driving to the office?" In contrast, in hypnoanalysis the fantasy used may involve suggestions such as, "If this were part of a dream, how would the dream proceed?" or "Imagine yourself someplace else, saying several times to yourself, 'I have nothing to say.' Fill the mental scene: Where are you? With whom? Who hears you? Who do you want not to hear you?" and so forth.

The essential difference between psychoanalysis and hypnoanalysis (using New Hypnosis approaches) is the attention paid to fantasy productions with a more active use of fantasy. It is extremely important to remember that, with New Hypnosis, any nonintellectual way of using one's thinking, and any form of any fantasy thinking, is considered hypnotic.

Consequently, this to me is eminently practical, always keeping in mind the positive outcome of the patient's change and detailing the introspective methods of hypnoanalysis to be used in order to obtain that effect. My assertion that hypnoanalysis is an important clinical modality of psychoanalysis is founded on three main interconnected arguments. The first is centered on fantasy. Because of the intimate relationship of hypnosis with fantasy, the patient starts to pay more attention to her fantasies, to understand them as a sign of unconscious creativity and as a problem-solving tool (Knafo & Feiner, 2006). Once this happens (usually after a few hypnosis sessions) the patient is encouraged to practice auto-hypnosis on her own as a follow up to the regular sessions.

The second argument, derived from the first, is that the hypnotic elements effectively shorten the number of sessions without detracting in any way from the benefits of traditional psychoanalysis, because psychodynamic connections are made more easily, insights come quicker, and resistance and fear are handled experientially. With hypnoanalysis, patients can get full psychoanalytic treatment even with only one weekly session (and occasionally more than one). The reduction of the number of sessions is, of course, presented either as an advantage or a disadvantage, depending on which side the debater stands. The difference seems to be that, during the last five decades, those who have used hypnoanalysis have clinical evidence of its success, whereas many traditionalists reject hypnotic methods without evidence of failures, based on the misconceptions mentioned earlier. I present hypnoanalysis as an advantage regarding the length of treatment, but never agreeing with the prevalent attitude of the "medical-industrial complex" that psychiatrist Gourguechon (2007) so soberly criticizes, explaining the uneducated enthusiasm of our culture for the instant cure of the pill, which has more of magic than of responsible health care.

The third argument for the advantages of hypnoanalysis is that the increased frequent introspection gained by the patient thanks to the hypnoanalytic experience, in the session and repeated at home, becomes more rapidly effective as part of his or her life. With hypnoanalysis, introspection leads to the limits of sanity and insanity, of possible and impossible, of true and false, of good and evil, of all or nothing. The patient truly experiences himself, including his Dionysian side. Here is where neuroplasticity concepts help us have a better understanding of what hypnosis really is and how it affects our "thinking" when "the mind changes the brain."

My intention is to share what the long years of practice have taught me and what I have found useful to help people change for the better and reach a deeper enjoyment of life. In my prolonged and very informal research (inevitably connected with the practice of hypnoanalysis), I had patients, individually and in groups, treated exclusively with one modality (psychoanalysis) for about a year, compared with similar patients treated only with the other modality (hypnoanalysis). I also had patients who, after a few months in traditional psychoanalysis, were switched to hypnoanalysis. In every case, the advantages of hypnotherapy became evident. Research-validated methods are not only those that can be measured in a scientific laboratory. A method that repeatedly has proven effective in transforming the lives of people cognitively, affectively, socially, relationally, spiritually, and, in general, behaviorally proves its solid value as an improvement method without subjecting it to the tests and statistical analyses of traditional research.

When I mention the benefits and results of hypnoanalysis, I remind myself that psychoanalysis has always been goal oriented (starting from what is expressed in the famous Freudian goal of *making the unconscious conscious*), focusing on the goal of interpretation, which Fink (2007) summarizes. We may enlarge his description by adding that this goal has consistently been to empower patients so they can become freer of past negative beliefs, illusions, expectations, and influences in general, in order to avoid the repetition compulsion, and to be one's true self so that one can make independent choices that are productive and enjoyable. This includes improving personal relationships; utilizing one's own talents and abilities; becoming more conscious of one's relationships with all other humans and the cosmos as a whole but establishing realistic priorities; being in an open attitude toward the truth with a willingness to modify one's biases, myths, and prejudices with a genuine acceptance of one's true limitations; and being sensitive to the nonmaterial aspects of our existence. All these gains of self-empowerment are included in my thinking about attaining the goals of psychoanalysis and of enriching it with New Hypnosis.

From the neuroplasticity perspective, which refers to the adult brain's ability and power to physically change, the intensity of focusing both reason and imagination on new changes establishes a much more vivid possibility of growing as human beings. Hamlet's "thinking makes it so" is not just a superficial statement anymore and does not refer merely to intellectual thinking. The Shakespearean statement was a forerunner of what science has discovered in the last few decades, that the healthy human brain continues to reconstruct itself until death. Therefore, if we add to rational thinking our experiential, emotional, and fantasy thinking, we physically create new neurological pathways that establish firmly the changes we are making due to being in psychoanalysis. Rewording a basic Buddhist teaching, we can remember that "if we want to change our world, we must change our thinking of life in general" and we'll be surprised.

## Daily Living Applications

It is not difficult to transfer all of the above to one's personal practice. Just by following the instructions mentioned so far, a seriously intended person will be able to become more sensitive to her imagination and will recognize good results from practicing auto-hypnosis. Just to give a couple of examples, the tense person can use her breathing and the subsequent muscle relaxation to experience a change of less tension and greater well-being. Another application can affect physical pain beneficially, especially if positive visualization is added. By visualizing the pain and focusing on that image, she can experience it becoming weaker with every breath until it is completely gone. The client can select a special place that she likes and in which she feels secure and content. She then visualizes herself there, taking note of as many details are possible: what she sees close by and the sounds she hears, what she feels because of the temperature in the place and the comfort of where she is, etc. The warning for this client is that doing auto-hypnosis is learning a new skill and therefore it requires repetition and patience. Unfortunately, some give up because they tried it once and "nothing happened." This is the reason it is important to have several sessions with patients before encouraging them to practice by themselves. The idea of repetition is nowadays validated with the discovery that new neuronal pathways are formed and established by reiterating the same mental activity.

CHAPTER 2

# Therapeutic Hypnosis

This chapter reviews material that has filled many volumes. Among the topics are the nature of hypnosis, producing psychologically and neurologically a special ego state; hypnosis in its historical perspective; its practical variations; its relationship to suggestibility and projection, mental images, and fantasy with its heavy sexual content; levels of awareness from unconscious to conscious; the phenomenon of dissociation in hypnosis; and Creative Imagination (CI), with its relationship to focusing and concentration. Finally, we will touch on the principles of hypnosis induction and ways of using induction without changing the rhythm of the session.

Before proceeding, it might be helpful to avoid confusion by distinguishing between *hypnotism* and *hypnosis*, as Weitzenhoffer (2000) does, although this distinction is far from being universally accepted. The former refers to the science of the latter, or hypnotism is the scientific understanding of hypnosis. On the other hand, hypnosis as Creative Imagination (CI) is the technique to produce a different manner of using the mind that subjectively gives the (hypnotized) individual the experience of an alternate (and altered) state of being and thinking. Autohypnosis takes place when the patient has experienced and learned this method and starts practicing it individually or independently.

## The Nature of Hypnosis

In the past, the use of direct suggestions in hypnosis made it much more authoritarian than it is now. Hypnosis was rather rigid in its techniques and practice, and centered on the commands given by the hypnotist. Nowadays New Hypnosis (Araoz, 1982) gives the client choices, and is patient-centered, starting from her spontaneous productions (verbal output and mood, gestures, facial and bodily expressions, and the like). For instance, in the traditional approach the hypnotist "hypnotizes" the patient, while in the new method the client herself "gets into hypnosis" through the guidance and suggestions of the clinician: the subject is *in hypnosis*, not *under hypnosis*, or under anybody else's control. The differences came from the earlier understandings of Mesmer's animal magnetism and of Charcot's hypnosis as a manifestation of hysteria, to the later view of Bernheim (1884) at the end of the nineteenth century and of Erickson's view (Rossi, 1980) from the 1950s to the 1980s, both of whom leaned on suggestibility and imagination, leading to normal dissociation toward the end of the twentieth century. Erickson made hypnosis a *naturalistic* possibility that would be stopped only by conscious opposition or unconscious resistance. Because of this important change in attitude and practice, we have another reason to avoid the term *hypnosis*, and to refer to "active imagination" in the spirit of Jung (1963) or "imaginative thought concentration." Unfortunately, the term *hypnosis* is so popular that, instead of clarifying what it means, a new expression might only create more confusion. This is my reason for referring to CI but not to abandon the old term, to help people understand that I am using a new expression for an old concept.

There are two main opinions that form the general theories currently in vogue. The most commonly accepted is the *state theory*, meaning first, "state of inwardly turned attention" (Yapko, 1990). To this we must add a state of *dissociation*, as Janet (1889) at the end of the nineteenth century and Hilgard in 1978 discovered and taught. Bernheim (1884) added the state of *suggestibility*. Finally, Watkins (1978) specified the "activated ego states." Thus the *ego state theory* of New Hypnosis with Creative Imagination encompasses introspection, dissociation, suggestibility, and different ego states—in other words, an alternate ego state. This theory is also referred to as *personality parts*.

The other group of theories to explain hypnosis/CI includes *a form of sleep* or a state of relaxation and concentrated attention, as well as *somnambulism* and *trance*. For the purpose of this book, I discard the latter group of theories and remain with the ego state theory mentioned above and discussed more in depth later. Weitzenhoffer's (2000) work is one of the very best sources for understanding and familiarizing oneself with theories of hypnosis.

## Variations in Using Hypnosis

The many practical variations on hypnosis/CI in clinical practice, to be discussed later on, come from the practitioner's understanding and belief based on one of two basic and different positions. The first belief, a behavioral one, is that the symptom is all there is to the problem, and that, by concentrating the hypnotic effort on the symptom and its removal, the problem is resolved. This view of hypnosis is the prevalent one in our culture at this time (the medical model?), as I have discussed elsewhere (Araoz, 2006a). The opposite belief, the psychodynamic one, is that "the symptom is not the whole story," and unconscious dynamics that are related to the patient's personality and character must be considered in order to resolve the underlying problem, which explains and is responsible for the entire symptomatology. This latter approach has given renewed meaning to psychopathology in the *Psychodynamic Diagnostic Manual* (PDM Task Force, 2006), complementing the non-diagnostic classification and categorization approach of the *DSM*, which has increasingly prevailed in the U.S. since its first edition in 1952. However, the *PDM* complements the *DSM* by focusing intently on the individual (personality, general mental functioning) who develops symptoms, not on the symptoms themselves, regardless of the person who has them. The *DSM* stays with the pseudo-obvious: this (symptom) is a sign of this ("disorder"), therefore apply this label, this medication, or these behavioral techniques to cure the symptom. On the contrary, the *PDM* looks for the hidden element, that this type of personality tends to develop a kind of symptom that is specific. We focus on the personality problem by means of psychodynamic therapy in order to truly cure what causes the symptom.

## Suggestibility

Of all the different ways of distinguishing the uses of hypnosis (Weitzenhoffer, 2000), the above general classification — behavioral vs. psychodynamic — is the most practical for the purposes of this book. Because of the power of suggestibility on human thought and action, which Erika Fromm (1977) calls *ego receptivity*, the removal (or at least amelioration) of many symptoms, either physical and medical or psychological and social, is surprisingly direct and quick. But if the symptom is directly related to the patient's personality, for example, due to negative developmental experiences, there is really no complete cure if all we do is focus on the symptom. We shall return to the symptom and its psychodynamics, but for now I would like to return to suggestibility or ego receptivity, which is a main characteristic of hypnosis. Many, starting with the Abbé Faría in the late 1700s, suspected that the main psychic mechanism in hypnosis is human suggestibility. This hypothesis was close to universally recognized as valid after Bernheim's (1884) comprehensive book, which became a classic (for which Freud wrote the preface to the German translation in 1888) and is still considered eminent. Thanks to Bernheim's work with Liebault in Nancy, France, a whole new trend was definitely established in hypnosis centered on suggestion.

The meaning of *suggestion* seems to include somehow an element of "non-awareness" on the part of the "suggestee." Thus an event, such as a movie, a conference, or a sociopolitical development may produce a strong emotional reaction in a person. When it comes to hypnosis, the practitioner deliberately proposes a message (formerly called a *suggestion*) to the "subject" in order to elicit in her responses that would otherwise not occur. This "message" might be to visualize herself in great detail reacting differently to a painful situation, to do or be what she considers unattainable goals, or variations on these themes. The visual images become more meaningful when the person is deeply relaxed. For instance, the anxious person is reminded that his slow breathing can help diminish his anxiety until it is practically gone At the end of this Creative Imagination exercise, the person feels different, relaxed and overall better than before without intellectually realizing what was instrumental in his change of physical or affective state. Now the original anxiety can be analyzed.

Suggestion is closely related to *positive transference*: An idea makes an emotional impact on a person because the individual proposing that idea is unconsciously connected with earlier (beneficial!) persons and situations in her life. In other words, the experts mentioned above discovered that suggestions work because the client unconsciously connects the setting of the suggestion (the person giving the suggestion, the message itself, the benign intention, the emotional comforts, etc.) with some important, though consciously forgotten or truly repressed, experience in her earlier development. Like the infant with his parents, the patient accepts the new idea without examining or questioning it. In this form of regression there is an unconscious quasi-identification with the analyst as it existed with the good parent. Without this positive transference, suggestions do not work. Therefore, the natural insecurity and parental dependence of the child is revived because of the transference, and the therapist becomes the unquestioned source of the suggestion. Chapter 6 will explain this as one of the many regressions in the service of the ego used in hypnoanalysis.

Another explanation of the power of suggestions comes from the heuristic concept of the two brain hemispheres, as Shore (2002) studied in his research on deregulation of the right brain and traumatic attachment. Suggestions in hypnosis lower the left hemispheric activities of logical/critical thinking, analysis, and conceptualization, while right hemispheric mental activities take over. These are, among others, inner experiencing, time distortion, mental images accepted as real, and predominance of subjectivity. An example of hypnotic suggestion that I use often as a test in the early stages of analysis is to propose that the patient imagine herself "changed," dealing with others, facing difficulties, doing what she was unable to do before, enjoying life more productively, and so on. This becomes a sort of test that shows the patient's ability to use her imagination, her motivation to change, the people in her life who might obstruct the emergence of the "new self," and other significant information on the patient together with the corresponding feelings. It also subtly conveys a message of hope, and moves away from pathology. Incidentally, this technique is already an example of New Hypnosis because of the predominance of right hemispheric activity required for its performance.

Therefore, the hypnoanalyst uses the transference to make it possible for the client to accept his messages, which initially focus on feeling relaxed through slow breathing, and to provide the therapist detailed feedback of what is going on in her inner mind. This preparatory approach fortifies the positive transference. To ask, "How do you feel after this relaxation exercise?" is not enough. The feedback that builds a strong positive transference comes from questions like, "Can you mentally check your body and notice what part is feeling more relaxed than the rest as a result of this exercise?" or "Do you remember any recent time when you felt so good just from breathing slowly?" Then the patient is encouraged to relive that past good experience and strengthen the current relaxation with the fresh memory. If there is no recent memory, the psychotherapist asks her to *imagine* a situation where she is becoming extremely relaxed and to compare her relaxation fantasy to what just happened. If the patient is afraid of even imagining such deep relaxation, it is helpful to analyze the fantasies she may have of what might happen if she were so relaxed.

Finally, a meaningful and crucial topic is *indirect suggestions*, which the disciples of Milton Erickson have been discussing for a long time, as Weitzenhoffer (2000) explains in detail, based mostly on Rossi (1980), who is one of the most scientific students of Erickson. We realize that anything that the analyst does or does not do can become an indirect suggestion. It is not what he does or intends but the way in which the patient receives, perceives, and interprets the actions of the analyst. One of the Scholastic principles of communication and interaction states that "everything is received according to the modality (or the needs) of the recipient" (*Quidquid recipitur ad modum recipientis recipitur*), a fascinating forerunner of the concept of transference and also of *indirect suggestion*. Later we will deal more with indirect suggestions as part of the New Hypnosis.

All human beings are suggestible, for the transferential reasons just explained. The clinician uses this proclivity to propose indirect suggestions as a respected person of authority in order to attain therapeutic goals. *Direct suggestions* ("You will enjoy being more aware of other people's good intentions") and *indirect suggestions* ("At some point your unconscious may allow you to see another side of the problem") are distinguished from each other because of the level of consciousness on the part of the patient. In some cases, the patient does not perceive the message as a suggestion. The less awareness, the more indirect is the suggestion. Later in this chapter we shall begin to discuss how to frame and phrase suggestions in hypnoanalysis, especially when there is suspicion or evidence of resistance. It is worthy of note that many of the contributors to Safran's (2003) book also find indirect suggestion a common trend in Buddhism.

# Conscious and Unconscious Fantasy

By *unconscious* fantasies (more difficult to understand than the conscious type) we mean those that seem to appear "out of nowhere" in one's mind, which Erika Fromm (Fromm & Nash, 1997) refers to as *primary process*, although the fantasies are triggered by circumstances, either biological (basic desires like hunger, sex, sleep, etc.), psychological (a strong emotion like erotic attraction, frustration, anger, or other such affect), social (a good or bad situation in which the individual perceives herself in a unique opportunity for improvement, or in a dangerous situation of damage), or physical pain. (See Jacob Arlow's [1983] chapter, which is still a classic on unconscious fantasies.)

Mental images, on the other hand, refer usually to conscious fantasies we deliberately allow to form, fantasies that are often creative and artistic. (Some Kleinians still prefer to refer to conscious *fantasies* and to unconscious *phantasies*.) Freud (1908) used symptoms to uncover fantasies, having discovered that the symptom reflects the fantasy otherwise not conscious to the patient. Knafo and Feiner (2006) point out that Freud's new idea that a "repressed thought could consist of a fantasy rather than a memory" (p. 12) was a crucial point in the understanding of the cause of psychological disorders. However, when dealing with therapeutic hypnosis we realize that unconscious fantasies often are also constructive, positive, and good, playing an important part in the process of healing and self-growth, as it is in Buddhism (see Safran, 2003). For instance, suggesting to a patient in hypnosis that night dreams, reveries, and daydreams might become empowering to him has proven to be beneficial for the process of healing in hypnoanalysis, according to the careful research of Barber (1976, 1979).

In the New Hypnosis, mental imagery or fantasy is considered central. First, this is because it seems that all human thinking is imaginative. Even abstract concepts like "beauty" or "intelligence" in most people elicit mental pictures, usually of a concrete situation or of a person whom we connect with the concept. Second, in psychoanalysis we hope that patients convince themselves of possibilities that they had found previously difficult to identify with. The evidence is quite strong (from Maslow, 1968, to Seligman's followers, like Linley & Joseph, 2004) that the natural way of bringing a possibility closer to one's reality is through a vivid mental representation of that reality or a *vivencia*, which is a vivid and detailed mental representation (Araoz & Goldin, 2004). From such a mental image, the person can start to add other "realistic" experiences such as feelings and emotional reactions. Simpkins and Simpkins (2010) discuss suggestions combining neuroscience and Buddhism when dealing with change. We know that dreaming always starts with fantasies of memories that often lead to strong emotional reactions (Lippmann, 2000). Finally, echoing Virgil's (1989) well-known statement in *The Aeneid*, "*Possunt quia posse videntur*" (translated in posters and greeting cards as "They can because they think they can"), we hope that the hypnotic experience is a new start for the patient to use fantasy for her improvement, enrichment, and growth. Virgil's phrase is actually much more fantasy-centered: "They have the power to change [their being] because they visualize themselves changing." More generally, he proclaims that "Only those change [their being] who mentally see themselves changing." Virgil is obviously talking about the conscious use of fantasy, which is essential in the process of therapeutic hypnosis because it acts as the ego, displacing the id. And for this type of fantasy humans need focus or concentration (to be discussed later). It is of great interest to realize that researchers in neuroplasticity (Schwartz & Begley, 2002) found that deliberately visited vivid images of what one wants to be or do start to construct a new neurologic pathway that changes the brain, thus scientifically corroborating Virgil's statement. Of course, before him, Buddhism focused on imagination as the indispensable means to self-improvement. It is surprising that in Safran's (2003) book, the index does not list *imagination* or *fantasy*, though Simpkins and Simpkins (2010) give it an important place in the process of focusing.

Fantasy and reality interact in human thought, mostly unconsciously but sometimes consciously, as if we were dreaming even while transacting our daily activities in the real objective world, as in the belief of Borges (1952), in his prolific imaginative literature. Loewald (1974) used the phrase "the fantasy character of the analytic situation" (p. 305) as part of the title of one of his important papers dealing with this issue. These unconscious fantasies are practically always present, combining rationality and feelings. In fantasy, the two brain hemispheres seem to be acting simultaneously, sometimes in harmony or cooperation, sometimes contradicting each other, as Schwartz (2002) explains. Our fantasies influence our positive or negative adaptation to reality, our perceptions, our reactions, our behavior, and our choices. And reciprocally, our fantasies are also constantly influenced by the external world and by our experiences. This explains the erratic and changing nature of our unconscious fantasies, which can act against our well-being if we allow the id to control our fantasies. In this case, as in many others, we try to attain through hypnosis Freud's goal of giving room to the ego in places (behaviors, beliefs, interactions) where the id was. Arlow (1969) raised this issue a long time ago, and recent research, for instance with addictions, has repeatedly confirmed it.

In summary, there is no hypnosis without imagery; whatever the practitioner does produces fantasies in the patient. But the clinician depends on fantasy to help the client change. All the methods of inducing hypnosis are practically indirect suggestions that elicit fantasies. In practice the hypnoanalyst avoids purely abstract language and uses images, mental pictures, and figures of speech that can be visualized. (For instance, instead of "being tired," he may use "feeling all washed out.") The sooner the patient starts thinking in images and fantasies, the quicker the changes of attitudes, values, reactions, feelings, and the like can take place in hypnoanalysis, because the emphasis on hypnotic fantasy bypasses neurotic rationalization, projection, and other defenses.

## Focusing and Concentration

Another condition or prerequisite for hypnosis is the ability (and willingness!) to concentrate, so much so that its practice, like that of Buddhist meditation, has been described as an exercise in focused attention. Using hypnosis, we seek something that facilitates focusing and leads to it naturally, but even then will power is needed. Thus, among other concentration techniques, "traditional" hypnosis uses strong voice commands or the swinging of a brilliant pendulum in front of the patient's eyes in order to induce hypnosis. New Hypnosis, on the other hand, may take hold of something important the patient has said, or ask her to repeat a gesture just made, requesting her to concentrate on it, or may simply suggest that she focus on her breathing in order to fix her attention on the process of entering hypnosis. In all instances, free association is suggested to concentrate sharply on something important for the patient.

There are situations facilitative of hypnosis that naturally force the individual to focus, such as intense physical pain or fear, an accident, or the danger of great harm to self or others. But for psychological work, we must create the circumstances that lead the patient to concentrate on the possibility and advantage of using hypnosis. As a matter of fact, often the patient enters this different state of awareness without even thinking of hypnosis, but actually is in hypnosis without realizing the cognitive change. This may happen when the patient is describing a situation that is emotionally laden for her. She may become so involved in describing it that she finds herself as if she were living it again. (I shall call this a *vivencia*.)

Concentration, therefore, is the environment in which hypnosis takes place. In ordinary language, many seem to equate the two—hypnosis and focusing—and refer to someone being hypnotized, deep in thought, or mesmerized when he is highly focused on what he is doing, as in some physical exercises or in martial arts. This is an important question from neuroscience, which Rossi (1986) has been researching for decades, trying to find the physiology. He came up with a four-stage model of mind-body communication (Rossi, 2002), which throws some light on the very complex mechanisms at work. This is a definite aspect of neuroplasticity. If our thoughts can modify our brains, others' (parents, for instance) insistent comments can do the same, for our benefit or for our detriment.

# Dissociation

Earlier in this chapter I referred to dissociation in connection with hypnosis as an altered ego state. Several authors have studied this and came up with slightly different conclusions. For our purposes, we may recall Hilgard's (1977) "hidden observer," a part of the self that is aware of what happens to another part of which we are not aware, as in the case of local anesthesia produced by chemical means or by hypnosis, where he found that there is a part that perceives the pain but represses it and, as a consequence, acts as if it did not have any pain. Also in hypnosis, the intent is to create a form of dissociation by which the person "separates" himself from the surrounding physical reality of time and space and concentrates on the inner "reality of fantasy" that usually is being suggested by the clinician. Dissociation is experienced as "not being where the person is physically" but being where his fantasy creations have placed him. Dissociation, therefore, is essential for hypnosis and can be considered requisite to the experience the inner reality of fantasy.

The levels of intensity in hypnotic work become corollaries of dissociation. Erickson insisted on *naturalistic induction* of hypnosis, meaning that the patient's uniqueness is the means to elicit the hypnotic experience, as he did in the case of *The February Man* (Erickson & Rossi, 1989), among others. The use of dissociation techniques, considered part of hypnosis, activates the patient's personality as the center for hypnotic work, because all his attention is directed to the aspect of himself that is being worked on, so that his mental energies are fixed on it and, in a sense, nothing else matters at the time. It is a dissociation from the external world. In the successful and ideal hypnotic experience, he is conscious of the hypnotic process and becomes "non-conscious" of the surrounding reality, including his body.

To define hypnosis, we must keep in mind Bernheim's (1884) surprising statement that "hypnosis does not exist. What exists is the interaction between a given context [in imagination or fantasy] and the aptitude of the subject to respond to that context" (p. 394). Elsewhere, intending to keep all the essential hypnotic elements in line, I defined hypnosis as "the experience of a new awareness of self, based mainly on the use of fantasy and imagination, which facilitates a modified and concentrated attention that allows the subject to engage in new ways of thinking and of experiencing new possibilities of self-control" (Araoz, 2005–2006, p. 125).

## Physiological Aspects of Hypnosis

Among those who have addressed themselves to the brain changes in the hypnotic state, Hilgard (1978) and Rossi (1986, 2002) developed concepts that are especially meaningful because of the multitude of studies conducted by them with hypnotic subjects, specifically on the physiology of hypnosis, and for the serious and careful approach of their work. Significant evidence of alterations in brain functioning were reported also in diverse scientific circles, for instance, by the New York Academy of Sciences (1977), and in a special issue on Hypnosis and Psychopathology of the *Journal of Abnormal Psychology* (American Psychological Association, 1979). In an indirect way, the new scientific concern with *neuroplasticity* (Doidge, 2007; Kandel, 2006; Schwartz & Begley, 2002) completes the scientific picture. I intend to refer to the valuable knowledge that all these researchers have found and reported, emphasizing the fascinating recent discoveries explained by Doidge. The reader may also peruse the book by Rossi and Cheek (1988). I also like to clarify that many others who have conducted significant research on hypnosis, like Barber (1979), did not specifically concentrate as such on the physiological aspects of it.

The essence of neuroplasticity is that the living human brain is constantly changing and accommodating to new circumstances, input, and experiences. Two old beliefs are involved here. The first is that the healthy human brain has specific and fixed rigid locations for the control of different organs and activities of the body; this has been proven untrue as an inflexible rule. The second belief, that of the power of positive thinking or positive psychology, has been given scientific status thanks to growing research and findings (Linley & Joseph, 2004; Seligman & Csikszentmihalyi, 2000). For hypnoanalysis to be effective, it is important to understand how people change and how hypnosis facilitates the process. This research has shown that we change cognitively and emotionally as a result of alterations in the neural networks. This alteration comes from strengthening new synaptic connections by focusing on positive and constructive ideas, thus weakening the old, destructive, and negative ideas to which we were holding on in the past. Holding on to unproductive beliefs, attitudes, prejudices, and fears is what I designated *negative self-hypnosis* (NSH) (Araoz, 1981, 1985a). We knew from clinical experience that it was therapeutic to encourage the change from negative to positive thoughts. Now we know the biological reason for it.

Hilgard's (1978) "hidden observer" refers to divided consciousness. Consciousness has been connected with the hypothalamus, which is part of the limbic system, as is the amygdala. It follows then that the parts of the brain involved in consciousness are affected by hypnosis. Because hypnosis affects consciousness (the subject experiencing herself differently than out of hypnosis), it follows that hypnosis modifies the functioning of the brain. Consciousness, in the Janet dissociation model discussed by Hilgard (1978), reveals itself when some part of the personality disconnects from the primary part, as in the case of multiple personalities, not because that part is deeper than the primary, as in Freud's model, but in the sense of it being a division of the primary. This division is the result of forgetfulness for Janet, and of repression for Freud.

Rossi and Cheek's (1988) studies, buttressed by Pert's (1987) neuroscience research, confirm and refine the above explanation. They stress the holistic aspects of biology and explain the psychosomatic network theory of how "alternating states of the receptor may be a psychobiological mechanism whereby energy and information could be converted into one another in living systems" (Rossi & Cheek, 1988, p. 211). They also remind us of the old Mesmerian theory of *animal magnetism,* which was a precursor of what science has demonstrated regarding the effect in the entire body of powerful words and fantasies perceived by the organism. In other words, hypnosis produces cognitive-emotional reactions in the subject, and thus alters the functioning of different biosystems, including the immune system, the gastrointestinal system, and the sexual system, in addition to the normal function of the brain. Throughout this book, therefore, we are taking for granted the physiological aspects of hypnosis.

# "Induction" of Hypnosis

All the explanations and references mentioned thus far are intended to clarify our view of hypnosis in order to discuss hypnoanalysis or hypnotherapy. Thus I intend to address myself to concepts that I, among many others, minimize, which can become confusing when trying to understand hypnoanalysis and which we can do without. There are quite a few of these but these five are, perhaps, the important ones: induction, hypnotizability, hypnotic depth, hypnotic amnesia, and specific hypnotic techniques.

*Induction* refers to the mental process of moving from the ordinary way of thinking to the special modality of Creative Imagination and mind training. In traditional hypnosis, inductions are rather ritualized, but New Hypnosis uses *utilization,* which means the employment of unexpected things that may happen, like noises, or the gestures and words of the client, that are naturalistic, patient-centered, and spontaneous. The change from ordinary thinking to the hypnotic modality should be individualized, and should never be based on any ideas, mental images, concepts, or expressions that have not come from the patient's previous behavior and conversation. Thus, we do not use formal inductions. This is especially the case with patients who are not familiar with hypnosis, and are even apprehensive of it. Thus, the traditional methods portrayed in movies and used in nightclub acts, like arm levitation, fixing one's sight on a specific point, using a Chevreul pendulum, and the like, are not routinely employed. All the methods to start the hypnotic experience are *naturalistic*. Therefore, the other four concerns mentioned above, namely *hypnotizability* (the ability to benefit from hypnosis), *hypnotic depth* (how completely the person gets into the experience of hypnosis), *amnesia* (the lack of memory for what just happened during hypnosis), and *rigid techniques* for inducing hypnosis are minimized and given little if any consideration in hypnoanalytic work. My belief is that *any person who dreams is hypnotizable* and, since we all dream, we can all use and benefit from hypnosis. Unlike in the laboratory, if the patient does not respond to one induction method, another is used. Hypnotizing ability or the flexibility of the analyst in using different approaches is more important than hypnotizability. Expressions related to "hypnotizing" are avoided, so as not to revive the old idea that the "hypnotist" has some mysterious power over the patient. To introduce hypnosis, the hypnoanalyst proceeds with *utilization*, seeking what I call the *point of entry*. He will take advantage of the client's words, movements, changes in physical position, and any facial expression or gesture and find out if he can use this point of entry to lead to hypnosis. Thus, if the patient says something that seems to be easy to visualize (like "I'm in the dark" or "I feel at the end of my rope"), that is tried as a point of entry. Let us assume that the expression used by the patient is, "I can't swallow his nonsense any longer." The hypnotic induction starts when the clinician invites her to imagine herself swallowing, and helps her make that mental image as real an inner experience as possible. For this she is helped to involve all the mind senses related to normal swallowing, so that she can reproduce the experience in her thinking as if it were truly happening.

If the patient is nervous or anxious, the hypnoanalyst "utilizes" this as well to make the patient aware of how the mind influences the body. To do this he spends a brief moment guiding her to relax by concentrating on her calm and rhythmic breathing, while linking inhaling with relaxation, good energy, or something positive, and exhaling with "getting rid of things the patient does not need" (including thoughts, worries, and other negative mental activities).

The same general approach is used with any spontaneous output of gestures, body language, or words on the part of the patient. This output may be opening or closing her arms or hands, pointing her finger, crossing her legs, facial expressions, and the like. The analyst's instructions direct the client to imagine herself somewhere, alone, with someone, or with others, making that same gesture. Once "there" the patient is asked to pay attention to any and all things that come to her mind, to anything (colors, scents, temperature, sounds or lack of them, etc.) she is aware of in the hypnotic state. Another way of using gestures or physical movements is to suggest that she repeat them several times to see if any association, memory, or feeling comes up. Then, typical analytic questions are directed at what was discovered, such as, "In what way do you understand this [what came from the hypnotic practice] to be connected with what we were talking about before?" I try to minimize the ritualistic part of hypnosis and stress the experiential aspect of it.

As can be seen, and unlike other methods, in this approach we *do not make a clear distinction between induction and hypnosis proper*. We echo Bernheim's (1884) statement that nothing is hypnosis and, again, everything is hypnosis, when one switches from left to right cerebral hemispheres. As a matter of fact, we consider that *from the moment one enters the world of fantasy, one is in hypnosis*. Therefore, contradictory as it may sound, induction itself is natural hypnosis because the subject allows herself to experience without trying to analyze and understand.

To recapitulate the steps for helping someone into the hypnotic state: the first step is to keep in mind the possible *point of entry* as any chosen element of patient output (keeping in mind the principle of patient-centeredness) that the analyst tries to use in order to start the hypnosis experience. The directions given to the patient stress focusing on the point of induction through *visualization* and allowing oneself *"to be there"* in one's mind. The more inner senses we can include in the induction, the quicker the person *disassociates* from the surrounding reality and thus enters into hypnosis. Notice that we who use this type of hypnosis do not use the common expressions of "going deeper into sleep" or "being under hypnosis," because the patient is actively involved in the procedure. The hypnoanalyst remembers that if there are any difficulties in induction, relaxation through breathing facilitates the switch from ordinary thinking to the very special way of hypnosis thinking.

In spite of the above warning regarding the basic nature of hypnosis that in clinical practice makes induction and hypnosis itself essentially the same, nevertheless it is heuristically important to distinguish between the two. The former gets the person into the latter and, technically, the hypnoanalytic work cannot start without the former. Because the number of *points of entry* is infinite, here I focus briefly on the "bridge" between the two: how induction places the patient in hypnosis. What induction does is to help the patient change a memory or any repressed material into an inner experience—from facts and data to *vivencia*, the Spanish noun mentioned earlier, meaning a vivid, detailed, affect-laden, and uniquely individualistic mental re-creation (Araoz & Goldin, 2004).

Regarding specific methods, a convenient universal way to help the patient enter hypnosis was also mentioned, consisting in asking her to repeat the word uttered, or the gesture she has produced that the therapist has chosen as the point of induction. This is done to check if any memory, mental picture, bodily sensation, tension, or such comes to mind or is experienced internally while concentrating on the point of entry.

A more specific point of entry is used when a patient mentions a positive place, a person, a set of circumstances, or a particular event. Hypnoanalysis tries to help the patient re-experience it emotionally as vividly as possible. What he is talking about should not remain merely a fact, a statistical occurrence, or an objective reality, but should become a personal, individualistic, subjective experience, a revivification or vivid reliving of a personal experience—a *vivencia*. Therefore, when the patient mentions any of the things listed above, the analyst asks him to be there in his mind, to notice all the details of what he sees, feels, smells, or senses. For example, the patient is reporting on an argument with a girlfriend and says, "We were getting closer to her house." The hypnoanalyst may reply, "In your mind, you can be there again right now. Would you do that? Would you be with her right now getting closer to her house?" Then, he adds, "Check your feelings. Connect with your feelings, the bad ones but also the good feelings, everything you are feeling as you are getting closer to her house." This mental exercise of reliving the memory in a vivid fantasy manner is the most spontaneous, perhaps, and effective manner of induction when dealing with memories—everything that one remembers. Consequently, the subsequent analysis becomes very meaningful.

The third method is used with repressed material that is not primarily a memory. For example, the patient states, talking about a new business that she is planning, "Everything is ready to go, I've spent a

## 2. Therapeutic Hypnosis

long time going over all possible details but I still feel strange and insecure." Here the hypnoanalyst may do one of two things in order to start using hypnosis. One choice is for her to focus on the feelings: identify one or two of them, where in the body are they felt, or define how they may have shape, color, weight, etc. The other choice is to imagine vividly and in detail the success of her new business. Then whatever is elicited is analyzed.

It is useful to remember that in all cases the experienced clinician has choices of techniques, even in the early stages of trying this new therapeutic approach, to connect with the unconscious psychodynamics of the patient. Keeping close observation of the patient, typical of psychoanalysis, allows the induction procedure always to be centered on the patient, without having to use any artificial maneuvers or rituals that may make the patient feel under the control of the hypnotist, as happens in the traditional use of hypnosis. Fantasy and spontaneous inner experience, yes; rituals and forced behavior, no.

To summarize, in clinical work we introduce hypnosis without any announcements that may be confusing and frightening. We remember that New Hypnosis considers hypnotic any experiential, nonintellectual mind activity. Therefore, the *first step* is to look for points of entry provided unconsciously by the patient. These are her words and figures of speech, important statements, movements. and gestures that we think may trigger unconscious material. When we decide on a point of entry, we enter the *second step*, applying the brief introductory preparation of eye closing, and concentration on *breathing* and *relaxation*. When the patient has become more relaxed than she was before, we move on to the *third step*, to "test" that the patient is in hypnosis. We encourage her to pay attention to anything that comes into mind and to accept it, even though it may not seem to make sense. The less logical and sequential her active imagination is, the more chances we have that the person is tuned to the "special thinking channel" that we call hypnosis. Obviously, this is not a scientific test at all, but it is clinically indicative. If the patient is still in the "ordinary mental channel" of reality orientation, we need to spend more time in the two previous activities of breathing and relaxation. Otherwise we can proceed to the third step. For example, if the patient says, "I feel lost," we ask her to stay with this statement and to allow any images and fantasies, memories, and past experiences to come to her mind. The initial "I feel lost," used in reference to how to deal with her boss, may change into images of being lost in a forest or in a dangerous neighborhood in a big city. To activate further unconscious material, we encourage the patient to repeat to herself the "I feel lost" statement and check the feelings it elicits: fear, anger, self-pity, and so on. Rather than to rush the patient to "tell us about those feelings," we encourage her to genuinely experience as fully as possible those feelings, and to pay attention to other details that may come up: people, places, events, and so on, that may trigger other feelings. This is the *fourth step*, the induced dream of Chapter 5, and we may use words like "as if it were a dream" to emphasize that she should allow herself to be fully involved in the fantasies. I find that *induced dreams* are helpful in solving doubts, questions, and ambivalences, even though, from the New Hypnosis perspective, the technical difference among dreams, daydreams, induced dreams, active imagination, and fantasies becomes practically minor in the clinical arena. Finally, the *fifth step* is for the patient to promise to repeat on her own this mind practice. The analyst has to decide honestly what word to use to describe this practice, because hypnosis often brings up fantasies, in many people, of someone taking control over another. As mentioned earlier, we have many choices, like *active imagination* (Jung's term) that do not have negative connotations. The analyst can come up with any term that indicates a true aspect of hypnosis.

## Summary

New Hypnosis originates in psychoanalysis (as psychoanalysis started with hypnosis á la Charcot) and fits very neatly into it, because it is centered on the patient as well as what is happening to him or her at the time, and also because it helps to deal with the unconscious psychodynamics underlying the symptoms that bother the client. The nature of hypnosis lies in a different experience of one's ego with greater *concentration* turned inward. This alone places the patient in a special form of *dissociation* and separation from the external, sensory world. The combination of these experiences makes the person more susceptible to *suggestions*, which are maximally effective when indirect and are possible in hypnosis because of a unique *transferential* experience. All suggestions involve fantasy, and the execution of change in perception, attitude, values, and behavior is possible because of fantasy. There is a mutual influence here: fantasy is produced effectively because of dissociation, so that dissociation makes fantasy possible, and dissociation is easier thanks to fantasy, as my definition of hypnosis shows, indicating an effective manner for the ego to take the place of the id, as classical psychoanalysis states.

Induction in New Hypnosis is always a utilization of something that the client has said or done in the analytic session. We avoid the artificial, theatrical, and magical mental pirouettes preferred by others who use hypnosis, thus keeping induction *naturalistic* in order to continue the entire hypnotic work in the same spirit. Induction methods describe how to use hypnoanalysis.

## Daily Living Applications

Ordinary people can learn to take advantage of induction, which is a form of distancing oneself from the bothersome events or thoughts that make it very difficult, if not impossible, to think clearly and to get out of the tense and stressful situation. By using induction and getting into the hypnotic experience, the person is able to utilize his or her best inner resources. He can learn to activate his inner strengths when he feels diminished. After the concentration on breathing and the experience of relaxation, he will refocus—now on his strengths, successes, and good results—and abandon the concentration on negative, painful, and unpleasant realities. By refocusing he will be able to think of solutions and ways of coping with his problems. The person who wants to take advantage of auto-hypnosis may follow the induction steps, always remembering that it takes some time to learn and to feel comfortable with this new mental activity.

All this can be labeled Buddhist, because the core of its teaching is one's control of thinking.

CHAPTER 3

# Development of Understanding of Hypnosis

It is quite well known that Freud became interested in psychodynamics during his visit to Paris in the late 1880s. On that occasion, he attended lectures and demonstrations by Jean-Martin Charcot, prominent psychiatrist at the time and enthusiastic practitioner of hypnosis in cases of "hysteria." Upon his return to Vienna, Freud started to use hypnosis, collaborating with his older colleague and friend Breuer, as reported in the book *Studies on Hysteria,* authored by both (Breuer & Freud, 1893). Freud's admiration of hypnosis continued all his life, even after he ceased to use it explicitly (Araoz, 2006b, based on the documentation of Gravitz & Gerton, 1981). The office of his last few years in exile in London was personally arranged by him, and it is significant that the most prominent picture over the couch, on the central wall, is that of Charcot using hypnosis with a middle-aged woman patient, a picture frequently found in psychology and hypnosis textbooks. According to Eisen (1993), Freud understood that the person in hypnosis accepts the hypnotist as an idealized object, comparable to what happens in the experience of being in love (Freud, 1905a). Eisen explains Freud's concept of hypnosis, stating that "just as the loved object often stands in the place of the ideal aspect of the self, *the essence of hypnosis resides in an unconscious fixation of the subject's libido to the hypnotist as an ego ideal*" (p. 123, my emphasis). Thus, for Freud, hypnosis has an erotic root and reactivates the Oedipus complex, as Ferenczi (1955) explains. The altered perception that the patient has of the analyst constitutes a form of self-hypnosis. This experience has been separated from hypnosis and is traditionally considered transference in the psychoanalytic literature. Obviously then, hypnosis implied, for Freud in the early years of practice, a form of therapeutic regression. But, as happened with many of his theories, the understanding of hypnosis also evolved.

## Development of Psychoanalytic Thinking

In order to find the right place of hypnosis in psychoanalysis, it is helpful to recall that there are (at least) four "psychologies" or perspectives within psychoanalysis, as Pine (1990) explains in detail. We also must keep in mind that New Hypnosis (Araoz, 1985a) is closer to Zen Buddhist meditation, with its concentration on fantasy, than to the traditional way it was used in Freud's time and is still used today by many of those outside the New Hypnosis. Initially, then, the classical psychoanalysis of *drives* or the id, from which all energy was thought to derive, centered on libido and the pleasure principle. So in the late 1800s and early 1900s, hypnosis was used to bring to awareness the repressions that choked the libido. With *ego psychology* (from about 1917 to 1923), psychoanalysis focused on the individual's ways of coping with circumstances and people who were interfering with his enjoyment. Hypnosis was applied here to the defense mechanisms and to a strengthening of the ego. Still growing, in the late 1940s, psychoanalysis abandoned libido as the main drive in humans and emphasized *object relations*. The true libidinal goal is not merely pleasure coming from relief of tension; it is only fully achieved in trusting, respectful, and interdependent relationships with others who are the people important and close to us. The lifelong process of attachment, separation, and individuation is heavily emphasized in object relations theory. Therefore hypnosis became a convenient tool to work with object representations— the images we unconsciously form of others from our perceptions and interactions— to examine them, to correct them, to change them. Finally, In the 1960s, *self psychology* started to unify the different components of the individual (id, ego, superego, ego ideal) into a consistent identity called the *self*. Erika Fromm, in my view the most important modern advocate of hypnoanalysis, summarizes in one of her many publications (Brown & Fromm, 1986) the connection between hypnosis and psychoanalysis: "All four psychoanalytic theories can be used in hypnoanalysis, the emphasis on one or the other depending on the case. Frequently, more than one, or the four psychoanalytic theories, will underlie the hypnoanalytic treatment of the same case at different points" (p. 200).

Currently the trend that may become as important as the previous four "schools" within psychoanalysis is *relationality* (Mitchell, 2000), which overlaps with interpersonal analysis (in many ways a similar theory on how the self reveals itself in the here and now in all interactions, including and in a very special way in the analytic encounter). Some Eastern European analysts, following Ferenczi's "mutual analysis" ideas (Bókay, Giampieri-Deutsch, & Rudnytsky, 1996) have touched on many interpersonal/relational concepts. Hypnosis is helpful to bypass resistances and to recognize internal relational constructs.

The highlights of hypnoanalytic thinking in its historical development since Freud are presented by Erika Fromm and Nash (1997). In a manner resembling Erika Fromm's summary, the following elaborates the progress and modifications in the psychoanalytical thinking on hypnosis.

SIGMUND FREUD. Freud learned from Charcot's demonstrations in Paris in the year 1885, understood hypnosis as a method to manipulate people's behavior through direct suggestion. We shall come back to Freud's view of hypnosis throughout the volume.

SANDOR FERENCZI. Ferenczi (1909) saw hypnosis as reactivating the Oedipus complex and, thus, as a regression that transferentially awakens the child hidden in every adult. He makes a distinction between *maternal* and *paternal* hypnosis (permissive vs. authoritarian), stressing that the former was very rare in his time and advocating its use in psychoanalysis (1955).

PAUL SCHILDER. Schilder, following his master Ferenczi, insists on the power of the word in hypnotic regression, which increases and magnifies that power. Like the child's reaction to a fairy tale, hypnosis regresses the patient to primary process (magical) thinking, but with an important difference (Schilder & Kauders, 1926). In adult regression, the adult secondary process thinking is not completely lost and, in spite of the regression, there is awareness of the external reality at another psychic level. Is this the same phenomenon of the *hidden observer* discovered half a century later by Hilgard (1977) in his experiments with hypnosis? Schilder also claimed that transference and suggestibility have their roots in the libido and thus in the preoedipal and oedipal developmental stages.

Schilder's (1923) insistence on the active existence of ego drives beside the id drives is another important addition to the previous theories. It is interesting to note that 1923 was the same year Freud published *The Ego and the Id* in German. The significance of Schilder's theories—not full regression, ego drives, and personality parts—is that they build the bridge between drive and ego psychology to explain hypnosis.

OTTO FENICHEL. Fenichel (1945) views hypnosis as a regression to the time in our very early life when we felt "secure in a greater unit, while at the same time, losing our own individuality" (p. 561). But he reminds us that this "creates an artificial ego state" that is used in hypnoanalysis "to overcome the drawbacks of the ego's not facing its conflicts and its continued dependency" (p. 563). Thus, he is a forerunner of Kris (1952) with his concept of "regression in the service of the ego." He also discusses the paradox of hypnosis, which makes the patient dependent on the analyst in order to make him maturely independent.

THEODOR REIK. Nowhere does Reik (1948) mention hypnosis as such, but in many places, dealing with insight, fantasy, and memory, he describes what are hypnotic experiences, as he applies them in analysis—a point of great importance for the New Hypnosis. For example, when commenting on the Yiddish proverb, *Pain also makes you laugh* (pp. 190–191), he reminds us that laughter acts as a self-suggestion that helps the person move her attention away from the pain and suffering. Notice that in this case, like in many others, Reik is not using mere cognitive-behavioral techniques but strictly a psychodynamic method that acts on the self directly from the unconscious by encouraging *the experience* that makes the patient change. For some, it may look like stretching this too much, but in terms of *New Hypnosis*, regardless of what one names the method, it is hypnotic if it utilizes the unconscious and learning through experience, bypassing reason and intellectual understanding in order to influence one's emotions and behavior.

LEWIS WOLBERG. With the New York state of mind, Wolberg (1945) uses hypnoanalysis to shorten and to accelerate the psychoanalytical process. Starting from the premise that "progress in therapy goes hand in hand with strengthening of the ego" (p. 242), he uses hypnosis to help the ego "tolerate unconscious impulses and ... react to them in the light of present reality" (p. 241). Thus the uncovering stage of psychoanalysis finds less resistance and the "re-educative phase" becomes smoother; both actions contributing to shortening the time needed for the work of psychoanalysis. Wolberg insists on the patient taking an active role and explains that "replacing hypnotic passivity by activity probably has an important effect with respect to the basic image of authority as restrictive, repressive and insistent upon being right at all times" (p. 247). His approach is obviously ego psychological but it can easily be adapted to an object relational modality.

JOHN AND HELEN WATKINS. Both psychoanalysts and academicians, John and Helen Watkins developed several uses of hypnosis also from the ego psychology position. By *ego states* (Watkins, 1978) they mean different inner experiences of oneself. *Resistance*, for instance, is understood as the struggle of two ego states, one recognizing the benefit of bringing something repressed to the awareness level, the other afraid of further harm and pain and reluctant to bring up the repressed material. These ego states are constantly active, and with hypnosis they can be utilized therapeutically. The *hidden observer* (Watkins & Watkins, 1979–1980, 1992)), or *double consciousness* (Eisen, 1993), is another manifestation of ego states. For Watkins (1978) then, hypnosis is a means, practical and natural, of getting in touch with the psychodynamics responsible for our perceptions, expectations, feelings, reactions, fantasies, etc., and of making a clear distinction between id and ego functions. In this process the patient discovers the meaning and function of many symptoms (Watkins & Barabasz, 2008).

ERNEST HILGARD. Hilgard is recognized as one of the most prolific researchers on hypnosis over three decades. For him, hypnosis takes place when the subject has the experience of *divided consciousness*, that is, when she is in touch with her own self but, at the same time, allows herself to enter into a different possibility of the self. She may be rather morose and depressive but can experience herself as truly cheerful, gregarious, outgoing, and funny. He refers to *the hidden observer*, "the vertical split ... between what the hypnotized part experiences and what some other part of the person knows" (Hilgard, 1978, p. 26). His long research, summarized in 1992, has shown that there is hypnosis when, at least to some extent, seven characteristics can be observed:

1. Planning function diminishes.
2. Attention and inattention become selective.
3. There is an increase in fantasy production and past visual memories.

4. There is a tolerance of reality distortion and reduction of reality testing.
5. There is an increase in suggestibility.
6. There is an acceptance of diverse roles (being and acting like a child).
7. There is at least amnesia for what happened in hypnosis.

ERIKA FROMM.* Fromm developed her own ego psychological theory of hypnosis that she used in hypnoanalysis after carefully testing it in laboratory experiments at the University of Chicago. She saw hypnosis as an adaptive regression or, in Kris's (1952) words, "a regression in the service of the ego," as is the creative act. She enriched Rapaport's (1953) "ego modes" theory of ego activity and passivity by applying them to hypnosis. Ego activity corresponds to free choice and self-regulation, whereas ego passivity refers to the inability to cope with life's ordinary problems. In hypnosis, ego activity is "a volitional mental activity during trance" (Erika Fromm, 1992), as when the person in hypnosis agrees to do something suggested. On the other hand, ego passivity may be the result of demands from the id drives, from the cultural imperatives, or from the superego. Though ego-dystonic, the individual complies out of a sense of helplessness. In hypnosis, a person who has a weak ego may obey the suggestions of a hypnotist that are not ego-syntonic.

Later, *ego receptivity* was added to Rapaport's ego modes. Fromm (1992) applied it to hypnosis and discovered that it takes place every time the *general reality orientation* (GRO) clicks in: in hypnosis, ordinary reality becomes preconscious and recedes into the background. This is the important juncture when the patient is open to internal stimuli and to the one source he is connected to, the hypnosis practitioner. This is the state when the patient *lets himself go*, as Erickson (Havens, 1996) called it, and the patient allows preconscious and unconscious material to move easily and spontaneously into consciousness. Therefore, ego receptivity presupposes hypnotic relaxation (trance) and makes possible the type of suggestibility mentioned earlier. Because of this, the quicker process of psychoanalysis that Wolberg (1945) had promised takes place. Fromm and Nash (1997) make an important point about the change in

---

*To distinguish Erika Fromm from Erich Fromm, the former preferred to be referred to by her complete name. Consequently I will do so, except when it is obvious that I am referring to one or the other.

thinking that hypnosis promotes, from secondary process thinking to primary process thinking, from concepts to pictures, from words to images, from logic to experience — all part of regression in the service of the ego. As we will see in the next chapter, fantasy is the preferred mode of self-expression in hypnosis, as it is in the primary process. And because imagery is highly idiosyncratic, we have to propose this type of activity very gently and open-endedly. Instead of offering "guided imagery" chosen by us, we suggest that an image may appear in the patient's "mental screen" to give him a fresh view and make him understand the issue he wants to resolve.

Finally, Fromm's theory of hypnosis and its application to psychoanalysis comprises three summarizing concepts: *attention, absorption,* and *general reality orientation* (Fromm & Nash, 1997). We may add that these concepts simultaneously are the prerequisites and the result of the patient's cooperation or positive transference in the hypnotic work. Regarding this important cooperation, which strengthens the concept that hypnosis is not magic, Barber (1976), who is highly respected as a serious hypnosis researcher, found that *trust* in the operator, reasonable *expectations* of success, cooperative *attitude,* and personal *motivation* are required on the part of the patient (or subject) in order for hypnosis to take place. Elsewhere I composed the acronym TEAM (Araoz, 1982) to highlight these prerequisites. *Trust,* based on a positive transference, may start with an "act of faith" in the hypnoanalyst. *Expectation* must be reasonable, not based on hoped-for miracles. *Attitude* must be cooperative, with a willingness to work and learn. *Motivation* should be real and personal, not just to please a spouse or other family member. Fromm's *attention* and *absorption* are possible because of TEAM. On the other hand, general reality orientation is a result of absorption in the hypnotic work and, even though momentarily one lets go of the surrounding reality, as in ordinary sleep, there is a temporary "disconnection" in order to link more fully with reality later on.

**MICHAEL J. DIAMOND.** As indicated at the start of this chapter, the four so-called psychoanalytic psychologies may benefit from the use of hypnosis. In addition to *drive* and *ego,* already discussed, Diamond focuses on *object relations,* "think[ing] of hypnosis as being an object relationship in which two people are [interacting] ... more intensely than in any other kind of therapy" (Fromm & Nash, 1997, p. 54). According to the same authors, hypnoanalysis, in Diamond's (1987) thought, is "a *dual interaction* phenomenon of great intensity (with) four dimensions which constantly overlap: (1) the transference; (2) the therapeutic or working alliance; (3) the symbiotic or fusional alliance; (4) the realistic relationship between the patient and the therapist" (p. 53). Two warnings are given, first that these four dimensions often intermingle, becoming difficult to identify independently of the others, and second, that one or another may be predominant at any given moment in the hypnoanalytic experience without losing the basic influence of the other three in a truly interactive manner. Explaining Diamond, Fromm and Nash (1997) state, "From moment to moment within the hour (and even outside of it) these object relations interactions between the hypnoanalyst and the patient are interwoven and intertwined, sometimes changing in constellation and emphasis very quickly between the two partners in the dyad" (p. 54). For Diamond, hypnoanalysis creates a system between patient and analyst that unavoidably involves both. No blank slate, no objective observer, but both actively involved in what is going on in the relationship. This is what Diamond (1987) calls the *real relationship*. We see here clearly that this is a way of applying hypnosis in an object relations orientation, although it also has many elements of the relational trend. Because of this realistic interaction between the two components of the system Diamond speaks about, the progress is easily moved away from the purely transferential aspect to that of reality testing. And again, as Wolberg (1945) would want it, hypnoanalysis accelerates the analytic work.

Finally in his latest book (2007), Diamond does not discuss hypnosis as such but in Chapter Five uses hypnotic concepts like Jung's *dialectical procedure* (to be considered later), giving us a good example of the practical value of this form of thinking in enriching one's life.

**ELGAN BAKER.** Commenting on hypnosis within a self psychology framework, Baker (1981) shows that borderline and narcissistic patients benefit from hypnoanalysis, as long as the psychoanalyst continues to stand by the patient so that she can be assured that the therapist will not abandon or betray her. This is done by means of the hypnotic state, mentally rehearsing closeness and distancing, being one with the therapist and slowly separating from him until both are at a distance but still relating through the good memories and feelings of the past. The different types of transference (selfobject, mirroring, borderline, psychotic) become a challenge to the psychoanalyst, who has to take on a very active and sensitive role in allowing himself to become a transference object to make up for the deficiencies these patients have suffered in their early development. This effort on the part of the analyst is necessary to overcome the developmental deficit that has interfered with the patient's growth and development. In an important sense, Elgan Baker completes the hypnoanalytical edifice, thus giving contemporary hypnosis a very different role than what it had at the very beginning of psychoanalysis.

**CARL JUNG.** Last but by no means least, Jung contributes to the understanding and clinical use of hypnosis in psychoanalysis. He (1973) referred to the practice of auto-hypnosis as *active imagination*, when the person activates her fantasies in a positive manner in order to live more fully and to enjoy it, or in order to separate the current self from the past with its mistakes. His method is not difficult to adapt to interactive hypnosis, as in hypnotherapy. Jung (1973) states, "You must step into the fantasy yourself and compel the figures to give you an answer" (p. 561). He calls this method a *dialectical procedure*, because it is "a dialogue between your (conscious) self and the unconscious figures" (Jung, 1977, p. 119). He realizes that our fantasies and the messages we read into them can make us unhappy and miserable or the complete opposite. He does warn us not to read into the fantasy figures any intellectual meaning, but to stay with the material of our imagination and experience it fully as it is. This is a form of what I earlier referred to as a *vivencia*. Because the therapeutic value of the dialectical procedure lies in merely experiencing the images, not in interpreting them, Jung insisted on having a conversation with the images that come to our minds. In other words (and I repeat the concept in order to join Jung in his emphasis), stay with the fantasy — don't let intellectualization take over and rob you of the therapeutic experience. He taught that we become what we allow to linger in our minds, and he recommended the hypnotic practice just described (not using the word hypnosis at all in order to stress the non-magical nature of this practice) to move from negative to positive living. If we change our "thinking" to constructive, optimistic, and happy, we can become that, for which current neurological science has given us proof. But "thinking" here does not mean reasoning, objective understanding, etc. It means allowing fantasies to stay at the center of our mental attention. This relates to the *fantasy principle* that, in the words of Adams (2000), is "the conviction that fantasy is logically prior to reality, that the psyche, or the imagination, constructs reality and that the image says what it means and means what it says" (p. 16). That "fantasy is prior to reality" is definitely true in the creative act (every human-made object was someone's fantasy before it became reality) but it happens also in our developmental experience, as the object relations school holds: we first perceive Mother in terms of our needs, not of her limitations. That "the psyche, or the imagination, constructs reality" may have many meanings. For instance, it may mean that our fantasy prepares us to face reality and we twist reality to encounter what we had fantasized, or become extremely disappointed not to find what we had dreamt, thus considering our fantasy a prophecy that must be fulfilled. We may also embellish a harsh reality, thanks to the fantasy that preceded our encounter with pleasant reality. Jung believed that we are always using fantasy by means of auto-hypnosis — for good or for bad — and that we can teach patients always to use their "thoughts" to be better and overcome the deficiencies of their upbringing and the pain of their living experiences. Finally, when Adams (2000) in the quote above says that "the image says what it means and means what it says," he refers to what Jungians call *amplification*. According to this Jungian concept, the image expresses always an ego-image, a reflection of an aspect of oneself: what aspect of my psyche does the image represent? Fantasy is seen as always being a projection of the self.

The last point emphasized in Jung's understanding of hypnosis is that, because of the universal unconscious, each one of us has the responsibility of avoiding thoughts of death, violence, pain, and destruction. By being positive, we help the rest of mankind. And that is one important lesson that we learn in psychoanalysis, to be realistically positive and optimistic. Therefore hypnosis, especially auto-hypnosis, refers to the *fantasy principle*, the analysis of the imagination that Adams (2000) describes.

To all these important figures within psychoanalysis, we could add others like Fritz Perls and Milton H. Erickson, who departed from practicing what is commonly designated as psychoanalysis, using many hypnotic approaches.

## Summary

This chapter has shown how hypnosis can be an enhancement and enrichment of psychoanalytic work, whether one is concerned with drives or the id, with coping styles or the ego, with interactions with others or object relations, with the self as the product of all of one's life experiences, or with the interrelationship of therapist and patient. Following Erika Fromm's systematic thinking, from which I benefited as her student, I mentioned several important hypnoanalysts, trying to understand their progressive view and use of hypnosis. In every case we realize that hypnosis can be a useful and beneficial technique to help people feel and get better. Because in hypnoanalysis the patient is given room to experience himself and his inner self directly, he reaps two benefits, among others. First, he takes more seriously his fantasy life, and second, he gets into the habit of connecting with his fantasy more often and for many things that he had previously separated from fantasy. In other words, he learns to practice self-hypnosis and to avoid the negative self-hypnosis that we often see in patients.

In all the theories listed we discover the early trend to be accepted, loved, cared for, and taken care of. Hypnosis helps us in this human need for attachment because it brings forth our own inner resources, strengths, talents, accomplishments, and positive traits, and it also helps us find the way to make them fit into our current life, occupation, and limitations. Every one of the theoreticians mentioned in this chapter agrees that hypnosis is a useful method to help people change from within and be happy with their creation of a new lifestyle.

To know more about the benefits of hypnosis, the references cited in this and the second chapter may be helpful. However, in addition to the required training in hypnotherapy, it will take time until one feels comfortable with this "new" approach for dealing with emotional pain and suffering. The final principle is clear. Every time we deal with another person, friend, relative, or patient, we can do whatever we may to activate his or her imagination and fantasy. The statement that "a picture is worth a thousand words" applies especially to human communication. In analysis we encourage people to share their fantasies with us, not first and foremost to interpret them but humbly to truly take them in and capture what they mean for the patient. In our psychoanalytic work, we put ourselves into their fantasy and try to make sense of the new fantasy from within. Hopefully, we do the same with our own fantasies outside the therapy work.

Hypnosis, as understood currently by many practitioners, occurs every time we enter the thinking mode that is mostly experiential (see Chapters 9 and 10), "as if we were there," and allow ourselves *not* to think rationally, critically, logically and analytically. The New Hypnosis—a larger umbrella than traditional hypnosis—covers all such situations, whether they happen because the person "is being hypnotized" or spontaneously, from night dreams to all sorts of reveries; whether we call them "hypnosis" or not, as we noted in the thinking of Theodor Reik and Carl Jung. As noted earlier, I suspect that their avoidance of the term *hypnosis* was due to the fact that, in those days, its use was too directive and authoritative, what Ferenczi called *paternal hypnosis*. This is especially useful to note in psychoanalysis because *maternal* hypnosis, in his view, facilitates the unconscious connection of current distress with past experiences, helping the patient to have a greater awareness of factors that have shaped his or her personality.

## Daily Living Applications

Mental rehearsal is a practical way of getting ready for something difficult or not wanted. The individual goes through in her mind the event she has to face, seeing herself doing it just right, relaxed, in perfect control, successful. This can be repeated until the person is convinced that she is "ready" to step into the real situation that before mental rehearsal seemed so hard.

Another hypnotic practice consists in activating two opposite parts of one's personality, the one that refuses to do something and the one that knows she can do it with some effort and determination. She may even give each a name or nickname, the "scaredy cat" and the "superwoman." She may visualize the two parts of her personality discussing the issue, why to do it, why not to do it. This practice makes the person own her strong qualities and overcome the weaknesses. As always, repetition is needed.

All the applications we bring up toward the end of each chapter require about 20 to 30 minutes of uninterrupted concentration in a private and secure place with the determination of leaving everything else for later.

CHAPTER 4

# Fantasy in Human Sexuality and Thinking

In every aspect of thinking there is fantasy — imagination, mental pictures, or visualization. In Sandler's (1975) view, Freud was convinced that daydreams, a clear manifestation of fantasy production, were very much like dreams, though in some ways different. In Sandler's words, "Thoughts, which include fantasies, differ from dreams in that in the latter only the concrete subject matter of thought is visually represented, not the relation between the various elements, the specific characteristic of thought" (p. 95). And he concludes that "fantasy ... is more than thinking in pictures, for it includes relations and hence is closely connected with verbal development" (p. 95). Some therapists applying hypnosis wrongly use expressions such as "going to sleep" or "waking up" that confuse the understanding of hypnosis. When we are in that different state of awareness, we are not asleep; we are closer to spontaneous daydreaming (Barber, 1979). In most cases fantasy precedes action or, conversely, nothing is done without fantasy. As stated earlier, it is impossible to think without some mental image in our mind.

Where do these fantasies come from? Sandler (1975) states that "Freud [no reference given] refers to fantasies as the product of a compromise in the struggle between what is repressed and what is dominant in the present" (p. 98). Earlier, Sandler had stressed the link between fantasy and the reality principle, citing *Two Principles of Mental Functioning* (Freud, 1911) and *The Introductory Lectures* (Freud, 1916).

Is fantasy so important because, as Jorge Luis Borges (1952) believed among many others following Freud (1908), we are always dreaming, asleep or awake, even in different levels of consciousness, preconsciousness, and mainly unconsciousness? Psychoanalysis realized, since the time of Freud, the importance and universality of fantasy, the indispensable component in mentalizations that have the power even to make or keep us sick or well. The mental causation of physical symptoms cannot be understood nor explained without the concept of fantasy. As a matter of fact, Gottlieb (2003) brilliantly explains that the whole idea of psychosomatic medicine, from Freud (1905a) and Janet (1889) to Simonton and Simonton (1978) and Rossi and Cheek (1988), relies heavily on fantasy. With Gottlieb (2003), we can summarize this key view of human behavior in the cryptic sentence, "Ideas can make us sick" (p. 875), as long as we understand, as he does, that the fundamental psychoanalytic question was set up by Groddeck (1923), "namely (what is for certain) the role of fantasy — primary unconscious fantasy — in the predisposition to, initiation of, and subsequent course of somatic diseases" (p. 875). Does fantasy also have an important role in healing? Alexander's (1943) theory of specificity offered an answer with the seven psychosomatic diseases he discussed, getting into which would take us too far away from our main concern. My wish is to emphasize the important role of fantasy in both mental as well as physical health and sickness. Scientifically, we know quite a bit about the role of fantasy in creativity and reality testing from the evidence of brain plasticity, though more research is needed to understand in detail how ideas make us sick or heal us from serious disease. Hypnosis activates fantasy, as the clinical experience of over a century has recorded, and thus it becomes a valuable method in psychotherapy.

    Because of this, it is unfortunate that behaviorists give little attention, if any, to "the unconscious in the obvious," to borrow the felicitous phrase of Ted Saretsky (2007) from Adelphi University, which often manifests itself in fantasies. Ordinary living experience, confirmed by philosophers and poets, tells us that the more we know about another person's fantasy, the better can we understand his personality and behavior. Obviously, this is not limited to psychoanalysis but applies also in dealing with friends or relatives, with corporate managers at any level, or with a boss in practically any business situation. In hypnosis, too, fantasy plays a pivotal role. By discovering the historical source of nonproductive fantasies we can modify them and make them positive and constructive. The New Hypnosis, facilitating the discovery of the origin of "negative self-hypnosis" (Araoz, 1981), called by Amen (1998) "automatic negative thoughts" or ANTs, helps patients to move gently into better places in thought and action. Finally, dreams are the free country of fantasy, as we shall see especially in the following two chapters.

## Human Sexuality and Fantasy

This chapter concentrates on the role of fantasy in realistic activities, especially in normal and spontaneous human sexuality, because patients can benefit from fantasy by using hypnosis. I am obviously excluding forced sex. Hanna Segal (1991) gives us a succinct formula: focus on fantasy in order to understand any human behavior, or in her own words, "Unconscious phantasy underlies and colours all our activities, however realistic" (p. 101). Regarding sexual behavior, even the most unlearned, healthy person realizes that fantasy makes sexuality exciting prior to the actual activity, during it, and later as a memory of the same. Without fantasy there is no sexual erotic stimulation. A stimulus becomes sexual because of the sexual fantasies it elicits in our mind. An example of the unique role of fantasy is the success of the pornography industry, because it triggers and facilitates fantasy in the consumer of pornography. The psychotic may not distinguish fantasy from reality, but others may benefit from fantasy to get themselves ready for activities that they are not sure about or even afraid of. Others (neurotics, according to Freud's list in his *Three Essays on the Theory of Human Sexuality* [1905b]) enjoy in fantasy activities that are completely forbidden in reality, from unprotected sex to bestiality and incest. Obviously, I am not focusing on diagnosis or on morality but simply on the presence of fantasy in sexual matters. For instance, many men in different cultures carry pictures of naked women who are typically complete strangers. This custom, in their belief, is a way of confirming their masculinity by activating their fantasy while looking at the pictures and experiencing some sexual excitement. These are examples of the power of fantasy in human sexuality, and of the fact that the sexuality Freud refers to is not necessarily biological but mostly the human attitude toward sex, which appears first and foremost in fantasy. These external objects, like a start button, trigger fantasies that produce some level of sexual arousal, thus reassuring the "practitioners" of their masculinity. This might be the advantage of distinguishing between symbolism and fantasy, because symbols, arising from objects, from symptoms, and from dreams, lead to many forms of

## 4. Fantasy in Human Sexuality and Thinking

artistic creation and are not necessarily expressions of repressed fantasies (Freud, 1900, 1923). Symbols are an idea in action. Thus, for instance, on the American one-dollar bill, the eagle of the Great Seal of the United States, looking to its right where he holds the laurels of peace, is a symbol representing the might of the country and the supposed preference for peace. The fantasy in pornography, however, is often the picture of the person with whom the "consumer" imagines himself involved in sexual activity. It might also be a memory or a mere fantasy of a sexual situation or partner. Fantasy, then, is the spice of human sexual behavior, from the very first exposure to any sexual feeling and, eventually, activity. A *New Yorker* cartoon presents a youngish couple in bed ready to end the day. He asks her, "What should we have sex about?" The activity is rather simple and direct, but the fantasy will give it a special meaning. The whole experience of the Oedipus complex, for most children, takes place just in imagination. Freud builds the case systematically. In an often-quoted letter to Fliess (Masson, 1985) from the year after Freud's father's death, he confesses, "I have found love of mother and jealousy of the father in my case too, and now believe it to be a general phenomenon of early childhood" (p. 223). Three years later he explains dreams (fantasy) based mostly on his own experience to generalize the Oedipus complex as existing in everybody. His scientific concern was suspended in this case.

On a different psychic level, sexual perversions could not exist without fantasy. According to Dor (1998), Lacan's emphasis on desire and his distinction among need, desire, and demand happens practically all in the realm of fantasy: "Because the subject first encounters his desire in a relationship to the other, based on the intentionality of need ... he will first experience his desire as *desire of the Other's desire*" (p. 182). Dor continues to explain that "the problematics of desire, formulated by Lacan in relation to need and demand, can be fully understood only with reference to Freud's theory of the first experience of satisfaction, in which Freud locates the essence of desire and the nature of its evolution" (p. 182). Dor elaborates this idea using the following Freudian sources, *A Project for a Scientific Psychology* (1895), *The Interpretation of Dreams* (1900), and *Instincts and Their Vicissitudes* (1915). We cannot forget that Lacan uses the noun *jouissance*, a sexual term in French street language, to designate the dynamics of desire. I suspect that he intends to remind us of the difficult aspect of sexual fantasy that makes many people uncomfortable. Many of the sexual fantasies do not coordinate with the individual's self-image.

Erotic transference and countertransference relate closely to sexual fantasy and the discomfort they all produce. Karlen (2008), with great wisdom, refers to this transferential experience as "conscious and unconscious erotic dynamics" (p. 20) and by this designation he means "the full spectrum of loving and sexual feeling, from affection, to devotion, to lust" (p. 20). Emphasizing the difficulty of dealing with sexual fantasy, he points out that Freud himself felt ambivalence about it. After "Freud called analysis a cure through love [he] saw erotic transference as a resistance to be subdued and erotic counter-transference a peril" (1915, p. 20). Karlen points out that this ambivalence was transformed by Freud's followers into dogma.

Therefore, when we mention fantasy, we always include sexual content, because fantasy makes human erotic expression possible and, unlike in other mammals, we are not moved to sexual action by drive or instinct alone. I have used hypnosis many times to help patients with sexual problems trigger sexual fantasies that may strengthen desire, activity, and satisfaction. I did this by fantasy alone, encouraging them to visualize themselves vividly in a concrete sexual situation, becoming aware of every detail, and allowing the lust and passion to increase, all in fantasy, with the added thought that all this could and probably would happen in reality with their preferred partner.

One of the reasons the analyst should train in sex hypnotherapy is the feeling of shame and embarrassment that has been accepted unconsciously by many patients and clinicians. Both avoid admitting sexual fantasies in themselves, based on the unconscious belief that sex is undignified, degrading, sinful, dirty, and so on. In hypnoanalysis, I often help patients to enjoy sex according to their values and, in doing so, to find pride and personality enrichment. Inviting them to "put themselves mentally in a sexual situation," they pre-live what they believed could not be. Hypnosis makes possible a new reality.

# Hidden Auto-hypnosis

Freud (1905b) had the courage to demonstrate that childhood sexual ignorance was a myth, thus making his name detestable in many circles of the Victorian era. Most myths are fantasy and, by destroying the myth of sexual innocence, Freud forces us to accept reality as it is and childhood sexuality as a natural element of human growth. Moreover, his concern with "the variations in form and structure that the sexual instinct takes" (1915, p. xxxiv), Freud compels us to recognize as natural forms of human sexuality that even he considered perversions, as Marcus Stevens (2000) wrote in the Introduction to the English version of *Three Essays* (1915). For Freud, perversions are "the general conditions under which mere variations of the sexual instinct pass over into pathological aberrations" (p. 27) and "the normal sexual aim is regarded as being the union of the genitals in the act known as copulation" (p. 15). Everything in sexual activity is understood by considering fantasy, always involved in what gives pleasure or "intensifies the excitation which should persist until the final sexual aim is attained" (p. 16). In other words, as the experience of normal, healthy people proves, mental images, spontaneous or helped by external stimuli, make possible sexual arousal, leading to sexual satisfaction.

In addition to the myth of childhood asexuality, there are still many myths related to female and male sexuality, or to sexual attraction and sexual fulfillment. Thus, common wisdom, buttressed by good research (e.g., Lips, 1997), declares that women score lower on the scale of primary sexual interest and curiosity, as well as in the degree of primary sexual needs, because women usually and universally consider sexual activity as part of the erotic and of adult love, whereas men, again generally, have the capacity to isolate sexual activity from emotional involvement in it. From our perspective, the interesting point is that all this fantasy in ordinary sexuality and even in nonsexual situations like psychotherapy, in pornography or virtual sex including perversions, as well as in factual perversions, is a form of self- or auto-hypnosis according to what I said in the Introduction regarding the designation of therapeutic hypnosis and negative self-hypnosis. It is through fantasy that the person gets to the point that he or she reacts to the mental productions *as if they were truly and genuinely reality situations*: what is in one's imagination becomes "real" in the sense that it produces the same or similar effects as reality would. The three elements of the psychoanalytic kaleidoscope—fantasy, hypnosis, and sexuality—become inseparable.

If all true hypnosis allows the person to focus so intently on one's mental images or fantasies that they become more vivid than the external reality from which one is momentarily disconnected, as Erickson taught and practiced (Rossi, 1980), pornography is often a natural "hypnotist" for those who use it with the intention of obtaining sexual pleasure. This may be the reason to justify the use of "virtual pornographic imagery" as part of the therapy of patients who are overly inhibited in sexual matters.

> This was the case of Jan, a man in his forties from a strict religious background who wanted to please his wife, who enjoyed cunnilingus. However, he could not shake the emotional belief that women who enjoyed this variety of sex were always "women of ill repute," as he put it in his careful vocabulary. I asked Jan if he had ever been with women of ill repute and he narrated the one occasion in his late teens in the military service, when he had been "weak enough" to let himself be convinced by his buddies to go to "one of those places." He had been scared and feeling so guilty that what was supposed to be pleasurable became mental torture. Jan regretted that experience even after many years. We discussed what he felt then toward the woman (a young, beautiful, innocent-looking girl) and his guilt came up. I used Watkins's (1954) hypnodynamic technique of *personality parts* or ego-state therapy in order to separate the current mature, adult self from the 19-year-old who felt he was sinning and taking advantage of an innocent girl. He was able to engage the two parts of his personality in a conversation (repeated several times in his hypnoanalysis) during which the adult self assisted the younger self to "forgive" himself. This intervention helped him discontinue the neurotic regression that had caused so much trouble in his mind and in his marriage.
> 
> After this significant step in therapy, Jan started to consider his wife completely different from that "innocent girl." His wife became the woman he loved, trusted, and with whom he happily shared his life and his pleasure. He himself came up with the notion that cunnilingus was another form — special, unique, and privileged — of kissing his wife. He believed that ordinary kissing, with all its sexual manifestations between two committed persons, is an honorable, spiritual expression of love and commitment. Cunnilingus, however, was a more complete celebratory expression of that love and commitment. The New Hypnosis made it possible for this patient to quickly move into a healthy frame of mind by identifying with the adult ego, thus liberating himself from the younger id drives as well as from his rigid superego, which had been controlling his thinking and his life. In the subsequent analytic work, he realized that he had been using religion as an excuse for resisting being himself, and cunnilingus as the excuse to avoid sexual contact, due to the long-unquestioned belief that abstinence was more meritorious and pleasing to God than sexual

pleasure. This insight made it possible for Jan to take realistic steps to be enriched by religion, giving up a literal understanding of his faith while holding on to the spirit of his religion, integrating sex into his values. The encouraging point in all this is that the patient himself "reframed" the situation and started to consider cunnilingus, which earlier he had regarded "sinful and dirty," as definitely honorable. In so doing he felt free from his use of religion as a resistance to full living and to taking responsibility for his choices. With this progress, his analysis continued with greater honesty, questioning his motivations, perceptions, and self-talk with greater freedom and courage than before his great sexual insight.

## Sexual Fantasy in Normal Human Development

Returning to the subject of normal human development, we realize that the entire phallic object in the castration complex takes place in fantasy, as Freud (1923) puts it: "We know how children react to the first impressions of the absence of a penis. They disavow the fact and believe that they *do* see a penis all the same. They gloss over the contradiction between observation and preconception by telling themselves that the penis is still small and will grow bigger presently; and they then come to the emotionally significant conclusion that after all, the penis had at least been there before and had been taken away afterwards" (p. 143). This clear explanation of the castration complex again emphasizes fantasy and describes a form of negative self-hypnosis. The child convinces himself of the castration reality as a deduction from a false premise and an explanation of what he sees. It is all fantasy, but because he takes it for real, it is also hypnotic. As mentioned earlier, negative self-hypnosis (NSH) takes place when a person focuses unconsciously so much on something negative (a failure, a sickness, a bad outcome, etc.) that the fantasy of it (thought, conviction, imagery) increases tremendously the chances of it going wrong. Seligman (1995), among many others, has shown how negative thinking does produce negative outcome. The opposite is fortunately also proven right (Begley, 2007). Positive thoughts facilitate positive results, and New Hypnosis, in Buddhist style, makes positive thoughts one's own. Therefore, if the child does not resolve the NSH of the castration complex, that mental reality will most probably be a source of unhappiness for the rest of his life.

## Is It Still Perversion?

Because fantasy happens as part of our development early in life, humans keep using fantasy in normal sexual development. This explains Freud's (1905b) placing the perverse process in the normal and universal unfolding of human sexuality. The difficulty for us, over a century after Freud, lies in the fact that he considered adult heterosexual genital copulation the only *ideally normal* or non-pathological sexual activity, excluding other choices that modern sexology does not consider necessarily perversions at all, such as homosexual sex, oral sex, sexual enjoyment with more than one partner, different sexual positions, anal sex, mutual masturbation, and the like.

Nowadays we would say that perversion is found when the person experiences an urgent and fixed desire to engage in any form of sexual behavior that deviates from the social norm, either in quality or in frequency. Thus, forcing sex on others (children, the mentally challenged, the imprisoned, etc.) and any other form of rape are definitely perversions. There is no perversion when any number of types of sexual activities are added to "normal" genital intercourse, by mutual consent of the adult partners, in the interpretation of Knafo and Feiner (2006), for instance.

This process of selecting sexual activities is done, in part, through repression, which seems to be the reason for Freud's assertion that neurotic symptoms are always related to the sexual drive. In his words, "these psychoneuroses are based on sexual instinctual forces" (1905b, p. 128). Freud emphasizes that the instinctual force is "the most important and only constant source of energy of the neurosis and that in consequence the sexual life of the persons in question is expressed ... in these symptoms" (p. 128). He concludes by stating that "symptoms are formed in part at the cost of *abnormal* sexuality; neuroses are, so to say, the negative of perversions" (1905b, p. 129). When fantasy becomes one's reality we are talking about hypnosis, with which the individual, unconsciously, is moved toward perversion or transforms it into neurotic symptoms. We owe to Freud the insight into many symptoms that are manifestations of repressed sexuality issues.

## 4. Fantasy in Human Sexuality and Thinking

# Fantasy as a Form of Auto-Hypnosis

This brings up again the question of natural hypnosis. If fantasy becomes one's reality, and if hypnosis makes this process naturally possible, we can say that the pervert unconsciously uses self-hypnosis when choosing perversions, as does the sexually healthy person with auto-hypnosis in any sexual activity. Freud (1905b) had mentioned "the mental factor in the perversions" (p. 126). This is nothing other than auto-hypnosis, specifically the new type of hypnosis as it is accepted nowadays, making it possible for the individual to create with auto-hypnosis his own reality in order to act on it. Here is an example.

> Ollie was a 59-year-old patient with sexual difficulties after a prostatectomy. He masturbated as he "imagined" a beautiful young woman whom he knew sitting naked in front of him, touching and fellating him. He "touched" her and gave her cunnilingus until "both" reached orgasm. He knew the girl was all fantasy. He used it as others use pornography with the aid of movies or magazines. This was his preference and, without his knowing it, he was practicing auto-hypnosis.
>
> Another case was Sanah, a 57-year-old woman, divorced and not wanting to remarry, who dated many men, most of them quite a lot younger than her. Even though she enjoyed sex with her partners, she also used fantasy to reexperience alone some of the situations she had savored with them. She also imagined them touching her, having oral sex with her, engaging in vaginal and anal sex, stimulating her nipples, until she reached a very exciting orgasm. And Sanah did not know that what she was doing was auto-hypnosis.

Are these perversions, from Freud's point of view, wishful thinking, psychotic hallucinations, or simply auto-hypnosis in the service of the ego? The point of this discussion is to stress the intimate connection between sexuality, fantasy, and hypnosis in order to remind us that the three components give us the psychoanalytic kaleidoscope of healthy sexuality based on fantasy and hypnosis. In the same kaleidoscopic form, if we focus on hypnosis, we realize that sexual fantasy makes self-hypnosis possible. To understand human sexuality, we must consider the individual's unconscious fantasies, and in order to use hypnosis effectively in psychoanalysis we must also recognize the pivotal role of fantasy with many sexual components in the hypnotic process.

## Suggestibility and Fantasy

Finally, we tie this to suggestibility, mentioned in Chapter 1. The message that the analyst conveys to a patient by means of New Hypnosis elicits a fantasy on the part of the latter. Otherwise, the message without the fantasy is purely intellectual. For instance, if the patient is invited to see himself as he is now helping the child he was when he suffered sexual abuse by an important adult, the probable image elicited by this invitation is what I just described: that of the adult self coming to the rescue of the child and protecting him from the abuser. The suggestion is for the patient to focus more sharply on positive aspects of his ego. This means that New Hypnosis activates the superego, encouraging the patient to live up to strong emotions like his own unconscious expectations of goodness, success, generosity, and such. These are traits that the ego had become distracted from, while not dealing well with the past abuse.

Hypnosis makes it easier for the patient to give up the influence of the id and to allow the ego to take over. But because of the transference elements of hypnotic suggestion, the ego is now already informed by the superego. In sequence, then, we may say that the hypnotic indirect suggestion creates unconscious fantasies that are part of the transferential process at work here. Because of the patient's suggestibility in the positive transference, the superego is not resisted but rather is allowed to become the ruler. This is the by now familiar process of creating a new neural pathway by repetition.

> Let me summarize the clinical case of Emmo, a 32-year-old patient who had been isolated from normal sexual development all his life, having started at 13 in the seminary to become a Catholic priest. He started analysis almost twenty years later, after five years working in a small church and in an administrative position in the Bishop's offices. Now still a virgin, he was bothered by fantasies of sexual play with young adolescents. Because he recognized that he had been deprived of normal social development, he felt a delayed need to have sexual experiences. Emmo came to the realization that his attraction to young men came out of fear of women, with whom he had had nothing romantic or sexual to do in his life. The only women who were harmless when he entered the seminary were his mother, his ten-year-older sister, and Mary, the mother of Jesus, who had become a frequent nonsexual fantasy that placed him in a mental state of sexlessness. These three females were Madonnas; all others were whores.

## 4. Fantasy in Human Sexuality and Thinking

In analysis, Emmo had said several times that he wished he could end all those sexual fantasies with youngsters. When asked what stopped him from acting on his fantasies, he answered that a force stronger than he pushed him to engage in sexual activities but another force "from God" stopped him, but left him depressed, unhappy, guilty, as well as physically weak and in pain after normal masturbation. He visualized this sexual force as an electric-like energy that started all by itself. This began a long exchange with me on his inner forces, concluding with his resolution to place his ego in the ruling position. He used hypnosis to clearly imagine "the change of governments" by which the id (and the strict superego) lost power while the ego took over. Many of these elements came up repeatedly in his free association.

In hypnosis as well, Emmo discovered new object relations. He saw himself reacting differently to young males and starting to become more sexually aware of young women. Several months went by before he recognized the distinction between sexual fantasies, often accompanied by the physical change of an erection in his body, and sexual action. This helped him accept the difference between voluntary and unconscious sexual reactions. This was the point of freedom for Emmo. Sexual fantasy and desire did not mean the inevitability of acting on them. In hypnosis, he saw himself as not having to stay with the mere fantasy of sex but also as not compelled to engage in sexual action. Therefore, feeling genuinely free for the first time in his life, he started enjoying heterosexual sex while still working as a priest. By now he was in his third year of analysis with two weekly sessions. The sexual aspect of Emmo's life led him to examine his entire existence, especially the changes he had experienced in the last years. He decided to take a one-year leave of absence that prolonged itself to three, before he retired from the priesthood to become a public relations officer in a large and active community service organization at his thirty-eighth birthday.

Taking a closer look at this case, we see the sequence of steps described earlier, which ended in the definite state of the ego refined and enriched by the benign superego taking control of Emmo's life and allowing him to act on his belief that no human can bar other humans from activities like sex that are natural, that is, a component part of being human. We may consider this real personal freedom, in accordance with Beres (1958), who views punishment in cases like this as a loss of self-esteem and as an expression of guilt. When Emmo had no true individual superego, he felt guilty thinking of breaking the no-sex command of the institution. After analysis, he accepted his own superego that encouraged him to be wholly himself, a sexual person. Sexuality became an important and very positive part of his life, accepted with the hypnotic activation of fantasy.

# Summary

Fantasy comes from what we experience in one way or another; in actuality or in our mind as desire or as apprehension. Because the body is "the vessel through which the infant mind gathers data and develops," in Pfeffer's (2006) beautiful and exact words, "sexuality embodies the earliest somatic experiences" (p. 14). This is the reason the experience of being human includes sexuality in a central and prominent place. As mentioned earlier in this chapter, there is no deliberate sexuality without fantasy and, more generally, there is no mentation or thinking without some form of sexual fantasy. This makes fantasy the essential element of experience as much in sexuality as in all other aspects of being human. In fact, this includes different ego states like dreaming or being in hypnosis, things which could not come to be without fantasy.

Fantasy and hypnosis go hand in hand. Hypnosis always includes fantasy and fantasy often becomes hypnotic, though mostly in an unconscious manner. Among the hidden hypnosis is negative self-hypnosis (NSH), which frequently sabotages what we want to do consciously. What hypnosis can do in psychoanalysis is to use and activate fantasy so that the patient can more quickly free herself from the grip of the id, as well as from negative unconscious elements and from the power of the death instinct in order to let the ego, enriched by the healthy superego, take over and help the patient enjoy her life. This change takes place through hypnoanalysis, using the natural suggestibility of the patient. But the indirect hypnotic suggestions do not originate from the analyst's fantasies, values, and hopes; they come from what the patient, becoming healthy in analysis, has decided is best for her. This could be the case of Emmo, or that of a woman considering divorce. In hypnosis she can experience what it feels like to be divorced, as opposed to being in an unsatisfying marriage and afraid of divorce.

One point to emphasize is that fantasy is always subjective, and thus a challenge for the analyst to truly enter into the fantasy of the patient. Pfeffer (2006) quotes Lewes (1998): "Since only the analysand

#### 4. Fantasy in Human Sexuality and Thinking

himself can provide information about the particular experience in his life, *the analyst must purge himself of all values and expectations*, including ... even the hope that the analysand improve, so that he might enter fully into the world of the patient" (Pfeffer, p.16, my emphasis). Pfeffer insists that "the analyst must have an awareness of what those values and expectations [of himself] are" (p. 16) so that the specifics of how the patient improves fall into the patient's categories, not into those of the analyst.

New Hypnosis is an experience in which one can detach from one's own values and beliefs, perceptions, and expectations. Therefore, when the analyst senses tension and difference between his and the patient's position, he can use self-hypnosis to "purge himself of all values and expectations," as Lewes said. We shall deal with this in the following two chapters. The next chapters present specific psychoanalytic techniques appropriate to hypnoanalysis. Before studying techniques it is beneficial to remember and welcome Fink's (2007) general and wise warning in his preface about the use of techniques, and his insightful comments about the difference between the treatment of neurotics, with whom "repression and the unconscious [should be] their guiding lights " (p. x), and of psychotics, with whom repression is absent. Especially with hypnotic techniques, it is prudent to be very discriminating, because popular authors often present these techniques almost as magical incantations that work with everybody, from the act itself, regardless of the patient's receptivity or of her diagnosis.

However, before proceeding, I would like to close this chapter by focusing on the culturally different and naturally open attitude of Buddhism toward sex. The masters of mind training, through hypnotic methods, developed healthy attitudes toward sexual activity, stressing sensuality, as in Tantric Buddhism. The main idea is that we are not fully human if we neglect and dismiss our sexuality, which is an unavoidable part of our nature. The "aberration" is to reject sensuality, avoiding sex. Buddhism insists that complete human sex is mostly "spiritual" (or not purely physical) but that we cannot enjoy the nonphysical dimension of sex without intense and persevering new hypnotic work in meditation. Chapter 12 will deal more with relevant Buddhist teachings for psychotherapy. That chapter offers many hypnotic possibilities that can be used and applied in daily living. They are not restricted to hypnoanalysis. Just the hypnotic activity of spending a few minutes rehearsing enjoyable and satisfying sex can bring improvement to what may have become almost an obligation.

CHAPTER 5

# Dreaming, Fantasy and Auto-hypnosis

Dreams are at the core of psychoanalytic clinical practice, especially for Jungian analysts. The topic has been discussed in depth since the early days of our profession, following the example of Freud (1900) himself in his first published book. I owe much to two contemporary dream experts, Paul Lippmann (2000), and Mark Blechner (2001), among several others, together with Bruce Fink (2007), whom I consider one of the best sources in English for understanding Lacan as a supreme Freudian. Each added valuable details to the initial Freudian concepts about dreams. From past sources in my early training, I learned about fantasy and dreaming from the writings of Theodor Reik (1948), Erich Fromm (1951), Harry Stack Sullivan (1973), and others. Both Freud and Jung, despite their disagreements, consider dreams the most direct way to the unconscious and, because dreams are quintessential fantasy, their relationship to hypnosis is immediate. As a matter of fact, it could be said that hypnosis is a particular type of dreaming.

## Scientific Value of Dream Study

Many among the self-anointed "scientific" psychologists dismiss dreams and the way we in psychoanalysis view and use them. They label them as irrational nonsense, to be considered only in the neurological aspect of dreaming. Among many examples, Rychlak (1968) demanded pure rationality that is objective, factual, and duplicable, in every psychological field, though he concentrated on personality development. Al Rubaie (2003), a scientist with medical and psychological degrees and with clinical experience in England, Spain, Austria, Caribbean America, and Iraq, attributes the problem of science and pseudoscience to the enormous influence of Descartes in Western thought, with his strict distinction between objectivity and subjectivity. I personally have found, talking to some behaviorists, that any mention of psychodynamics, especially dreams related to inner states, elicits smiles of condescension and even pity. But, as Al Rubaie (2003), citing Epstein (1981), reminds us, scholars in the field of hypnotherapy have confused the issue by allowing right cerebral hemispheric functioning to be described with left hemispheric terminology. Al Rubaie concludes by emphasizing that knowledge is not the same as science "nor can [all] knowledge be reduced to science" (p. 3), adding that processes of the right hemisphere, like dreams, are not irrational and illogical but rather are non-rational and non-logical. "The right cerebral hemisphere is considered as the anatomical host of the unconscious mind and its activity as the physiological correlate of the unconscious mode of thinking" (Al Rubaie, 2003, p. 3).

Because, as Tart (1965) has researched, there are four different responses to waking dreams, specifically to induced dreams — a dream-like hypnotic experience, intense hypnotic imagery, daydreaming, and little imagery but intense concentration on one idea — there is controversy and confusion regarding how and when to interpret the induced dream. Some (e.g., Waxman, 1989) claim that interpretation in the state of hypnosis is more effective. Others, like Haley (1993), seem to advise that the clinician be also in hypnosis. Finally, many (e.g., Boss, 1977) prefer the induced dream interpretation in the waking state, as I do.

## Induced Dreams

That the right hemisphere is mostly "responsible" for our unconscious activities does not mean that we cannot activate these functions, resulting in hypnotic or induced dreams. We do so, in and out of therapy, in daydreams, in vivid recollections, and in other ways. One of the methods to activate right hemispheric functions is by means of induced dreams. As a parenthesis, I would remind the reader that the phrase "wakened dream," used by Desoillé (1971), is a contradiction in terms if taken literally (which Desoillé does not) because "waken" implies conscious, and "dream" unconscious. This state of *rêve éveillé* could exist when one starts the induced dream, but could not be used for the dream itself.

Returning now to the dreams that are induced hypnotically, we need to remember that hypnoanalysis distinguishes between spontaneous or natural dreams and induced dreams (Sacerdote, 1967b), so that in practice much of the time spent in hypnoanalysis centers on "dreams." Induced dreams produce a hypnotic state. In other words, active imagination or active fantasy is the practical tool for working through in hypnoanalysis. And as Erika Fromm (1992) states in the introduction to Sacerdote's book, this therapeutic work becomes an "effective way of shortening treatment without sacrificing depth" (p. vii). In Erika Fromm's thinking, empowering the patient is essential to successful analysis. Therefore, the practical aspects of abbreviating the length of treatment proper, and teaching patients to use their dreams for self-analysis, first between sessions and later after formal termination, does not have to take anything away from psychoanalytic depth, utilizing the patient's unconscious for her benefit and growth. All the experiences had in psychoanalysis become more immediate and direct in hypnoanalysis, because the interference of rational thinking, frequently with its accompanying resistance, is avoided, and this makes the road from id to ego smoother.

What the patient discovers about the self, either in regular analysis or with hypnosis, is the same previous mystery of unconscious unknowns and, more often than not, of long repressed material, often sexual. In hypnoanalysis this discovery happens more directly, and is an especially moving experience. This is because the patient is taught to use auto-hypnosis outside of the session as an ongoing continuation of her analytic work.

Any fantasy the patient presents can be integrated into an induced hypnotic dream. Although later I will address myself to the induced dream in the process of psycho(hypno)analysis, here is an example.

> A therapist, Dr. B., in supervision with me, finds one of her patients very dull and boring. She says, "I would swear he is asleep, talking in his sleep." After a few minutes hearing more information about the patient, I asked her to close her eyes, pay attention to her breathing, and allow a dream about the patient to form. After a couple of minutes, Dr. B., now in the ego state of New Hypnosis or mind training, tells me that she is in an outdoor field that has a few trees grouped in different places. The day is exceptionally beautiful. She sees her

## 5. Dreaming, Fantasy and Auto-hypnosis

patient, though he does not see her. She feels angry, saying, "I can't get rid of him, even here." She hides behind a tree and looks back in the direction of the patient, who now has laid down to sleep. I suggest that she interpret her dream by returning to her ordinary way of thinking and she says that she knows what she dreamt and that it has meaning for her. She ends by saying, "It's my dream, but that's all there is to it."

This is reminiscent of Blechner's (2001) model of dream interpretation, which starts from the realization that "the dream is not concerned with communicability" (p. 9), which seems to be close to an important statement of Lacan (1977): "The real is what is impossible to speak" (p. 14). In my understanding, Dr. B. meant that her dream was primarily an idiosyncratic, existential experience with real meaning for her, and thus impossible to communicate verbally to others. The central point is *to acknowledge, accept, and understand the meaning* of the dream, not to explain it verbally. However, elements of the induced dream may be useful in the future. Dr. B., several months after the experience with the induced dream, commented on the fact that she felt invisible with this patient. I asked if she thought this had something to do with that detail in her dream when she was able to see him but he did not see her. Dr. B.'s insight in trying to respond truthfully to me had to do with her attitude that made it impossible for the patient "to see" her, that is, to know anything about her inner self.

To return to the induced dream itself, to my question whether she wanted me to know what the dream was all about, Dr. B. had responded that she could not tell me any more about what the dream was but that, thanks to the dream, she was now at peace with her negative feelings about her patient. Later, in the above scene, she realized that she was at least partly responsible for her negative feelings toward her patient. Initially, she had added that the dream made her understand that the patient was not with her to socialize, entertain her, or please her, that he had a depressive personality, and that she had to work with him the way he was, not the way she, countertransferentially, wanted him to be. Several months later she questioned the original insight as an excuse for not doing anything in order to diminish her negative reactions to the patient. In a sense, the induced dream had no mysterious meaning but *produced* a psychic change in Dr. B. It affected the way she related to this patient. As a psychoanalyst, Dr. B. used her dream about the patient efficiently, respectfully, and with humility, as if she had read the wonderful chapter of Lippmann's (2000) book in order to prevent "the analyst's neurotic style" from damaging the significance of the dream. Incidentally, this anecdote from my own experience is from the mid–1980s, about two decades before either Lippmann's or Blechner's books were published.

A concluding observation might be useful. Even though some may insist on differentiating fantasy and dreams, I find it difficult to do so in clinical practice. For me all dreams are fantasy, even though not all fantasy takes place in a dream state. However, if the person stays in his fantasy for a while, I believe that he enters the ego state of hypnosis, often without realizing that it becomes a dream-like state. And as we know from our clinical experience, often many references to sexuality appear spontaneously — again the psychoanalytic kaleidoscope of hypnosis, fantasy, and sexuality.

One theory justifying the use of a patient's fantasy to start a dream is that this method brings forth unconscious material with little effort and with much genuineness. With Sacerdote (1967b), I start from the premise that the dynamics of induced dreams are "equivalent" or practically the same as those of night dreams. His emphasis on "equivalence in psychological, intellectual and emotional, not necessarily in physiological terms" (p. 39) comes from what was known at the time from the EEG during natural dreams and in hypnosis. Almost four decades later, Blechner (2001) described what he calls "endoneuropsychic perception" (p. 270), expanding on Freud's (1933) endopsychic perception, the delusion of being judged, a psychotic symptom attributed to the superego during dreams. Blechner explains, "By that we mean that certain psychological phenomena may represent an insight into the organization of the brain" (p. 270). Freud (1900), in one of the very few places where he connects dream interpretation and hypnosis, refers to sexual symbolism in dreams and mentions an experiment by Schrotter, who had suggested the production of a dream to "deeply hypnotized" subjects. The fact that Freud mentions this and does not criticize it leads us to believe that he saw some value in this procedure. (For a wealth of neurological information regarding sleep, in wakened and dream states, see Blechner's [2001] Chapters 20 and 21.) Because the issue is still undefined, and because the subjective experience of hypnosis is likened to sleep by most people who experience hypnosis, I stay with Sacerdote's "equivalence theory" (see also Sacerdote, 1967a).

## 5. Dreaming, Fantasy and Auto-hypnosis

Thus throughout hypnoanalysis, the intellectual narrative and factual descriptions by the patient are minimized in favor of fantasy work, because in our dreams we are brutally honest with ourselves, but in symbolic ways whose meaning we have to discover, being careful of not intellectualizing the entire process, after Al Rubaie's (2003) advice. The effort on the part of the analyst is to help the patient "translate" into fantasy any thought or concept that can be expressed in mental images.

> This was the case of Alan, a 60-something married patient, who was talking intellectually about his "infatuation" with a woman less than half his age. She did not know about his attraction because he dealt with her very professionally in his business. I suggested then that Alan allow himself to have a dream in the session about the situation.

Note that the guideline proposed is very general, "a dream about the situation," not specifically about the young woman. To get into mind training or New Hypnosis, I used a hypnotic prop, mentioning an imaginary mental movie screen where images will appear. I have found this helpful, mostly with patients prone to intellectualize, in order to make the transition from ordinary thinking to the special hypnotic mode.

Alan's dream was about him and the young woman relaxing in her apartment, which he had never visited. However, it should be mentioned that this open-ended induced dream could have been about their making love, about the young woman rejecting him, about his wife finding out about the situation, etc. Or the induced dream might not be directly related to the young woman. It might have been more symbolic if Alan had dreamt that he was by the sea in the midst of a storm, or that his house was on fire and he was looking at it from the street, where he had ran to for safety. Whatever the topic or manifest content of the induced dream, the subsequent analytic discussion will focus on the patient's feelings, insights, and reality testing. The general principle is to use the images that come up spontaneously, or to convert a topic into a sequence of images. The goal is always the same: to get in touch with unconscious feelings and fantasies, both positive and negative, in order to gain deeper insight into oneself, with beneficial insights leading to freedom from unconscious repetition compulsion and from emotional reactions still tied to childhood events.

To the resistance of patients to participate in this type of analysis, presented as objections ("I can't force myself to dream," "I don't want to waste time fantasizing," etc.), my response might be to point out that many "images" about the situation are already in his unconscious and that it may become easier for him to decide how to proceed in reality if he becomes aware of these unconscious fantasies.

In a few cases of this type of resistance, with great caution, I have shared with the patient the fantasies that come to *my* mind elicited by his or her dream; they become my own induced dream. In Alan's case, my fantasy was of the patient sneaking into the young woman's apartment with a bottle of wine as a present, and she greeting him at the door with great affection, as if they had been lovers for a long time. On the contrary, I also might have "dreamt" that she tells him this cannot be, that she is sorry but this affair is a bad idea, apologizing and feeling afraid of losing her job for rejecting his wishes. Depending on how well we know our patient and at what point he is in his analysis, we may even share some of our own fantasies *as a fantasy*, not as a judgment or criticism of the patient. In several cases I had the opportunity of the patient seeking meaning in my own induced dream. The patient, as well as I, always has benefited from the insights derived from that analysis. We do not make up our "dream" consciously and later "analyze" with the patient.

Induced dreams are one of the better examples of New Hypnosis. The clinician does not use commands, as the old traditional hypnotist did, but gently suggests a change of thinking modality (the waking dream), switching from rational into experiential thinking, moving from ideas and words to spontaneous images and fantasy. Making sure that the patient is relaxed helps him avoid ordinary thinking, becoming more able to accept the images, memories, associations, and other inner and spontaneous productions without understanding them intellectually. Afterwards the patient will find the meaning — part of the movement toward ego functioning.

## Dynamics of Dreams

Perhaps Lippmann (2000) emphasizes the dynamic nature of dreams more than others, as if he is telling us that all the dreams we shall ever dream are already there, in the darkness of the unconscious because, as he puts it, "they live beneath the surface" (p. 160). Freud also considered dream dynamics but initially he saw the main purpose of the

## 5. Dreaming, Fantasy and Auto-hypnosis

dream as *wish fulfillment*. Slowly Freud modified his theory and added other meanings, such as fears, reflections continuing in the sleep state, or a creative thought, in the case of Dora (1905a), or attempted wish fulfillments in the *New Introductory Lectures* (1933). Finally, in the *Outline of Psychoanalysis* (1940), he made the distinction between dreams that make a demand upon the ego and those that originate from the id for the satisfaction of an instinct, and listed "solution of a conflict, removal of a doubt or the forming of an intention" (p. 169). In spite of his ideological developments, Freud always maintained the psychodynamic nature of dreams.

Hanna Segal (1991) summarizes Freud's position, starting from the premise that dreams express and elaborate unconscious fantasies and fulfill many functions. The dream

> provides a phantasy expression of unconscious conflict and seeks a phantasy solution — wish fulfillment. Dream-work is part of the elaboration of unconscious conflict. It provides also an intrapsychic communication between the unconscious and the conscious. When we remember a dream we retain communication with symbolic expressions of the unconscious. In the analytical process, this internal communication becomes also a means of communication with the analyst [Segal, 1991, p. 64].

In the way Segal understands wishful thinking as a fantasy solution, she joins Jung and many psychoanalysts who rejected the superficial understanding of wish fulfillment as "wanting what I cannot have." Segal's emphasis on fantasy explains what wish fulfillment truly means, although in Jung's (1934) thinking the fantasy in dreams "co-operates with an integral consciousness" (p. 104). This is Jung's theory of *compensation*, which is seen as opposed to Freud's of wish fulfillment. But according to Blechner (2001), "compensation itself always implies ... a wish for balance in one's life ... to bring to one's life that which one does not have" (p. 110).

All this is interesting because of the importance of fantasy, which seems to be meaningful and not random. Perhaps because of this aspect of the nature of fantasy, dreams have been considered prophetic and even predictors of health status (see Blechner, 2001; Lippmann, 2000).

The *dynamics* of dreams, therefore, refer to one aspect of what Yalom (1980) calls a model of mental functioning, which he considers "Freud's major contribution to the understanding of the human being"

(p. 6). Dreams confront us with the "forces in conflict within (us) and ... thought, emotion and behavior, both adaptive and psychopathological, are the resultant of these conflicts" (p. 6). Yalom emphasizes that *"these forces exist at various levels of awareness"* (p. 6, his emphasis). Because of this, and remembering Freud's statement that dreams are the royal road to the unconscious, hypnoanalysis was developed. By returning to night dreams in hypnosis, or by facilitating new hypnotic induced dreams in the hypnoanalytic sessions, we keep in constant touch with the unconscious and the personal dynamics it otherwise keeps from consciousness.

A final brief note of dream dynamics refers to sexual images or symbols in the dream. They are not, just because they are sexual, necessarily connected with the dreamer's real sexual activity. Many sexual dreams, or rather dreams of sexual content, are not related to one's real sexuality, as clinical experience has shown, but refer to dynamics that are symbolized with sexual images, such as power, lust, pleasure and joy, surrender or possession, anger, humiliation, freedom, rebellion, and so on.

## Clinical Use of Induced Dreams

From the previous introduction to the topic, it is easy to realize the possible clinical value of dream work. All the practical points that are made for ordinary dreams in terms of therapeutic effects apply also to induced hypnotic dreams. Because of the way induced dreams are hypnotically elicited, we reach the unconscious respectfully and unobtrusively. As in the case of Dr. B., the therapist who disliked her patient, I will suggest a dream about the topic at hand, without being more specific than that. In this case, without allying myself with any of the details of the various theories of dreaming synthesized by Blechner (2001), I help the patient obtain meaning from her dream. What the patient brings up is uniquely her own personalized material, keeping in mind Blechner's theory that in dreams we often express what cannot be expressed in words or "extralinguistic thinking" (p. 25). Instead of asking, "What does that mean?" I find it more effective to ask, "How does that make you feel?" or "What does that bring to your mind?" or "Notice your feeling reaction to that [aspect of the dream]," as we saw in the case of Dr B.

## 5. Dreaming, Fantasy and Auto-hypnosis

In practice, when we use induced dreams, we employ a form of hypnosis that is completely idiosyncratic and, again, very different from the general understanding of hypnosis. Without planning and with little effort on our part, it is always naturally tailored to fit the patient, because the induced dream always originates in the patient's unconscious. Unlike traditional hypnosis, which offered the hypnotist's interpretation as a suggestion, and thus its value lasted as long as the patient had faith in the hypnotist, this type of hypnosis centers on the patient, helps her accept her own interpretation *based on the individual meaning* it has for her, not on the power of the hypnoanalyst. This important point explains the benefits and success of hypnosis in analysis (Fink, 2007).

What moves us to use the elements of the induced or hypnotic dream therapeutically is the assumption that the induced dream material is a bit of data that is meaningful for the dreamer and that *the meaning is unconscious*. All the authors cited in this section show us that there are several effective modalities to uncover *the meaning* of our dreams in general and especially of induced dreams, remembering that the English translation from the German of Freud's title of his book on dreaming is not "interpretation" of dreams, but *Bedeutung*, that is "significance" or "meaning" of our dreams. Fink's (2007) Chapter 6 is a wonderful summary of the therapeutic use of dreams. One of these interpretation modalities is the *recipient* method, allowing the patient to stay with the dream (or with elements of it) in order to accept and savor the feelings it elicits until they become a uniquely personal experience. I realize that to talk about "savoring" one's feelings may be confusing, but words cannot express clearly how we can make a dream image genuinely our own and thus grow and benefit by it. In this way, helping the patient to stay with her dream, much can be accomplished, because the identification with her dream produces a form of shorter free association and brings out new *Bedeutung* from the dream.

The second modality is *associative*, asking the patient to allow associations to the dream or any of its parts. The more spontaneous these associations are, the more probably they are unconscious. The analyst stresses that they do not have to make sense at this stage.

The third method of finding *Bedeutung* to an induced dream is *active*, encouraging the patient to continue using what she remembers of the dream the way a writer would use those elements to write a short story, in other words, to complete the dream in a re-dreaming way.

Finally, the *feedback* method, one of Erich Fromm's (1951) ways of interacting with the patient honestly, and of confronting the patient with her resistance, consists of sharing with her one's own images, fantasies, and associations. The patient is asked for her reaction to the analyst's reactions to her dream.

Please notice that in hypnoanalysis we never start hypnotic work without the patient offering the first step (e.g., a small piece of a dream, a figure of speech, an important statement, gestures or any other body movement). Out of these, we start the hypnotic work there. If the patient does not respond after we give her time to do so, we move on, realizing that in the next few moments other opportunities will present themselves as entry points. Finally, when the patient reacts to her dream, we proceed by using one of the several methods or modalities appropriate to find the *Bedeutung* of the patient's dream.

In working with induced dreams, once the patient has been invited to allow a dream to form in her mind, the analyst may calmly repeat "a dream coming from *your* innermost mind" or a similar statement, until the dream starts to flow. As in night dreams, more often than not the patient comes up with snatches and dissociated images rather than with an ongoing story as in a movie. Later, one of the therapeutic techniques described above is applied to those partial elements in order to bring about wholeness, meaning, and sense for the patient. Variations and refinements of these approaches will come up in following chapters.

I do not know any analyst who conducts the entire session with the patient in the hypnotic state. To move from the id to the ego, the therapist cannot merely stay with the unconscious. *Reality testing* is a most appropriate term to describe the constant need for checking the individual's progress and general changes with the objective reality of her world. Therefore, after the hypnotic experience, I find it useful to allow the patient in her ordinary state of mind (not in hypnosis) to have reactions, comments, questions, and any afterthoughts. After the subjective right cerebral hemispheric experience of hypnosis, it is useful to integrate it with the objective left hemispheric function. The kaleidoscope I have adopted is therefore not arbitrary or artificial, but comes from what clinicians encounter in psychodynamic work with hypnosis. The three parts fall into each other and the final outcome will be the balanced life of the person who has completed his or her hypnoanalysis.

## 5. Dreaming, Fantasy and Auto-hypnosis

# Summary

This chapter focuses on three main points: first, that fantasy is our most frequent way of thinking; second, that much of fantasy is sexual; and third, that in using fantasy humans engage in natural self-hypnosis (positive or negative). The consequence of this is a justification for the use of hypnoanalysis with, among others, its technique of induced dreams. Because there is such a heavy dependence of one component on the other, the deliberate use of hypnosis in conducting psychoanalysis can produce the effects of traditional psychoanalysis efficiently and quickly. Moreover, many psychoanalysts in the course of their analyses are using New Hypnosis in the currently accepted sense that Erickson developed successfully in the 1960s and 1970s (see Araoz, 1985a; Rossi, 1980) without being aware of it. The old definition of hypnosis was centered on the hypnotist. Erickson, on the other hand, was eminently "client-centered" without ever having had any influence from Carl Rogers (1951), who conceptualized that modality (Araoz, 1986).

Because of the importance of fantasy in our daily living, we must recognize that much of our thinking may be self-deception, wishful thinking, illusion, self-fulfilling prophesies, or other cognitive distortions. The Buddhist warning about human thinking reminds us that "I am what I think." This is the reason for distinguishing auto-hypnosis, therapeutic and constructive, from negative self-hypnosis, which interferes with realistic thinking. The first impression one has of a person, positive or negative, is usually more fantasy than reality, unconsciously projecting on that person's hopes, expectations, or old prejudices about people of that race, age, gender, or occupation. We need practice in assessing our thoughts in order to use fantasy creatively for our benefit, without abandoning reality.

This chapter presented the introductory steps for employing hypnosis effectively in dream work as the first attempt at combining psychoanalysis and hypnosis in a methodical manner. It further offered techniques especially designed to work with induced hypnotic dreams. Because dreams are natural and spontaneous manifestations of the unconscious, and because they are highly respected in psychoanalysis, I present them as the model for the use of hypnosis in analytic work. In practically every case where a hypnotic technique is described in this book, we could have used dream induction. As a matter of fact, I know several analysts who use induced dreams almost exclusively without realizing that they are hypnotic.

The conclusion of this discussion may lead to a new insight for psychoanalysts into their work, which often includes the new form of hypnosis, and help them refine its use, as I shall try to do in the following chapters. Erika Fromm (1973) agreed with me, many years ago when I studied with her, that good psychoanalysis always includes hypnosis, even when the analyst does not call it such or does not even realize that he is using it. By this I do not mean, nor did she, the antiques of stage hypnosis that were in the past used in hypnotherapy. I mean the insistence on fantasy, working directly with it as if it were external reality (because it is the patient's direct experience either at that moment or regarding her situation or problem), helping patients to become familiar with the mysteries of fantasy that come from the unconscious, encouraging them to take their fantasy seriously, as manifestations of their innermost self. Thus we help patients recognize that the symptom is not the whole story (Araoz, 2006), and that, by recognizing the unconscious, we shall find *Bedeutung* in our most insignificant actions, including our dreams.

A final note: I deal with the *clinical* use of dreams and avoid the controversy about the nature of dreams between psychoanalysts and medical scientists presented by Hobson in *Dream Life* (2011), published after a dozen books on the subject. Hobson's (1989, 2011) discoveries should be integrated with Freud's, not used to condemn him.

CHAPTER 6

# Auto-hypnosis as Therapeutic Regression

The hypnosis we are discussing, New Hypnosis, is the way of thinking that makes us believe, not intellectually but from the experience itself, that our thoughts can become reality, knowing at the same time that they are thoughts and mental representations. With hypnosis we create our own reality, either consciously (as in therapy and analysis) or unconsciously (as in negative self-hypnosis). In the positive situation, we believe in ourselves and our inner resources for goodness, growth, happiness, inner satisfaction, and peace; for honesty, truth, and fairness with others; for respect for the entire universe and its laws, many still mysterious to us. In the negative situation, we are convinced that we are no good, that living is a waste, that we have nothing to offer others, and that the world would be better off without us. We see our glass half empty, or even almost completely empty. The healing effected by hypnosis takes place because it focuses us on our positive resources (our glass is half full), as Seligman's (1995) research on positive psychology teaches. These two forces at work in our psyche (Eros and Thanatos) appear in different ways and can be the resonance of a healthy ego and/or a benign superego or, on the contrary, of the id and/or a strict superego. In this chapter I will merely touch on three of the ways that our "inner dummy" (the I. D.) or our "energizer general operator" (the E. G. O.) show themselves (Weiner & Hefter, 1999) and are used in hypnoanalysis: (1) regression (with repetition compulsion as an important manifestation); (2) ego states therapy (an extension of which is the ideal self); and (3) primary and secondary thinking processes. I focus on these three manifestations because they can be universally applied in clinical work. Reviewing all the hypnotic techniques listed in the next chapter, for example, we find that practically every one of them falls into one of these three categories. These psychodynamics, so closely connected with fantasy, can be utilized in the process of psychoanalysis that then becomes *hypnoanalysis.*

## Regression in the Service of the Ego

Hypnotic regression is the first practical application. A voluntary release of control of one's thoughts is required in hypnosis, which in itself is a form of regression. The release of control in this case is similar to what Kris (1952) applied mainly to artistic creation and to what we humans naturally do in many instances—a sexual or musical experience, for example—where an outside element makes us lower our conscious and rational control of what we are doing or experiencing. The subject must allow herself to think in an "as if" mode, that is, as if she were taken by the music, or by the sexual passion.

> If Fanny, a middle-aged woman who consulted with me regarding her constant thoughts about previous lives, had refused "to let herself go," to use Erickson's (Erickson & Rossi, 1989) expression, and thus to regress as if she were a child playing a game, I would not have been able to help her so quickly and directly. She believed that she had been a slave among those who served a very powerful Egyptian magnate in the first century. She started by saying that she wanted to know the truth about this. I asked her to go into her own mind and experience herself as a slave of that important official. Initially she protested and complained that she did not need me to do that because she was able to do it any time she wanted. After a few moments, during which I refused to discuss this or argue with her, she took on the personality of a slave. At this point I requested that she tell me what her unique experience of having been a slave could do now to benefit her current condition of being a middle-aged woman. I encouraged her to take her time trying to feel realistically how she could profit now from having been a slave in the past. She was still in hypnosis when she said very slowly and in a whisper, "I see myself attacking and destroying the slave. I hear myself saying, 'I don't need the slave to face the truth.'" [A long silence with some tears followed.] "The truth is that I hate not being young and having the nice body I used to have. The truth is that I am lonely and I belong to no one. The truth is that I want someone to make love to me, not just to have sex." [With heavy tears now] "The truth is that I hate my life and the slave nonsense gives me a distraction from my misery."

We may notice how she showed two sides of herself, the one that created the slave and identified with her, and the other that lived the hard reality of her present situation. To become aware of what was bothering her, Fanny had to regress and place herself where she had been when she unconsciously invented the slave story and, in so doing, Fanny also discovered two parts of herself. These two dynamics from two parts in her nature (regression and mature personality) were a form of giving back to the ego the control that she had abdicated a couple of years earlier. Without realizing it, she was following Freud's (1923) famous advice, *Wo es war, da soll ich werden* (Where id was, there shall ego be).

In the case of Fanny, the slave fantasy became a dream and a call to honesty with herself. If this had not been done, Fanny would have talked about the slave fantasy probably for a long time, with the possibility that at some later point she might have become convinced of the truth of this fantasy. The New Hypnosis intervention made the direct insight possible. Without any prodding, Fanny left the fantasy behind and faced the truth about her current unhappiness, allowing her to analyze these repressed feelings without further exploring and uncovering. At the same time, she found herself enjoying and using her current mature self with pride and ease.

To recapitulate the concept of *regression in the service of the ego,* Erika Fromm (Fromm & Nash, 1997) tells us that "it is a combination of ... [an] increase of primary process thinking, a natural loosening of defenses and the fact that the general reality orientation with its customary logical thinking fades into the background of awareness" (p. 278). These three elements—thinking in images rather than in ideas, feeling free to be oneself without having to conform to expectations, and focusing on one's inner realities paying less attention, if any at all, to the surrounding environment—are essential elements of hypnosis that we have already mentioned. I find it of great interest that, in regard to the ability of hypnosis to calm the person, researchers like Amen (1998) have found that hypnosis directly affects the basal ganglia, a part of the brain around the deep limbic system, including the thalamus and the hypothalamus, responsible for our level of anxiety and our pleasure/fear balance, also affecting fine movements, motivation, and other functions.

## Ego States Therapy

As I mentioned earlier, John and Helen Watkins created this psychodynamic approach within the general domain of hypnosis in the mid–1940s. The thorough understanding of ego states is quite interesting, as explained in detail by Paul Federn (1952), but for the practical application of it in hypnoanalysis the following synthesis is, I hope, helpful and convenient. Ego states therapy is basically rooted in the Freudian tripartite theory of personality. The practitioners of this method may or may not explain it cognitively to the patient, but they always give the patient the opportunity to *experience* it. They may decide on ego states therapy, for example, when the patient becomes upset because she cannot have what she wants. In the case where the patient holds on to "things"—objects, people, occupations, places, and more—that are damaging to her, the analyst may suggest that the patient think of something she wants to have but cannot afford, for example, an expensive summer house on the French Riviera. Then the patient is encouraged to listen to the part of her that wants to have it and to the other part that reminds her of the realistic objections to it. An actual conversation, as in a dream, is developed after each part is clearly articulated as different from the other. The well-known cartoon of the little devil on one's left shoulder and the little angel on the right is a popular oversimplification of the same idea, and reminds us how it can be used naturally and with relaxed spontaneity. The active dialogue of the two parts is used to get to the point where each part is making a strong argument for itself and for its position. The patient is reminded that both parts are she, and that she has to decide which part is going to win and run her life. Because of this, it is helpful to let the patient give each personality part a name or nickname to be used while the hypnotic experience takes place and for the length of time it may take her to decide on the issue at hand. The two ego states or personality parts, in the hypnosis mode, are interacting and discussing the decision of which part will be the boss. Analytical work lends itself well to this approach, when often important facts, memories, emotions, and so on from the past appear with ease while doing personality parts work.

As is easy to imagine, the hypnotic technique of ego states or personality parts is useful in many situations, as in the technique of the ideal self, to be discussed in the next section, and can be used in many circumstances that patients may bring up. This was the case with a woman who had been seriously neglected as a toddler and as a child, and who was helped to give up the current fruitless lamentation of what happened to her a long time ago by hypnotically becoming the child who was comforted and validated by the adult self. Fanny's slave fantasy was also cured by using ego state therapy. In the following chapter you will find ways of using hypnotic techniques in the analysis of diverse categories, taken principally from the pathological personalities listed in the *Psychodynamic Diagnostic Manual* (Psychoanalytic Consortium, 2006).

## The Ideal Self

This technique, in truth an extension of ego states therapy, was one of Erika Fromm's (Fromm & Nash, 1997) favorites. It comes from the fairly universal human fantasy of being better than one is, or of having more talents and possessions than one has, quite evident in our capitalistic society but also present in so-called primitive groups. In the neurotic, this is either exaggerated and almost impossible to reach, or it is depressively absent. In the *ideal self* exercise that we are discussing, the patient who, for example, talks of what she wants to be or change into, is told to imagine attaining that goal vividly in her fantasy. Depending on the circumstances, she is helped to imagine the steps she must take, patiently and progressively, in order to reach her therapeutic goal. This is done hypnotically, after inviting her to relax initially through slow abdominal breathing, noticing how this kind of breathing affects her body beneficially, and then to focus on the goal image experientially, as if it were real — as if she were already enthusiastically taking the steps to attain her ideal. Once the fantasy is obtained, she can examine it and decide first if it is possible, and second, what steps does she have to take concretely in order to reach that possible goal. She also is encouraged to consider obstacles, difficulties, and oppositions, if any, and to "pre-live" her possible reactions to them. If it is not realistically possible to reach her goal, she is guided through the ways to give up an unrealistic dream. The entire formation process of the fantasy is subsequently examined and analyzed, out of hypnosis. This practice, an example of mind training, usually has to be repeated, frequently several times.

Mojo is a case in point. He was a 31-year-old patient diagnosed with Asperger's Syndrome, who started analysis twice a week because he believed he had not done all in his power to get well. But early in his therapy he realized that at the same time he was convinced that this was his nature and personality, disabled and never able to change. Practicing the *ideal self* technique repeatedly, he changed his view of himself in less than four months. Mojo's new resolution was to keep the Asperger's symptoms in his "sick self" under control by mentally experiencing himself completely normal and enjoying life as most people in his family did. This was his "ideal self." This took almost another six months, with resistance, transferential issues, and frequent changes of mind. However, he felt very encouraged by his progressive improvement, even though he had to be constantly vigilant to make sure his symptoms would not take over and rule his life again. The old reactions kept reappearing all during the day and even in dreams. This struggle became the main topic of analysis; he got to the point where he was able to keep his symptoms in the personality part that was his "sick" self, thus obtaining greater control over his life. In terms of brain plasticity, it makes perfect sense: the old neural circuits were so much part of him that he needed time and repeated effort to allow new brain circuits to be established. But by repetition and perseverance, the new pathways "overpowered" the old that, now neglected by him, weakened and died.

The *ideal self* technique is especially useful with people who, because of very early experiences, suffer from low self-esteem, or for those who have an overly strict superego. Consequently, it can help the patient discover and/or unfold her creativity.

This was the case of Zuli, a 51-year-old housewife with three grown children who, because of several dreams where she saw herself as a painter, decided that she wanted to learn how to paint. She had never painted in her life before. Her family laughed at her when she mentioned her desire to become a painter, and told her she was crazy. This motivated her to consult with one of my supervisees. He introduced her to the *ideal self* concept and technique. She experienced her ideal self as a masterful painter. The therapist and Zuli analyzed the meaning painting had for her, her need to change so drastically, the reactions she fantasized in others, and so on. Zuli registered for an art class for beginners and was the best in the group. In less than three years, she was selling her paintings and had several exhibits in local events. One of the comments she made was that, before the ideal self experience, she did not dare to think of herself as an artist; she was afraid of it, following the traumatic experiences from parents that were, as she expressed it, "very old-fashioned, especially with girls."

Now she considered painting part of her true self, and was very proud of what she had accomplished. The *ideal self* technique made it possible for her to be what she unconsciously was, but had remained hidden for so long. A few months after finishing her analysis, she mailed her therapist a painting of hers that he now has over his chair in the office. On the back she had written, "With gratitude. My ideal self, Zuli." She had become a beginning member of one of the most prestigious associations of watercolor artists, which has very high standards, requiring the candidate to present several of her paintings before accepting her as a full member. What happened in this case is that Zuli, in her analysis, realized that her parents raised her, like most girls in the 1950s, rather negatively, always emphasizing what she was not, what she could not accomplish, what was not part of her. As a child, she had accepted this limited philosophy of feminine defeat and, by the time in her life that she suspected it as being too radical, Zuli felt too dependent on her family to do anything about it. To change meant to be disloyal to her family. She had resigned herself to being as limited as her family expected her to be. Now, however, she wanted to be her true self and that motivation led her to hypnoanalysis.

As we see, the analytic work is basically the same with or without hypnosis. However, in hypnoanalysis the uncovering of repressed material and the focusing on a specific topic is more direct and to the point, thus moving therapy faster. Another advantage is that the patient deliberately rehearses mentally and thus is better prepared to undertake the difficult change she needs to grow and enrich her life.

## Primary and Secondary Process Thinking

I will begin by defining the primary and secondary thinking processes. In brief, we may say that *primary process thinking* is nonlinguistic, metaphorical, "imagogic" — the domain of fantasy — whereas *secondary process thinking* is more developmentally advanced, based in reality, and factually oriented — the domain of language. Primary process is guided by the pleasure principle, while secondary process is guided by the reality principle. Grandin (1995), who studied autism as well as animal communication, has shown evidence to prove that schizophrenia and autism are neurological disorders, and agrees with the psychoanalytic explanation of normal development that secondary process gradually takes precedence over primary process.

In situations where the patient is too literal (e.g., the worry that the preadolescent children on vacation do not love their mother because they don't want to communicate with her), she can be guided to vividly imagine saying to herself that this is a normal child reaction, and visualize that she is happy because her children are normal. Once she succeeds in interpreting the children's behavior with more detachment than before, her reaction can be analyzed and she can find out what elicited her panic.

> When a patient cannot give up her fantasy of something unrealistic, as in the case of a 73-year-old woman who fell in love with a 30-year-old man, imagining herself acting and having fun as if she were 29, hypnosis allows her to come back to reality. This happened when she began to imagine, as vividly as possible, that she had a magical power to truly know what was in the young man's brain and that she reviewed its contents and found in there interests, values, and preferences very different from her own. A second hypnotic fantasy was seeing herself with the young man in a social situation, with friends and with strangers, with her family and with his, realizing how truly uncomfortable she felt. A third hypnotic fantasy was of their lovemaking. Several more fantasies could have been constructed, always allowing the patient to select the one she would like to get into. After each, her feelings and emotional reactions are analyzed, her desire and wish to be with her lover are placed more fully into the reality of their lives.
>
> This patient also had weight control problems. She commented that, as in situations where food is always available, now the sexual wish was still there and the possibilities, at least in fantasy, abounded. She added, "Old age for me is difficult because I still feel hungry for sex with young men." What hypnosis can do in a case like this is save time, and help the patient change *for herself* from primary to secondary thinking, to come to decisions experientially, not merely cognitively. Hypnosis is therapeutic only when the patient can, experientially, be completely absorbed by her secondary process thinking. The old expression of "being in trance" referred to this experience. But New Hypnosis tries not to use the term because of the prevalent misunderstanding of trance being like general anesthesia. The ideal self is ultimately the *true* self, the self that one can be at this point in one's life.

# Summary

The hypnotic techniques to be used in psychoanalysis are many and, as is clear from the brief sample provided, overlap generously.

## 6. Auto-hypnosis as Therapeutic Regression

Rather than memorizing the names of the various hypnotic techniques, it is important to keep in mind the general principle of *utilization*. As I suggested earlier, it is up to the analyst to take advantage of statements and gestures that, with some prodding, may elicit spontaneous fantasies from the patient. The more nonintellectual and the more experiential is the interaction between the two people involved in the psychoanalytic relationship, the more opportunities will be found to utilize the patient's fantasies for her self-knowledge, growth, and happiness. Rational, objective learning is weaker than the unique, experiential learning attainable through hypnosis when it comes to human change and self-transformation, as we shall discuss in Chapter 9. Mystics like Lao Tzu, Ezra Ben Menahem (11th century), and Teresa of Avila, or philosophers like Plato, Socrates, Marcus Aurelius, or Santayana, agree that what satisfies the human spirit is to savor things internally, not to know many things—experience vs. purely intellectual knowledge.

Because fantasy is often sexual, symbolically or explicitly, as discussed in Chapter 4, the analyst has no choice but to expect this type of material. As we know, there is much repression in this area, in society at large as well as in the individual who internalizes what society teaches him. This is the reason for following the advice attributed to the great psychiatrist of Freud's time, Emile Charcot: "Always look for the sexual thing" (*Cherchez toujours la chose sexuelle*). Material that may create resistance and embarrassment is often handled by the patient in hypnosis in a relaxed and beneficial manner. The suggestion, "Follow the image. See what it brings up next," is especially useful with sexual material, although it has a universal use with any topic that comes up spontaneously in the psychoanalytic work.

CHAPTER 7

# The PDM Personality Types in Hypnoanalysis

Unlike the superficial classification and categorization of symptoms characteristic of the *DSM-IV-TR* (American Psychiatric Association, 2000), the *Psychodynamic Diagnostic Manual (PDM)* (Alliance of Psychoanalytic Organizations, 2006) tries to understand the symptom as an unconscious, unique expression of the individual. The principle enunciated by the *PDM* in the introduction to the section on "Personality Patterns and Behavior" succinctly states that "what [patients] are trying to change is tied up with who they are" (p. 17). Shortly thereafter, the authors emphasize that "[u]nderstanding individual people and their development can be more important to treating them than understanding specific disorders or mastering specific techniques" (p. 17). In agreement with this point of view, alien to the rigid labeling of the *DSM*, I assume that the hypnotic intervention to be mentioned in the case of each personality pathology is merely one of the multiple interventions the analyst can use in order to help patients out of the predicament that brought them to psychological treatment. Though I present techniques, I do not believe in them as such. All techniques are effective and all techniques are failures. It depends on how they are used within the relationship the clinician has established with the patient. If that relationship is good, almost any technique works.

When it comes to personality pathology, the *PDM* lists 15 different categories frequently encountered in clinical practice. They are: schizoid; paranoid; psychopathic or antisocial; narcissistic; sadistic and sadomasochistic; self-defeating or masochistic; depressive; somatizing; dependent; phobic or avoidant; anxious; obsessive-compulsive; hysterical or histrionic; dissociative; and mixed or "other." I will comment on

## 7. The PDM Personality Types in Hypnoanalysis

13 of them, in the same order they appear in the *PDM*. I omit the sadistic and the dissociative personality disorders, the first because of its similarity to the psychopathic (as I will explain later), and the second because its complexity would take us too far away from the focus of this book. The category of Sadistic Personality (listed in the *PDM*, p. 40) is very close to the psychopathic, though the sadist is not necessarily a psychopath and vice versa. Psychodynamic methods do not work well with sadists, because their introspection is minimal and their insight nil (Erich Fromm, 1973). Because these people do not "let go," and make an effort to be constantly under complete control of their experience, they do not get into hypnosis. Their non-cooperative attitude makes hypnosis impossible. Once the diagnosis of sadism has been reached, they must be exposed to clear behavioral techniques of punishment and rewards. McWilliams's (1994) book on psychoanalytic diagnosis does not even mention the sadistic personality.

My intention is to concentrate on the main behavioral and attitudinal characteristics of each personality disorder and, on that basis, I propose an hypnotic approach appropriate for each. I insist that there is no necessary or exclusive natural connection between the hypnotic technique suggested and used in the clinical vignettes to follow and the personality condition described. The brief vignettes show *examples* of effective hypnotic interventions. We remember that, if we look behind the behavioral and attitudinal sides of patients, we always find the psychodynamic. In the experience of New Hypnosis, the patient very often discovers connections between the current problem and past experiences, and this helps us to work on those psychodynamics. One advantage of hypnoanalysis is the ease with which it leads the patient to marvelous insights.

I will present a brief outline for each personality type, taken from the *PDM*, which, I hope, will serve as a mental trigger to the analyst. It should be remembered that in most cases an individual is not "pure" narcissistic, or paranoid, or anything else. Most people have mixed characteristics of two or more personality types. For each personality, I have selected an appropriate hypnotic technique, but *many other hypnotic methods, or a combination of them, should be kept in mind to try* if the first one tried does not give results in reasonable time. In each instance, the clinical vignette is either from my own practice or from those of psychotherapists who chose me as their supervisor during the last four decades.

The hypnoanalyst will never use New Hypnosis as the final cure, implying that when the symptom is no longer there the patient is finished with psychotherapy. On the contrary, once the symptom is weakened or even removed, the opportunity is available to work psychodynamically with the patient. The psychoanalytic questions that I proposed elsewhere (Araoz, 2006a) about the history of the symptom and its meaning can now be dealt with without the "distraction" of the symptom that the patient thought was the whole story.

# Personality Types

Please note that after each personality type the name for the hypnotic approach useful for each condition is placed in parentheses. These names are not official, nor are they used by most practitioners. Following these I give an explanation of how to apply that technique in the analytic work, before ending with a clinical vignette.

### Schizoid Personality (Mental Rehearsal)

According to McWilliams (1994), in her book on diagnosis, lack of conformity and disregard for conventional social expectations are "the most striking aspects" (p. 195) of patients with a schizoid personality diagnosis. In addition, the schizoid person avoids close contact with others or any emotional intimacy. Cognitive-behavioral therapy (CBT), much as does psychoanalysis, tends to elicit in the patient the argumentative reaction. If not very careful, the analyst gets involved in vexing and feckless intellectual discussions that accomplish little.

There are at least two ways of understanding this approach. First, in agreement with Wachtel (1977, 2008), integration of diverse approaches is the wise way to go. We can and should use methods of behavioral and cognitive schools, as long as we later analyze the patient's inner life while engaged in the non-psychodynamic techniques, as well as subsequent feelings after the Creative Imagination experience.

Second, from the neuroplasticity perspective, the growing research data (Doidge, 2007) confirm that the plasticity of the adult brain allows it to establish fresh neural pathways on the demand, conscious or unconscious, of the subject. These become more definite with the repeated activity or thought that originated the pathway. By encouraging the patient to counteract his symptoms, we help his brain define and strengthen new patterns that, with repetition, will weaken the abandoned neural pathways until they disappear through mere disuse.

The possible hypnotic approach, among several others in this case, is to use *mental rehearsal*, combined with the *personality parts* technique. The hypnoanalyst points out, giving honest feedback, that there seems to be a reality of two "parts" in the patient's personality, the one who engages in the undesirable behavior and the other who is now talking about it as something to be changed. Once the patient has accepted non-intrusive and respectful feedback about the two personality parts and the reality of the neural pathways, he is guided to enter into the fantasy of himself under the influence of the ego, namely the part of him that knows his behavior hurts him socially and in terms of his self-image. The *mental rehearsal* consists of inviting him to concentrate on seeing himself in fantasy, with great detail, acting normally and staying in this possibility. Once into this fantasy, he is asked to get in touch with his feelings of accomplishment, pride, and joy. In this case, "ego" is not an all-or-nothing concept, so that it is incumbent on the analyst to assess the patient's ego strength from the ease or difficulty he shows in mentally seeing himself being and acting normally. All this is done as a fantasy exercise, without any mention of hypnosis. This approach gives the patient an opportunity to transferentially "test" the analyst, feeling more protected than if he was out of fantasy. Anything too bizarre can be "explained" as fantasy. On the other hand, with hypnosis, the analyst can be very close emotionally to the patient through fantasy, without any sense of threat, so that a constructive therapeutic relationship can be built. All these dynamics will be easier to analyze after the hypnotic experience, because the schizoid patient, both desirous and afraid of intimacy, has experienced in hypnosis the therapist's genuine and honest way of relating to him. Hypnosis is like a playful, though serious, rehearsal of the relationship, human to human, that the schizoid person fears but needs.

In general, but especially with these patients, the analyst will not use the word *hypnosis*, a confusing term, and will not give any suggestions unless they are clearly connected with what the patient is saying or doing. On the basis of something the patient gives out "without thinking" or preconsciously (physical movement, verbal hesitation, and the like), the analyst introduces what he knows is hypnotic.

The following clinical vignette may clarify this. His nickname was Brownie, and he was 55. He was a retired civic employee, who was single and had never lived with anybody else as an adult. He was an advanced diabetic, very smart, sarcastic, angry, looking down on everybody, but trying to help others through volunteer work in hospitals or schools. His most positive memories were of a baseball team, first as a player, years later as a trainer, and finally as a consultant. This team had become his second home, where he spent countless hours over more than two decades. His main concern was death. He did not want to die alone. After discussing his options, Brownie emphatically stated that he did not want to live in an assisted living home the last days of his life. The thought of a nursing home triggered nightmares. He wanted to settle this now, "before I become senile," even though there were no indications of any form of senility.

I introduced hypnosis as Creative Imagination by asking, "What images come to your mind when you think of living in a home for seniors?" After some resistance, Brownie started describing a very gloomy place, with antiquated furniture and many old and dysfunctional people. I interrupted and asked him to close his eyes so he could concentrate better. After a few attempts and suggestions of abdominal breathing, so he could relax and focus sharply on his fantasy, he became more involved in his mental images, using a slower and softer voice and responding well to my requests for more fantasy details directed at getting feedback on his hypnotic experience, which is always required. I asked where he was in his fantasy. He said that he was the only one standing and walking, looking down (in the literal and symbolic sense) on all the disabled seniors. His response to my question, "What are you saying to yourself?" was that they should all be "put to sleep," as we do with our old pets.

At this point I inquired if, as a test, he could fake being there with a different, more positive attitude. To make the transition, I spent a couple of minutes focusing on his breathing and relaxation. Then he said, "O.K., I'll fake it." He started very sarcastically and I reminded him that this was like a test and he could fake it properly, "as if he truly had an optimistic attitude." This was successful. Brownie found many good things: being cared for, having three healthy meals a day, etc. As a matter of fact, the place in his fantasy was now different: seemingly the same building but bright with light, very clean, modern furniture, soft classical music playing, etc. When we finished, Brownie asked, almost in a friendly tone of voice, what this test was all about. Smiling, I simply said, "You passed it. You can have a different, more positive attitude toward an assisted living place." He protested that he had been faking it and I emphasized that nevertheless he was able to do it.

Later we analyzed his negative attitude toward this type of facility, which was centered on his "repugnance" to becoming friendly with any of the people there and liking them. The hypnotic exercise, which was repeated twice in the same session, made it possible to move smoothly into the possibility of making arrangements to be in such a residence in the future, when he needed to do so. In the process, Brownie realized the importance of using his fantasies to be able to enjoy his life more. Just by changing his mental pictures, he could change his feelings and outlook on things. The patient referred to this "formula" as useful to think differently about the possibility of being in a nursing home. As the analysis progressed, the patient reverted to fantasy several times in order to clarify his feelings and decide on options.

This case also shows how denial can help create a negative fantasy, which for the patient becomes his true reality, contributing to his unhappiness and negativity. Moving away in hypnosis from the damaging self-made reality is a form of reality testing, which makes it possible to give up self-constructed negative fantasy made into reality.

As in all psychotherapy cases, though the symptom is not the whole story, the improvement of the target symptom indicates success or failure of the analytic work. The old psychoanalytic teachings on technique included ignoring the symptom and seeing it only as another manifestation of the unconscious in need of analysis that will change or disappear, as parts of the process of personality change and improvement. In the strong statement of Owen Renik (2006), "Failure to keep track of therapeutic benefit and to make technical choices on the basis on whether symptom relief is being achieved leaves an analyst wide open to dangerous complacency about his or her own work. It spares the analyst accountability at the patient's expense" (p. 36).

## Paranoid Personality (Hypnotic Reversal)

The expression *paranoid* is used in common language to describe someone who suspects malicious intentions in others without factual evidence for his fears. The technical meaning is much more subtle, this being one of the most severe personality disorders. People suffering from paranoid personality use projection as the main defense, it is true, but, in addition to blaming others for evil designs on them, they take unusual and extraordinary measures of protection against the suspected and hidden enemies. There is still no clear explanation for the paranoid formation, which probably involves a genetic predisposition to irritability and anger, with fear and envy, shame and guilt (see *PDM*, 2006, and Meissner, 1978). However, the early family experiences may have much to do with what later shows up as paranoid personality. Here we find childhood exposure to threat and humiliation, unfair accusations, parental double messages that made the patient very anxious, all contributing to a contradictory early sense of self: helpless and vulnerable, destructive but insecure out of grandiose fantasies, always questioning oneself. The paranoid personality patient shows acute anger in transferential situations, to the point that clinicians dealing with these patients need training and supervision to help these people successfully. It should be noted, as McWilliams (1994) does, that paranoid personality patients may be misdiagnosed and confused with psychopathic, obsessive, or even dissociative personalities.

Because these patients are so suspicious, hypnosis must be employed very carefully. If used in a matter-of-fact way, *hypnotic reversal* is usually accepted readily by the patient. The patient is asked to tell the analyst his or her most common fantasy (not as fantasy but as the patient's common thoughts). It is typically a situation of fear, lack of confidence, or threat and danger to self, with strong anger. Then he or she is asked to think that, for a moment only, he or she could imagine (just imagine) the complete opposite. It is helpful to reassure the patient that the opposite fantasy is only in his or her mind, in no way denying the previous negative fantasy. Often it is less threatening to ask these patients to "see" it in their mind as a flash, very briefly. The patient does this and, in most cases, the initial try takes barely a few seconds. After analyzing his or her inner dynamics during this experience, the patient is invited to try this again. This time the analyst tries to extend the "good" fantasy experience a couple of minutes. Again, this is analyzed afterward. This sequence is repeated several times, prolonging it each time, until the patient feels comfortable going in and out of the "good experience" on his or her own. The effectiveness of this method seems to be directly related to the important research of Bach-y-Rita (1972, 1980), described in detail by Doidge (2007), about the plasticity of the brain. Repetition of the beneficial activity or thought strengthens the corresponding brain circuit and weakens the opposite one that is being ignored.

> The case of Marla, 43, may illustrate the paranoid personality condition. She had recently lost her job in a prestigious legal firm because

of her paranoia, as her boss had told her. However, he added that she could reapply when her condition was cured. This, in a similar way, had happened once before in another firm, three years earlier, but without the promise of rehiring her. At that time her gynecologist had prescribed Ativan, 6 mg. a day, monitoring it every two or three months. She was still taking it with barely good results. Marla was obviously quite intelligent, her qualifications were excellent, her job ethic was superior, her interaction with both lawyers and clients was masterful. But she could not hide, as she said in her first session, her constant suspicion of clients and other firms' lawyers "who had plans to destroy the work done by her in her firm." On the other hand, she realized that she was "overreacting" without having enough evidence. She added that this overwhelming paranoia affected her private life, and her relationships with friends and relatives, making her existence miserable with constant worry.

Her childhood family experiences were "sad in general" and extremely confusing. She only remembered that she was always accused and found guilty of minor and major infractions that affected her family. From her description, her parents seem to have been alcoholics who neglected her and gave her neither attention nor affection. When she was older, she dated several men who were around her own age, but always found reasons not to see them for a second time, and had never been romantically or sexually intimate with anyone. Now she did not date at all. A similar pattern had occurred in her relationships with therapists, two men and four women, only one of whom she had seen more than two times. With another male therapist she had two sessions, and the other four analysts she had visited only one time each.

She said she did not know what my intentions toward her were, but she had to be careful because I might also try to hurt her, although she respected, liked and, yes, trusted the elderly former teacher whom she had consulted after being fired, and who had highly recommended me. In the second session I suggested *hypnotic reversal* (thinking of the opposite of what she thinks consciously), imagining that I had positive goals for her, asking her to test me based on my professional standards, reputation, and legal or ethical consequences of my behavior, as well as my standing with her former teacher, whom she respected as much as I did. Perhaps because true paranoids live in a habitual state of negative self-hypnosis (NSH), she entered the known hypnotic mental activity easily and promptly, staying relaxed for the entire exercise of less than twenty minutes duration. When she returned to the ordinary manner of using her conscious mind, she agreed that she had been very relaxed and free from worry, but now she was afraid that I had hypnotized her without her realizing it so that she would feel so good; perhaps I was playing with her and manipulating her mind. I simply asked, "How could you know this and be sure?" She responded that she could not be sure. I reverted to the previous points of my professionalism. While she seemed to be thinking about it, I guided her again to the hypnotic state and asked her to stay there, relaxing and using her mind to find out what my intentions were. This lasted about ten minutes. At the end of this, Marla opened her eyes, smiled, and said, "I must give you a good try," and she mentioned again her former teacher, whom I would not want to make angry by hurting her. The session ended there and I felt uncertain of its results.

The following session was three days later. She reported that during that time she had felt well, relaxed, and had had fewer disturbing thoughts. Without explaining what we were doing, I invited her to activate her Creative Imagination by practicing hypnotic reversal in her mind with one of the legal clients that she felt bad about, then with one of the lawyers. We repeated this practice with several other people in the firm and I suggested that she do this alone at home. The rest of the session was spent analyzing her paranoia. At the next session she mentioned that she had done the mental exercise every day and that her general anxiety was much less than before. She also reassured me that she trusted me, and she had reported this to her former teacher in a phone conversation after the last session. The symptom was weakening and she was even more convinced that she had to continue working on her paranoid personality. The analysis continued.

The point of the above vignette, like that of all the others in this chapter, is to illustrate the advantage of using hypnosis as Creative Imagination in specific psychoanalytic personality diagnoses. This is not the place to enter the area of paranoia as a disorder similar to OCD or repeat the neuroplasticity explanation of its cure.

## Psychopathic/Antisocial Personality (Superego Attunement)

Psychopaths are people without a conscience (malformed or distorted superego) and often without the common sense to study the entire situation before they launch into action. The *PDM* (2006) and McWilliams (1994) describe clearly how to identify a true psychopath. My purpose in this book, however, is to understand how hypnotic Creative Imagination can be useful with these patients, so that their psychodynamic treatment becomes more effective using hypnoanalysis. A helpful hypnotic technique for psychopaths is *attunement of the superego*. Psychopaths who seek therapy are often those who have failed in their wonderful plans to beat the system, or to conquer the world, or to become billionaires, or to be discovered by an important celebrity who will depend on them, and the like. In this case, with hypnosis, we can get them to imagine what would have happened if they had succeeded. We slow down here, allowing them to absorb the big success that did not happen because of "a little detail" that went wrong, or due to lack of attention to one point. But one of those minuscule details made all the difference. I encourage patients to imagine what would have happened if they had taken care of the detail. With Creative Imagination in hypnosis, using their fantasy and with appropriate questions, I help them get to *the voice in them* that reminds them, "You could have paid attention to that, and to the consequences of failure. You acted like a fool." Then, still in hypnosis, I ask them to find out where that *voice* is from, to realize that this voice comes *from a part of them* that wants to protect them and make them happy. This voice comes from their true, honest, and especially mature and responsible self. This way of thinking and experiencing oneself makes it possible to recognize that "my superego is my higher self. There is more to me than what I am familiar with." It may take several months and many tries before they accept the superego's beneficent function in their thinking and behavior. Once psychopaths identify with the superego, I suggest an experiment letting the higher self take over *for a little while* in the Creative Imagination practice: What happens? What are they aware of? What would they have done differently under the influence of the superego? What will they do differently in the future? Can they imagine now, in hypnosis, what they would do? The sequel of this new consideration of themselves is, in most cases, that the patient starts to question sincerely the wisdom of acting in psychopathic ways and becomes moved to constructive life alterations.

> This was the case of Lorraine, who had spent most of her married life involved with men other than her husband, even though she saw him as very controlling, possessive, and jealous. She, a pharmaceutical representative, had lived in a state of excitement, looking forward to the risky adventure of the next affair with the possibility of being discovered. In nine years of marriage this had never happened, which was for her a source of great pride. However, the last affair almost blew up in her face. Thanks to her sister, who had lied and protected her for such a long time, at the last minute Lorraine was able to change the entire scenario so that her husband never even suspected what happened. The reason for Lorraine's seeking psychotherapy at

the time she did was the same sister's threat of blowing the cover of what had happened unless Lorraine got herself into therapy right away. Most of the time in the first few sessions was spent with her resistance, ambivalence, and denial, as expected. In the sixth session she accepted the possibility of the idea of a superego and of engaging, though disinclined, in the above-mentioned "experiment" for the hypnotic adjustment of the superego. This laborious effort led Lorraine to a committed psychoanalysis that helped her recognize the mistaken evaluation of her personality, which now she recognized as psychopathic and in need of urgent correction.

The necessary steps to change lasted over four years of hypnotherapy, using almost exclusively free association and dream analysis even on the couch. She divorced her husband and started to lead a normal single life. Three years after the end of her hypnoanalysis Lorraine remarried. She had become comfortably familiar with her superego as a positive and enriching part of her life. She was proud of her "new brain" and happy to understand what she had made to happen with her persevering focused attention that literally changed her neurology for her own good.

## *Narcissistic Personality (Filling the Void)*

The *DSM-IV-TR* (200) refers to narcissism as if it were a clear and serious disorder. It ignores the fact that narcissism is a continuum from mild to severe. On the contrary, the milder narcissists, according to the *PDM* (2006), are far from psychotic. They move "toward the *neurotic* end of the severity spectrum ... may be socially appropriate, personally successful, charming and, although somewhat deficient in their capacity for intimacy, reasonably well adapted to their family circumstances, work and interests" (p. 38). Those at the other extreme, however, "suffer from frank identity diffusion, lack of consistent sense of inner-directed morality, and may behave in highly destructive ways." (p. 38). These are close to the psychopathic personality that Kernberg (1984) labeled "malignant." Because narcissistic patients feel empty inside, they try to fill that vacuum with attention and fame, honors and distinctions, wealth and possessions, feeling good when they defeat or even devalue others. On this basis, distinctions have been proposed such as "phallic narcissistic character" (Reich, 1933), "malignant narcissism" (Kernberg, 1984), "oblivious character" and "hypervigilant narcissist" (Gabbard, 1989), or "covert" and "thick-skinned narcissism" (Akhtar, 1989).

One of the Creative Imagination or hypnotic interventions that is appropriate with narcissistic personality patients is *filling the void*. The patient is asked to check if her unhappiness is connected to her feeling of emptiness and to her efforts trying to find the opposite feeling of fullness depending on external events, material possessions, and people's reactions to her that she expects must always be positive. To become less dependent on external factors, the patient can learn to fill the emptiness from inside. In this technique, the patient in hypnosis reviews her lifelong accomplishments (from learning to walk and speak, to any other social, mental, or mechanical skills), taking credit for what she has done from childhood to the present. While the hypnotized patient is doing this, she reminds herself that all this is her doing. The analyst encourages her to relive in fantasy (hypnotically) the good moments of specific successes. The reliving should comprise the good feelings experienced in the past while going through the particular positive memories. Mitchell (1986) addresses this general issue of fantasy, illusion, and narcissism. In this hypnotic approach, both steps (remembrance and reliving) are essential for its positive outcome. The two mental activities, first the intellectual/cognitive recollection of events that can make the patient proud of him- or herself, together with the second, experiential/affective reliving of the good feeling those events generated in the past, make this approach effective. The following case illustrates this method.

> Bob came to hypnoanalysis at the age of 53 expecting magical results. He recognized that his constant striving for attention, praise, acknowledgement, and reward was taking away from the energy he needed to truly succeed. We analyzed his background and his constant need to be recognized, emphasizing the fact that he was neglecting to consider many real successes he had had in his life by limiting what he called "success" to external, glamorous, and material events, ignoring personal acts of goodness, generosity, understanding, and kindness of others toward him and on his own part toward others. In the state of hypnosis, while working with Creative Imagination, he agreed to relive some of the best moments in his life that he could genuinely attribute to his own doing. He lingered on these until he felt convinced that he deserved to give himself credit for them, since they were his own accomplishments. In the course of analysis, he was encouraged to practice on his own, at home, this new way of looking at himself. Once in a while, in the analytic sessions, we repeated the same exercise. I found it interesting to realize that, every time we did this, Bob found new instances or situations that he truly could attribute to himself. One of the comments he made was, "I have enough to be proud of. I don't need others to convince me of it."

His diagnosis changed from Narcissistic Personality Disorder to mild neurotic self-absorption, with a new type of rigidity shown mostly in his need always to find new reasons, based on historical facts of his own life, to convince him that he was all right and that he did not need external factors to make him feel successful. He continued what he considered his second analysis—after he had resolved the presenting symptom—and dealt mostly with this rigidity. Bob celebrated his 58th birthday by ending his analysis. I agreed with him that he was ready to put into practice everything he had learned in his hypnoanalysis. In this case, too, the use of activation of his Creative Imagination, resulting in the New Hypnosis state, enriched his analytic experience.

## Masochistic Personality (Mental Cleaning)

These people are self-defeatists (*PDM*, 2006), not limited to sexual situations with physical pain and psychological humiliation, as common language implies. They strangely find ways of ending up in situations where they experience suffering, inconvenience, abuse, others taking advantage of them, and so on. They are not happy people; rather their entire attitude is depressive and negativistic. There are variations of the masochistic personality, from those who accumulate misfortunes and calamities seeking sympathy, understanding, and help, especially in psychotherapy (moral masochists), to those who find pain and sorrow in all close relationships (relational masochists). The first group overlaps with narcissism (Cooper, 1988) and the second with borderline personality (Berliner, 1958).

Using New Hypnosis through Creative Imagination, masochistic patients can train themselves to cleanse the memories that torture them by not focusing on negative events of the past. As neuroscience has shown us (Bach-y-Rita, 1972), they need to establish new neural circuits that are positive and constructive, merely by changing their thinking with intense and sharp focusing, fantasizing positively and constructively. More mind training, obviously: the new positive neural pathways, as they become stronger with repetition, let the old ones fade away completely. In order to do this in hypnosis, borrowing from Buddhism, patients learn to connect breathing with renewal. Some imagine their fingers and toes as stress escape valves. With every exhalation they visualize a small amount of negative memory leaving their bodies, and with every inhalation a good memory appears or advances slowly up front.

In the place of the "bad" memories, their mind is now full of light and the patient enjoys the cleanliness and shiny appearance of his mind. I call this hypnotic technique *mental cleansing*.

The masochistic patient who sounds pessimistic and finds all sorts of unhappiness in close relationships, based on tragedies that could happen or emotional negative changes of the other person toward the patient, is helped by making use of New Hypnosis in the Creative Imagination modality, in order to find the motivation of the part in him that rejects happiness and deprives him of it. That this part of the patient, and the unconscious motivation to change, do exist comes from what is happening to the patient symptomatically. The way to find this part is by encouraging the patient to remember negative messages given by others, especially those from early life, that the negative part of him might have taken seriously. When he starts uncovering some of these self-destructive messages, the patient is advised to quickly assess if there is any beneficial value in that type of message. This is what is called *relabeling of a thought* (Schwartz & Begley, 2002). When he now does not accept the negative message, he visualizes getting rid of it in any dramatic, cartoon-like manner that may come to mind—like shooting the negative message into space in a powerful rocket. The patient is encouraged to use the same or a similar fantasy technique whenever any of these negative messages starts to intrude in ordinary life. The fantasy to be used comes from Doidge's (2007) neuroplastic application, consisting of the complete opposite of masochism; the message of one's worth, dignity, respect, and value is imagined growing in the brain and beautifying every corner of one's inner self.

> The following vignette is illustrative of the two types of masochism, moral and relational. Tolo, a man in his late 50s, had missed several important opportunities in life because at the moment of making the final decision he had backed off. The last few years had been spent driving a limousine but Tolo, though he felt he deserved this, knew that he was capable of much more and that his current job was not for him but for retired people. What had shaken him out of his complacency was a woman in whom he had become very interested and with whom, he imagined, he could spend the rest of his life. He practiced the hypnotic cleansing exercise successfully, and in doing so he discovered his negative self, who was still punishing him for mistakes that he had made when he was a child and an adolescent.
> This was a case in which several other hypnotic techniques, like

mental rehearsal, adjustment of the superego, and inner friends meeting (to be explained in the next section) were applied to strengthen his resolution to make a go of this relationship that was still new and fragile. Important discoveries with practical consequences came to light in his analysis. For instance, he recognized his father in him, who seems to have resented him from the moment he was born, finding the baby boy a threat to him and using every opportunity he had to put him down and humiliate him. Even at his death, he cursed the son, who was 34 at the time, saying that he was good for nothing, adding that he was ashamed of having such worthless son. Tolo's analysis allowed him to disassociate himself from his father. Eventually, when he realized the relationship would not be a source of suffering, he moved in with his girlfriend and both were happy together.

## Depressive Personality (Inner Friends)

With these patients, in addition to regular psychoanalysis and even medication (depending on the severity of the depressive symptoms), a Creative Imagination or hypnosis intervention that can be helpful may be called *joining your inner friends* or simply *your inner friends*. The reason is that most studies with depressives (e.g., Seligman, 1995a) show that they have gotten into the habit of being depressed and of ignoring good events and supportive people in their lives. The patient is given the psychological prescription of making a list of people who have been optimistic, encouraging, inspiring, validating, and well intentioned in their relationship with the patient at different times over his or her lifespan. At the next session, when the list is ready, the analyst instructs the patient to imagine (again, mind training through fantasy, this time by means of hypnotic Creative Imagination) all these people coming together, concerned about the patient's unhappiness. Details, such as where they meet, are left to the patient. After the preliminary preparation of abdominal breathing and body relaxation, when the patient is sufficiently concentrated on her mental image of the meeting with her friends, to the point that she does not react to external distractions like noises, including telephone, traffic, etc., and uses minimal verbal output, she is told to listen to what the friends are saying about her, consistent with the positive memory the patient has of that person in the past. We must be prepared for some patients who prefer to have several individual encounters, instead of one large meeting with all their friends. Our prompt change of plan by agreeing to that will only benefit the patient.

The following seems to have a special advantage: the patient fantasizes that with each positive statement of her "friends" a new neural connection of positivism is established in her brain. She can imagine that her entire brain starts to shine with a new glow. She may hear soft music that confirms in fantasy what is happening in her brain. Still in fantasy, all these new connections of hope start to move very slowly through her entire body and touch all the vital organs: heart, kidneys, liver, spleen, etc. Because she is in the state of hypnosis, she is experiencing it, feeling and believing that this is happening.

The patient is urged to repeat this practice on her own every day until the next psychoanalytic session. The audio tape or CD that I often make specifically for the patient strengthens the positive transference, becoming a type of transitional object in the process of regression in the service of the ego, which Winnicott (1953) regarded as promoting autonomy in the toddler, given that the object is under the direct control of the infant, unlike the mother. So too is the case with the audio-tape or CD with which the patient will re-enter at will the therapeutic session.

> Libby is a good case in point. At 47, she had a steady job that she liked and did well, and paid without effort for her expenses. The main complaint was that she was lonely, without a special person in her life. The last long-term relationship had broken up four or five years earlier, and Libby was still friends with her former lover. She was now living in a small city apartment, ordinary and poor compared to those of her many friends who were better off than she was. They included her in get-togethers and parties, but she was ashamed of inviting them to her very modest place, which she described as "boring." She had felt depressed since her last birthday, seeing herself growing old, lonely, and economically not very comfortable. She refused medication for depression, saying that the depression was not so bad because she had not lost one day of work.
>
> In the tenth session, when Libby said that she did not know why her friends still cared about her, I suggested the "inner friends" technique. In practicing it, Libby recognized that she had good and reliable friends. She also realized that her mistrust came from her early years (two to seven) in the relationship with a mother, seemingly borderline, who felt rejected by her own mother and who expected Libby to be loving to her in the midst of drastic mood swings—from tender and caring one moment to spiteful, angry, and nasty the next. Two or three sessions after we used this hypnotic technique she told me that often, when she found herself starting a depressed mood, she would take a few minutes and "enter the inner friends circle," where she

always had such a good time that the depression disappeared. All along, we were analyzing her shame, her serious attachment issues, her life orientation, and other such issues, until she found peace in simply being, without the anxiety of finding a life companion or living in a place beneath her preference.

Paradoxically, a very good man appeared in her life and, after a reasonable amount of time, they decided to stay together. The paradox was that Libby had resigned herself to be alone when, unexpectedly, she found this man. Curious about her inner self, she continued analysis "to know myself thoroughly and truly."

## *Somatizing Personality (Feelings in One's Body)*

People with this condition have difficulty expressing their feelings verbally due, in part, to poor fantasy, self-detachment, or masochistic self-attachment and rigid superegos. They are distinguished from hypochondriacs, from those with psychosomatic or conversion disorders, and from the sufferers of chronic fatigue syndrome. In general, somatizers are those who develop generalized physical symptoms when bothered by emotional turmoil, truly a form of regression and, in neurological thinking, an indication that they have created a neural pathway, perhaps through many years of detouring feelings into somatic manifestations. Extreme cases come close to the fascinating patients that Ramachandran (1998) describes as having phantoms in their brains, making them believe incredible things about their physical selves. The studies reported by Begley (2007) explain the improvement in attachment style that hypnosis creates as due to ignoring the old, habitual pathway as the patient develops new neural pathways by verbalizing feelings.

The hypnotic technique of *identifying feelings in one's body* starts by reminding the patient that feelings can be felt in one's body. To the question of "How do you feel now?" patients often respond that they feel "all right." When responding to "Where in your body do you feel all right?" they are forced to connect feeling with the body. In New Hypnosis, they often are guided to do a quick mental body check, focusing on different parts of the body, to discover how the body is expressing feelings. First, they are invited to check how the body was behaving when they were talking in therapy of painful things. Finally, they are asked to think of something else that makes them sad, worried, anxious, or any other unpleasant feeling, and to check how the body expresses it. This experiential awareness helps the patient know what the bodily sensations tell about feelings, and also to recognize that not all sensations are expressions of feelings. The purpose of this exercise is to give patients enough confidence in how the body works, so that it becomes easier for them to stop thoughts of weakness or helplessness, and to recognize other thoughts as useful or indifferent.

> Will was 52, and had a long list of somatic complaints. He had been to many specialists and had gone through numerous medical interventions. There had been no agreement on his diagnosis, other than what several physicians had told him: "It's all in your head." When Will contacted me he had not had psychodynamic therapy. I said I could promise a total improvement for all his physical problems only if he was willing to enter psychoanalysis. About two months into his analysis, mostly two sessions a week, I started using hypnotic Creative Imagination, and he responded well. He lent himself to practicing faithfully "identifying feelings" and reported that, every time after doing the exercise, he felt a sense of liberation and freedom. By that time, he was becoming quite accurate in verbally identifying his feelings and inner states. Will learned other forms of hypnotic work described earlier in this chapter, and attributed to them the increase in inner peace and contentment that he was experiencing. He also learned Buddhist meditation, which from my perspective of Creative Imagination is considered a form of hypnosis (see Chapter 12). The experience of hypnoanalysis changed his outlook on health and sickness, increasing his confidence in the wisdom of the healing power of his body, while at the same time he recognized that he (and all humans) have the power to train their minds to change their brains, a process that the use of Creative Imagination makes effective and easier than it is without therapeutic hypnosis.

## *Dependent Personality (Inner Wisdom)*

Although there are various subtypes, patients with this personality disorder were in the past labeled childish, inadequate, and insecure — anaclitic. The "dependency" comes from their habitual self-definition in terms of others. In order for them to be happy, they also need to make sure that others important to them are approving of them, praising them, ready to help them. They solicit the opinion and advice of others, unconsciously believing that they are inadequate and ineffectual. Because of this belief, they find it more difficult than do normal individuals to be alone without contacting one of the "others" they depend on. They seek psychological help when they have lost contact with a person they depended on although, as the *PDM* (2006) indicates, a diagnosis of dependency requires the therapist's awareness of cultural demands and expectations that elsewhere may be very different than our Western, and especially American, advocacy of independence and self-reliance.

With the Creative Imagination of clinical New Hypnosis, the patient may discover real areas of strength and positive resources to cope with life without overdependence on others. The technique used may be called *inner wisdom*. The patient, as always, is asked to breath, relax, and concentrate before she is instructed to remember some situation when she was surprised by her own coping, even though she had expected not to be able to do so. She is asked to concentrate on her ability, and to recognize her wisdom as a result of her life experience. Many things in life have added to her wisdom, so that it is possible to accept experientially a richer wisdom than what the patient could see before. Perhaps the wisdom appears in a symbolic, unexpected way, like an animal or a flower or an angel or a wise old person talking to her. If her wisdom comes up as a fantasy, the analyst advises her to listen carefully to what her wisdom is saying. The patient is invited to mentally talk to the wisdom that is part of her. Often the patient touches on long repressed material, finds meaningful insights, and becomes ready to take action and to change.

However, if the patient cannot think of any such situation, we go back to *mental rehearsal*, used above with schizoid personalities. By a process of approximation, we encourage her to imagine herself coping with a rather easy situation. Slowly, we propose progressively difficult situations until she can see herself acting quite effectively and with normal anxiety in difficult situations.

> This is what happened to Silvio, the editor of a literary publication in his late fifties, whose 38-years-younger partner, Juan, had died less than two years earlier. Even though Silvio was not a classic dependent personality, he was so affected by his partner's death that he was unable to think clearly. They had been practically inseparable for the last seven years. Working on relaxation, he eventually connected with his "inner wisdom," which appeared in his imagination as Juan as a spiritual being (naked but not sensual, extremely kind and gentle, beautiful in a new state of being), and came to the realization that he had done many things on his own even after Juan entered his life. Juan had always encouraged him "to use his mind and decide for

himself." Silvio imagined his inner wisdom saying that Juan was doing the same thing now and was giving him the energy he needed to try to make it on his own. The fantasy of his inner wisdom was a tunnel entrance, very dark, out of which Silvio heard Juan's voice, energetic, self-assured, and cheerful. This gave Silvio a very positive feeling, telling him to enjoy life by using his talents, thus living a full life and honoring Juan's memory. After several months of this "spiritual presence of Juan" in Silvio's life, as he called it, and of realizing in analysis where his dependency had come from in infancy, the patient considered himself cured but continued in psychoanalysis, in his own words, "in order to take full advantage of the wisdom I did not know I had." This happened after a long discussion on the "reality" of Juan's presence in Silvio's life now. The "reality" of Juan's presence after his death I consider *constructive self-deception*, which many use unconsciously, strongly believing it to be real. Juan is dead and gone but his memory in Silvio is still strong and vivid so that he, without being aware of it, imagines Juan talking to him and helping him. And this experience is enriching to Silvio. He decided to start oil painting at age 62, never having done this earlier, and he attributed this to Juan's influence and discovered with joy a talent new to him. I also see this as a benefit of constructive self-deception.

## *Phobic Personality (Inner Healer)*

There is no complete agreement on what constitutes this personality type. What psychoanalysis has called phobic, the *DSM* designates as avoidant. But regardless of the label, these patients use passive-aggressive defenses to feel safe and secure. Clinical experience teaches that many phobics who seek the help of psychotherapy for one particular phobia turn out to have been phobic for a long time in many other areas of their life. The phobic person feels restricted by his reaction to the "object" that bothers him and acts with fear and magical thinking, believing that he will be safe as long as he avoids certain specific things, people, places, actions, and the like.

In this case the *inner healer* is a hypnotic intervention that emphasizes one's unconscious ability to undo or resolve neurotic complexes in order to function well. The patient starts by paying attention to her heartbeat or her pulse, becoming aware of it. She spends a couple of minutes focusing on that manifestation of the non-conscious part of her brain controlling her heart. This same primitive brain takes care of the innumerable functions that are happening even when one is not aware of its activities, like body temperature, production of blood cells, digestion, etc., including the self-healing that is going on every minute of our existence in our physical body. Once she is in touch with this reality, she can think that this same part of her brain can help her use her own strengths and resources to be more self-sufficient and less dependent on others and on external circumstances. She can say and repeat statements like, "Yes, I can do it," visualizing herself in great detail doing what she wants to accomplish in spite of her phobia, and involving in her fantasy as many senses as possible. As with all hypnotic practices described in this book, and in Buddhist practice, repetition is essential, as the research on neuroplasticity, including Amen's (1998), has taught us. Brief instructions are given the patient to practice every day, as in the vignette below. The daily practice is strongly emphasized, as if it were a prescription medication to be taken regularly. However, often there is a conjunction of two or more personality types in the same individual, which makes it convenient to combine techniques. In this next case, traits of dependency and phobia are intertwined.

> Celeste had been brought up in the old-fashioned way, when females had no identity of their own and obtained their "being" from their marriage. Her numerous fears were well disguised. At the age of 46, she was still acting as if she were a sweet teenager and everything nice appeared in every aspect of her life. She never showed annoyance, impatience, or anger. She did not drive, she did not write checks, she spoke on the phone only with relatives or friends, she did not leave the house in the evening without her husband, she did not use public transportation or cabs. The list of phobias was very long. Now her husband was sick with leukemia, and the top specialist had told her that he probably would not have more than six to eight months to live. Celeste was desperate.
>
> Right after the diagnosis, one of her friends persuaded her to start psychotherapy, and drove her to the office for an initial double session. Celeste kept crying and asking, "What am I going to do without him?" She added that her husband was the only person she trusted. After listening to her helpless complaining for about half an hour, the clinician insisted on her paying attention to her pulse, which she finally did, slowly starting to become relaxed and comfortable while doing this. Then the analyst suggested that while this was happening her body was starting to enjoy the fullness of life. All this proceeded very slowly at first and went on in the next ten to twelve sessions, as Celeste began feeling less agitated and more comfortable. She realized and accepted that her body was healing her pain and freeing all the

inner resources she needed to become stronger. She perceived her healing forces as powerful but gentle waves that were giving her strength with every breath she took. The repetition of this mind exercise started to change her outlook, and she began to feel able to cope in that painful critical time. She started to believe that she had the needed resources and that she had the strength and capacity to become self-sufficient. She visualized breaking the self-imposed limitations, and had a fresh sensation of a freedom to be everything she was and had not been before.

Celeste's husband died seven months after he was given the cancer diagnosis. Despite the sadness, she handled the whole situation very adequately in her own estimation and to the relieved surprise of her two sons, one daughter, and many family and friends. She realized that she was a stronger woman than she had believed throughout her adult years, and continued in analysis to "change my childish helplessness." Applying what she learned about her mind through the use of New Hypnosis, she used fantasy and focused visualization very often when she started to feel frightened or insecure.

## Anxious Personality (Stop Negative Self-Hypnosis)

The *PDM* (2006) makes a statement that may surprise some: "Most individuals currently diagnosed with Generalized Anxiety Disorder are better understood as having a personality disorder in which anxiety is the psychologically organizing experience" (p. 36), adding that the omission of this personality category in most texts is "unfortunate." Anxiety ranges from mild neurosis to acute psychosis. It affects the character of the neurotic patient with symptoms of hysteria or obsessive-compulsive behavior, and it often increases the symptoms to paranoia in the latter condition. The differential diagnosis lies in two facts: first, that patients with Anxious Personality Disorder are aware of their anxiety and unable to stop it, and second, that they feel different types of anxiety such as separation, moral, signal, and so on, in contrast with patients who suffer from only one of these. Anxious patients function normally except in the one restricted situation, thus are diagnosed specifically, while those with Anxious Personality Disorder truly feel universal general anxiety.

Because these patients are masters of negative self-hypnosis (NSH), constantly reinforcing their fears and conviction of danger, even from mysterious (magical?) forces not based on reality, the awareness of their own NSH becomes a practical means for their treatment. This is the first step to improvement and cure. As we may recommend that the analysand pay attention to her dreams, we recommend her catching herself using NSH and to stop it by forcing herself to change her thoughts. Usually in the next session she will report at least awareness, and at best real progress, in the diminished use of NSH. Analysis continues in order to discover the genesis and meaning of this symptom while the concept of positive auto-hypnosis is brought to her attention. I like to explain it to patients simply as learning to use our thoughts (especially fantasies and mental images) for our benefit. Then the patient is helped to get into hypnosis, where she chooses thoughts, scenes, and people who give her a sense of peace, trust, and happiness. This is done to obtain a sense of saturation, so that she can truly believe and say to herself, "Yes, this is me. I can enjoy peace and serenity." In this type of Creative Imagination work, I like to involve as many details as possible in a dreamlike manner. I may ask, "Is there any sound close by or far away?" or "Do you notice a change in clarity and light?" or "Check if your body feels any change." In the last comment, I am looking for increased relaxation, in order to bring this up in the following step of the analytic work, in which I hope the patient realizes that her thoughts make a difference in her affect and well-being, as the following clinical vignette shows.

> Roberto, a 45-year-old bachelor, had named his Labrador after himself. Now he was convinced that this had been a mistake, and was thinking constantly about this "problem." He thought of getting rid of Roberto, but he was lovingly attached to the dog, believing that if he did so, he (the master) would die due to some mysterious, hidden forces that controlled his life. Roberto, the dog, was healthy and did not show any signs of maladaptation or unhappiness. In the first session the patient said that he was driving himself crazy with this, that he knew he was creating his own anxiety, and that this is what happened to him with everything. When his mother died of a liver disease, Roberto convinced himself that he had killed her. When his girlfriend of five years started dating a younger woman, he assured himself that it was all his fault, even though there was no evidence of anything Roberto had done or not done to bring this about. I remarked, "It appears to me that you are the first explanation you have for anything negative in your life." I mentioned, almost in passing, that this was NSH. "It seems to me that now, Roberto (the dog) will be a victim of your NSH." It looked quite obvious that there was a neurotic identification with his dog and I wanted to understand it. Because his NSH had taken the form of magical thinking, I suggested "counter-NSH" and he agreed to it enthusiastically. I asked him to use his imagination to act as if he were Roberto (the dog) talking

about his master. In spite of his initial enthusiasm, his mood changed, and he said to me that I was treating him as if he were the dog, his first expression of a transferential reaction. I asked him if anyone else had treated him that way. Roberto explained that his mother was a dog lady, and often, in a spirit of closeness, would call him "my little doggie," an expression that he despised deeply in his childhood and adolescence, but about which he said nothing because he enjoyed his mother's closeness and love. He added that often, when she called him that, he would growl and bark, sounds he hated but she loved. This behavior brought him more love; in spite of the degradation he felt when he did it. He realized then that I did not treat him like a dog, but that my suggestion of entering the dog's mind, as it were, reminded him of his childhood experiences with his mother.

What I hoped for happened. Talking as if he were the dog, he emphasized the positives and had Roberto, the dog, express how happy he was, how secure he felt, how well he was treated by his master, how fortunate he was to be called like his master, and so on. After the hypnotic experience, the patient said spontaneously that the part of him that was talking about getting rid of the dog was his "sick part" and that he was here to stop the anxiety about everything in his life. He went back into an hypnotic ego state so he could "own" the good things "the dog" had expressed. I suggested that he remember what happened in this session until the next one. In the next session he reported that he had repeated on his own many times the positive self-hypnosis "the dog had taught" him. With this insight into the meaning of dogs in his development, the analysis progressed, keeping in sight the link between his current anxiety and his early affective needs. The change takes place, as we have already seen before, when, through hypnotic focusing and repetition, a new neural pathway starts to be built slowly in the person's brain.

## *Obsessive-Compulsive Personality (Ten-Point Scale)*

To succeed in our capitalistic society, we have to be goal-directed, organized, determined, and sacrificing, that is, we must have obsessive and compulsive characteristics. Wilhelm Reich (1933) referred to the people who abide by these rules as "living machines." They are overly serious about work and do not accept affection, external expressions of caring, playing, having fun, and relaxing unless they have "justification" to do so. They are in tension between submission to authority and rebellion against authority, with its rules and limitations of freedom. Those with obsessive-compulsive personality, in their fear of losing control of their impulses, find it difficult to consider the light side of things. Humor is mostly absent. Obsessives are intellectually over involved in their "obligations." Compulsives are concerned about the smallest details and spend the time trying to do everything perfectly (as they understand "perfection"). Medications seldom cure this problem. But the method proposed by Schwartz (Schwartz and Begley, 2002) when dealing with "brain lock," which is rooted in the three parts of the brain involved in obsessions, does replace OCD behaviors with functional ones. To outline the process in simple form, the three parts of the brain are the *orbital frontal cortex*, which is activated above normal in obsessive patients, which triggers the *cingulate gyrus* (the second part) to start acute anxiety, which causes the *caudate nucleus* (the third part) to affect the body with feelings of fear and anxiety.

If hypnosis is mentioned, obsessives tend to worry about doing the right thing. They try too hard "to be hypnotized," but paradoxically resist letting go of conscious control with trust in their own unconscious, which is a requirement to enter the hypnotic experience. This is why Creative Imagination, instead of traditional hypnosis, is used successfully with obsessive-compulsive personality patients, and extra time is granted to help them relax. In order to accomplish this, methods of Buddhist meditation can be used, like a gentle and very slow rubbing of one's hands, reminding them to concentrate on every sensation and feeling that this activity elicits. Because of these patients' obsessive-compulsiveness, the clinician may suggest an imaginary ten-point scale "to measure" their concentration on their hands, encouraging a patient to increase the scale number from where she finds herself now. To do it successfully, the patient, already relaxed, imagines a ten-point scale and allows any number to pop up. Once the analysand has succeeded in letting go of other thoughts in order to concentrate on her hands, she has attained the goal of concentration and focus required for CI work. Then she is reminded that in sleep she lets herself go, simulating sleep if she prefers. The suggestions may center on freedom from "the tyranny of the should," as Horney (1950) called it, freedom to be herself, freedom to be more spontaneous and genuine. But this is not an abstract idea; she has to imagine herself enjoying the new freedom in different situations that she reviews experientially in her mind thanks to hypnosis, as Lucre did.

Lucre had just celebrated her 31st birthday and had been promoted in her job, with the new responsibility of a dozen employees. She worked in a large and important malpractice insurance company that served physicians. She realized that because of her obsessive-compulsive behavior she was wasting much time, neglecting some of the employees under her and delaying tasks that needed immediate attention. In the first session she described these patterns, saying she knew this was self-destructive behavior but that she was unable to stop herself. I responded that we would analyze her masochistic tendencies, but only after she had controlled her obsessive-compulsiveness. So, in Lucre's case, we started behaviorally in order to clear the way for the psychodynamic work. My efforts were centered on the *letting yourself go* mindset explained earlier. She firmly resisted in the first three sessions, which was her unconscious effort to get to know and trust me. Then she really tried to "let go" and practiced between sessions, initially with great intensity but after two weeks with a much more relaxed attitude, as a break in her routine and as a game, not as an obligation. After 23 weeks Lucre was convinced that she would change drastically and was able to focus on the analysis of her obsessive-compulsive personality.

## *Hysterical Personality (Self-love)*

What psychoanalysts have called *hysterical*, and the *DSM* (American Psychiatric Association, 2000) labels *histrionic*, refers, among other things, to patients with unconscious gender problems, which manifest themselves in their sexuality and personal power issues. In the succinct description of the *PDM* (2006), "unlike transgendered individuals, the hysterical or histrionic person accepts his or her biological gender, but feels that it confers significant disadvantages" (p. 60). These patients are uncomfortable with their own sexuality and gender, which they judge negatively (castration complex) in themselves and in others of the same sex. On the other hand, they believe that those of the other sex are better, stronger, more exciting, and consequently dangerous and a threat to them. The typical feelings have much to do with shame for being what they are, with fear of the other sex and, in competing with the other half, with a sense of guilt.

*Self-love* is an hypnotic intervention that emphasizes one's own personal value and that of one's own life with its uniqueness. In hypnosis the patient is guided to experientially review, gently and slowly, the values, the good deeds, the positive experiences had individually and with other people, the accomplishments (those of normal development, like talking, taking care of oneself, etc., and those more specialized that assume self-choice, like skills, aptitudes, and accomplishments). The patient may visualize herself in hypnosis participating in these situations and reminding herself that these mental images are true of her life. She may even be told to try to say to herself, "I love myself," in order to test how this statement feels and what impact it has on her, both physically and psychologically. This Creative Imagination practice has to be reiterated until she is perfectly at peace while she thinks of loving herself. This method of ego enhancement is intended to give the patient a new sense of self-worth, strength, and pride. The clinical work must insist on the fact that these positive aspects are owned by her. Repetition is essential, as new neural circuits are formed in the brain. Analyzing later her hysterical personality, with all the typical negativism, elicits less resistance because she is able to have a taste of the opposite feeling about herself. And, once more, repetition will create the new neural circuit that will take the place of the previous one., thus facilitating the analysis. A brief vignette of what happened to Kelsey illustrates the *self-love* technique.

> Kelsey was a bright, ebullient, sensitive, and giving 41-year-old woman who had lived with the habitual feeling of being worthless because she was not a man. She sought psychoanalysis because her 18-year-old daughter, "a carbon copy" of Kelsey, in her words, was showing many signs of discontent with herself. Like the mother, she hid her unhappiness and negative feelings, drawing people's interest to her and being the center of attention at parties with her friendly, loud talk and jokes. Kelsey wanted to change for herself and for her daughter, who had made comments on different occasions about the disadvantage of not being a man, hoping that her own change would help the daughter avoid many years of unhappiness like the mother had had. Kelsey added that she wanted to learn to be proud of being a woman.
>
> I presented the hypnotic experience of Creative Imagination as a "test" for her, to find out how widespread her negative feelings and dissatisfaction with herself as a woman were. Initially, Kelsey interrupted herself, even in hypnosis, every time she mentioned anything good about herself, qualifying it in order to make it appear less good. After a few times, she started correcting herself and saying things like, "Yes, that is true, I did this myself," or similar statements. Finally she was able to go over a long list of accomplishments while in the hypnotic state, and enjoyed recalling scenes from the past. With each

incident she recalled, she learned to relive it in great detail. The analyst helped her relive the memory by gently saying something like, "Go back to that moment (or scene). Be there and capture all the details, sounds, scent, temperature, objects, and persons you see. Enjoy all the good feelings," and other such statements. Kelsey repeated this practice many times between sessions. Her hysterical personality analysis lasted 15 months before we could move on to other aspects of her life.

## Dissociative Personality (Independence)

This disorder, also known as Multiple Personality, is the result of complicated defense mechanisms against severe early abuse that have become "characterological in the same way that any other defense can become locked into personality" (*PDM*, 2006, p. 62). At the time of its inception this syndrome was beneficial for the person's emotional survival but, once the individual becomes free from the traumatic situation, Dissociative Personality becomes a disorder. These people have a natural capacity for hypnosis and any form of Creative Imagination because the "multiples" appear real to them as if the person had purposely been hypnotized. In treatment, negative self-hypnosis (NSH) can change into therapeutic (auto-) hypnosis. The treatment method is to help the patient identify the affect that each multiple (personality) enacts, assisting her to find a mature and realistic way of expressing that feeling, without the prop of the "other." This makes unnecessary the "existence" and presence of the multiples, one by one. In other words, with New Hypnosis we help them to de-hypnotize themselves from the multiples as "real" people who take over their personality.

These are difficult patients and require clinicians with much patience, experience, and solid training in psychoanalysis, in therapeutic hypnosis, and in dissociative identity disorders. It is possible to address hypnotically one or another alter in order to reinforce first the healthier ones and eventually concentrate on the alter most connected with reality. The point of bringing up this rather unusual disorder is to emphasize that hypnoanalysis using New Hypnosis is effective with them, as these patients are quite expert in self-hypnotic work without realizing that this is what they have been doing for many years. The old neurological pathways have to be replaced by those that respect the patient's affective needs bypassing the symbolism of the alters' presence.

## Summary

Hypnoanalysis is always an adaptive regression (see Chapter 3, under Erika Fromm). It is regression because, for the duration of the hypnosis, the patient *gives up rational thinking* and he or she temporarily *abandons ordinary control* allowing another person, the analyst who is trusted both as a decent person and as an expert, to take over. The concept of regression in hypnosis may be clarified by thinking of dreams as expressions of what happens in a regressive state. On the other side of the coin, hypnosis is *adaptive regression,* according to Erika Fromm (Fromm & Nash, 1997), because the patient "uses" the hypnoanalyst for her benefit, idealizing him or her unconsciously. And it is also adaptive in the sense that in hypnosis the patient "sees herself" being or doing what, out of hypnosis, she believed to be impossible. I have described therapeutic hypnosis as "constructive self-deception," which is another way of talking about *adaptive regression*. But because the noun *deception* is mostly negative in our daily vocabulary, I prefer Erika Fromm's expression of adaptive regression, especially realizing that hypnoanalysis is always *a help to the ego* in order to function with greater power, satisfaction, and joy.

Another way of explaining *adaptive regression* is what Flemons (2008) elaborates in terms of boundaries between "the observing-i and the observed-me," where the distinction between the two ego states or personality parts is abandoned, in the way that the observing-i is deactivated and the observed-me blooms. "Indifferentiation," or the weakening of boundaries, extends also to the interaction between self and clinician, between self and problem, as well as between representations of different times in one's history. These terms are, obviously, similar to the *experiencing ego* and the *observing ego*, terms often used by Erika Fromm (1977).

Therefore, the hypnotic interventions described in this chapter are never ends in themselves, but are aids to uncover the truth of feelings and memories that had been repressed for a long time. The question that needs a clear answer is, "Why use hypnosis at all?" The answer is that we humans are constantly using fantasy, and it makes sense to "train" ourselves to employ fantasy for our own benefit. Freud (1897) studied unconscious fantasy and concluded that psychopathology often developed from that dynamic. Thanks to his discovery of the unconscious, he started a new science that became public with his major work, *The Interpretation of Dreams*. Later (Freud, 1908) paid attention to myths, fairy tales, and legends, as expressions of "wish fantasies of whole nations" (p. 182) (see also Bettelheim, 1977; Gieser & Stein, 1999; Knafo & Feiner, 2006). Unconscious fantasy frequently has toxic effects, but it may be used differently to obtain positive outcomes. This is what the pioneers of hypnoanalysis were after, as we explained in Chapter 3. From this point of view, not to use New Hypnosis is to neglect the potential benefit that facilitates and makes more practical the analytic work.

The next chapter deals with the principles of hypnoanalysis. I hope that reflecting on them will enlarge our tolerance and help us accept the value of New Hypnosis in psychoanalysis.

CHAPTER 8

# Principles of Hypnoanalysis

By *principles* I mean the foundations or bases, from the Latin word *principium*, which means "beginning." These principles are the component parts, the actions and attitudes without which we cannot have hypnoanalysis. I was tempted to use *kaleidoscope* in this book's title because these principles mingle with each other, overlap and enrich each other, creating new therapeutic realities—a true kaleidoscope. In the Golden Age of the Roman Empire, *principia* were mostly real, universal, practical *ideas*, not speculations, theories, or opinions. This is the reason *Lex Romana*, the Roman law, was not based on precedent and concrete cases, as the Common Law of the Anglo-Saxons was. This is also why *the spirit of the law* (the reason for its existence) rather than *the letter of the law* (what the law concretely states) was considered by the Romans in order to decide if the law had been kept or broken. Even today we see this attitude in many European countries where the Roman Empire existed, as well as in Latin American countries, which inherited their legal system from Spain and Portugal. In these countries, the spirit of the law always trumps the letter of the law, and the 60 minutes of the Anglo-Saxon hour becomes 45 to 75 minutes and it is still one hour.

With this in mind, we discuss here the *principia* of hypnoanalysis. There are two categories: *essence* principles and *practice* principles. The first category, initially discussed in Chapter 2, refers to the nature of hypnosis and is centered on fantasy with its heavy weight on sexuality, on the unconscious, on suggestibility, and on dissociation, which is impossible without understanding focusing. The practice (or utilization) principles (what conditions are required for hypnosis to be effective) are the do's and don'ts in the clinical use of hypnoanalysis for the patient and for the analyst, in order to make hypnosis effective in psychotherapy, subscribing to Renik's (2006) spirit of clinical practicality.

## 8. Principles of Hypnoanalysis

Also in Chapter 2 we touched upon *concentration, fantasy, suggestibility,* and *dissociation,* each a topic that has been dealt with by prominent authors in many volumes. *Focusing* is part of conscious fantasy in a closed self-feeding cycle, because often fantasy compels one to focus on inner reliving or pre-living of an event, and the focusing enriches the fantasy with more details. I left focusing for this point in order to emphasize the essential principles of hypnoanalysis, which are better understood as we expand our knowledge of traditional hypnosis with the modifications of New (Ericksonian) Hypnosis and the emphasis on Creative Imagination. Thus, much interest is shown today in Buddhist meditation and mindfulness, even though since Freud's time only a few psychoanalysts have paid attention to Buddhist practices, especially meditation. Among these we find Jung (1963), Erich Fromm (Fromm, Suzuki, & DeMartino, 1960), Molino (1998) and Safran (2003) among others. Meditation consists basically of focusing, and focusing leads to meditation, because it requires a change of mental attention, centering on images of tranquility and mindfulness, leading to images of something that the individual wants to experience, at least mentally. This is what Erickson's (Rossi, 1980) "letting oneself go" and Flemons's (2008) "weakening of boundaries" refer to. Focusing is always indispensable to having a vivid inner experience. For example, if someone's self-confidence is weak, the person shows it unconsciously in his behavior. But New Hypnosis can change his mental attention to the complete opposite behavior, and he can be so focused on it that, at least for a moment, he'll experience himself full of confidence. I am trying to emphasize that the Creative Imagination type of hypnosis affects focusing, often making focusing possible, but also that without focusing there cannot be any type of hypnosis.

This issue of mind affecting matter, or in Begley's (2007) words, "the causal power of purely internal mental processes [giving] rise to a biological effect" (p. 156), which is the centerpiece of Ramachandran's (1998) patient research, requires an understanding of the importance of focusing, concentrating, or simply paying attention. Science has discovered that "paying attention physically damps down activity in neurons other than those involved in focusing on the target of your attention" (Begley, 2007, p. 157). "Attention, then, pumps up neuronal activity" (p. 158) and "experience coupled with attention leads to physical changes in the structure and future functioning of the nervous system" (p. 159).

This explains the many extraordinary effects of Creative Imagination work, such as suspension of physical pain, relief of emotional distress, and many other similar results.

## Essence Principles

If we accept that New Hypnosis is a powerful means for experiential learning (a point the next chapter will elaborate), we realize also that the hypnosis elements mentioned in the first chapter — the unconscious, fantasy, suggestibility, dissociation, and focusing — are indispensable for experiential learning. The key question remains: Learning what? Ultimately the answer is always centered in Socrates's "Know thyself," out of which comes mental health and enjoyment of living to the fullest, accepting one's true limitations, and developing one's potential, the love of wisdom — philosophy. The "Know thyself" is a strong echo of the old Chinese wisdom that makes "man realize he is this true self, the Tao, and [his task is] to unite his with it again" (Cooper, 1988, p. 58). Learners must first have a fairly clear mental image of what they want to learn. Second, they must be open to the suggestion conveyed by the object to be learned, or by the person who introduces the learner to that object — the Master (guru) in most Buddhist disciplines. Third, in order to do this, they must separate or disassociate from other concerns and distractions. These elements comprise *focusing*, the activity required to learn. To express it differently, mental concentration is indispensable to using the power of the mind in order to establish new neural pathways that make permanent change possible.

Using in psychoanalysis the Creative Imagination methods of New Hypnosis we are discussing here, the patient, guided by the analyst, tries or tests effortlessly, first in her mind, what she is now confident she can do. A brief example might be helpful.

> Faustine was a 67-year-old widow with two grown, independent children when she came to the conclusion that her constant concern about pleasing her 100-year-old mother was limiting her, and made her feel owned by her mother. This was especially true since her father's recent death and the fact that her mother had now become a lonely senior, though she was healthy in mind and body. After talking for a while in a session, Faustine repeated that she was unable to stop calling and visiting the mother daily. Her rationalization was that,

## 8. Principles of Hypnoanalysis

because she refused to move in with Faustine and there was nobody else in the family to take care of her mother, she had to keep an eye on her. But, at the same time, she realized that she overdid the caring and had become obsessed with her mother's well-being. Faustine had a clear insight regarding her own insecurity, guilt, and dependency but felt trapped and unable to change.

At this point the analyst asked Faustine to imagine herself acting less intensely. She objected, saying that she was able to think of it but then, when it came to changing her behavior toward her mother, she was helpless. The clinician told Faustine that she could think in such a way that she would feel strongly that the change in her behavior was the right thing to do. He then helped her get into the state of hypnosis. Thanks to the Creative Imagination activity, Faustine did experience herself as very relaxed. She spontaneously visualized a little rosebush that she was watering and feeding, while calling her mother only every other day and visiting her only three times a week, a big reduction in daily contact. She accepted the suggestion to practice this mind activity privately every day. Faustine's analysis continued concentrating on her exaggerated feelings of responsibility toward her mother, while she was now free of the symptom that had brought her to psychoanalysis and that had been an unconscious distraction that helped her not to concentrate on her real, underlying personality problems of dependency and insecurity.

Emphasizing the goal of self-knowledge, the basic essential principle in psychoanalysis, as it is in other types of therapy, is to help the patient know herself better, more in depth, to recognize her own repressions before having the courage to face them, and to work in order to improve and eventually to free herself of the values, attitudes, perceptions, and behavior that limit her existence. Cure, often meaning freedom to be herself and happiness in her life both personal and public, is one of the basic essential principles of psychoanalysis.

Instead of wasting analytic time with the external symptom, recognizing that it is not the whole problem, hypnoanalysis proceeds by first dealing with the symptom, trying to get it out of the way. Then the psychodynamic work continues by analyzing its origins, its consequences in many aspects of the patient's behavior, its symbolism, the fantasies about the effects its absence will have on her life, and other psychodynamics.

In the above case we see some of the conditions and practices of New Hypnosis in psychoanalysis. Most are *utilization* or *practice* principles, as the next section will remind us by listing the many attitudes and behaviors that the two people involved in Creative Imagination work have to have. But the *essence* principles cannot be dismissed, and are mostly matters of common sense. Typically, the person starts with the common therapeutic conviction that she cannot attain a goal by herself but simultaneously has some hope of changing. She is also receptive to mind activities, principally of fantasy and imagination, to help her change. This is not *guided* imagery as it is commonly understood. It is rather a way of teaching the patient to use her fantasy for her own greater benefit. Whether we call this hypnosis or Creative Imagination, is less relevant than what we do activating her imagination, which is *mind training*.

## Practice Principles

The first and perhaps the most important practice principle that applies to hypnoanalysis is that the analyst should have had the benefit of some serious training as well as supervision in the use of New Hypnosis in psychotherapy. I repeat what I have emphasized earlier (Araoz, 1982), that New Hypnosis is patient-centered, even in evaluating it (Tart, 1964). The clinician is merely a facilitator who helps and encourages patients to activate their Creative Imagination and to let go of mental controls, so that mental images start flowing freely. In New Hypnosis, in Jungian fashion, the analyst steps into the fantasy with the analysand in order to facilitate the flow of idiosyncratic and Creative Imagination products. Any techniques used, like those listed in Chapter 7, have psychoanalytic value if they are genuinely eliciting personal and spontaneous (unconscious) material in the patient, as happens in dreams. I just mentioned that the analyst is "merely a facilitator" and that he "steps into the dream" that the patient experiences. In other words, there is an interaction that the therapist ignores only to his detriment and loss.

Creative Imagination or New Hypnosis work is eminently clinical, and idiosyncratically to be used in psychotherapy, not in experimental work. This is the reason for the lack of concern with constructs such as hypnotizability, posthypnotic amnesia, or hypnotic depth, among several others. This is because New Hypnosis starts from the premise that if the patient dreams, he can use hypnosis—again the emphasis on fantasy—and that the patient finds the "depth" or intensity of hypnotic

## 8. Principles of Hypnoanalysis

experience that is comfortable and helpful for him after the initial resistance is overcome.

A second practice principle for the analyst is not to introduce New Hypnosis as a change in the psychoanalytic process. The efficient way of using Creative Imagination or New Hypnosis is by mentioning fantasy or imagination. As I have explained, I prefer to use the expression Creative Imagination rather than hypnosis to avoid many misunderstandings. Thus, I find myself saying things like, "You can take advantage of your creative fantasy that produces mental images." The usual response is "How?" Only then will I go into the induction, described in Chapter 2, without further mini-lectures on the procedure.

The third practice principle refers to countertransference. It consists in staying focused and centered on the patient. The hypnoanalyst knows where to go, and often must ignore the fact that the patient moves slower in his awareness and general acceptance of the hypnotic treatment than the clinician. In supervision I notice often a sense of unconscious hurry and impatience on the part of the analyst. The more the analyst pushes, the worse it gets for the patient; he becomes more resistant. Therefore the practice principle here is not to lose touch with the patient's tempo, and to become tolerant of the patient's speed.

The fourth practice principle is also countertransferential. It is humility, or the recognition that we do not cure or produce change, but we simply guide the patient to do it. We are facilitators, a humble role, not like that of the surgeon who does not need the cooperation of the anesthetized patient. Consequently, when we use hypnoanalysis or New Hypnosis in the practice of psychoanalysis, we must be careful not to let our grandiosity take over and lead us to believe that patients react as well as they do with hypnosis because of our wonderful skills.

The fifth practice principle is the recognition that New Hypnosis is used in the service of psychoanalysis. It is effective because we use it as part of the entire treatment, not as if it had any value in and of itself. An analyst is not going to be better using New Hypnosis if he is not a good therapist without hypnosis. My assumption is that Creative Imagination helps us do better what we can do without New Hypnosis because the patient, like all humans, is almost always using fantasy. In supervision I have met practitioners disenchanted with psychoanalysis who use New Hypnosis believing that it (hypnosis) will justify the otherwise "tedious work of psychoanalysis," which they are starting to despise. I advise them to go back into personal psychoanalysis before they decide what to do. They have spent much time, energy, and money to become psychoanalysts, and if they want to discontinue that work, they must be sure that this is the right thing for them to do. This last practice principle may be called *facing the truth about oneself*. If one really feels tired of psychoanalysis, one should not use New Hypnosis to distract and entertain oneself but should face the reality of this existential moment in life and act accordingly: quit, take a break, change careers, but always re-examine honestly what one is doing—for which one must return to the couch.

Finally, I offer a brief list of do's and don'ts as practical principles.

- The place where hypnosis takes place, especially in the early stages of practicing this method, should be quiet and free from distractions.
- The room should not be too cold or too hot.
- The subject must be able to lie down or sit comfortably.
- The patient should not be hungry, thirsty, or too tired. (This applies also to the practitioner.)
- The patient is not to be chewing gum, eating, or drinking anything.

We are aware that too many patients' requests for change may be indications of resistance or a way of testing us. It may tell us that the patient is not ready to use fantasy productively, and we have to be patient, postponing Creative Imagination work for another time.

In every case it is useful to find out what concept of hypnosis the patient has, or what experience (hers or of friends or relatives) she has of hypnosis. This would be the time to find out any fears the patient may harbor of the experience. Once a patient asserted that she believed hypnosis was a greater risk than brain surgery. Ignorance of hypnosis is widespread, even among professionals, so we cannot be quick to interpret any objection as resistance, and consequently it is to our advantage to be ready with brief and clear answers when patients bring up questions or objections.

## Involving the Body

A very important principle of hypnoanalysis, which will be discussed further in the next chapter, is that the main purpose of using

## 8. Principles of Hypnoanalysis

New Hypnosis is to provide the patient with experiential learning about herself. In Buddhism, "the way" is found by practice involving the body. Thus, in every example of hypnotic technique mentioned in this entire volume, we may ask the patient to identify *the place in her body* where she feels the affect that accompanies what she is talking about, be it anger, depression, fear, or any other emotion. The justification for this procedure starts from the fact that for many people a psychological pain is less concrete than physical suffering. By using the method of Creative Imagination, the patient feels less helpless and becomes naturally aware of the intimate connection between mind and body. Consequently, she can do something about her pain, and she learns to use the method on her own. Anxiety, so frequently a complaint, serves well to illustrate somatic involvement. When the person mentions that she suffers from anxiety, the needed preliminary information is to find out if she is going through this right now. If so, I find it helpful to suggest, as in the case of obsessive-compulsive personality in Chapter 7, a ten-point fantasy scale of anxiety, in order to ask her where she finds herself now on that scale. The first question is to ask where in her body she feels the anxiety more specifically at this point. Let's assume she indicates her chest. Next we ask her to visualize the anxiety lodging in her chest: its size, its texture, its color, etc. Is the anxiety moving at all? Is it changing its shape? Then we suggest that she direct her breathing, again using her fantasy, to that area, saying to herself that the mind controls the body and she wants to use that power for her well-being. So, for a couple of minutes, every time she inhales, she tries to remind herself of her mental power to arrest the anxiety, while she visualizes her anxiety, as described before, melting away or shrinking, so that after a few minutes she feels the anxiety weaken, as indicated by a smaller number on the scale.

Summarizing the method to attain somatic involvement, we have the following steps (not to be covered literally but to keep in mind as a general guide).

1. Is the patient suffering from his condition in the present?
2. If so, how intense is the suffering? (Use the ten-point scale.)
3. Where in the body does he feel that affect?
4. What is the fantasy nature of the (suffering) experience? How does his suffering appear in fantasy?

5. Direct breathing in fantasy to that part of the body. How does the feeling appear in fantasy and how does it change?
6. Monitor the change in sensation by using the patient's mind power.
7. Continue with #5 and #6 (above) until there is evidence of change.

For the involvement of the body in the hypnotic experience, the starting question is always #3. And then we proceed as just indicated. The patient has to recognize that his psychological suffering has unconscious meaning. This meaning is analyzed after it has shown itself in the body.

## The Case of Mr. P.

He was in his mid-forties, in a medical profession, a well-educated and hard-working person. He had the admiration of his family and friends, and was well liked by all his acquaintances. When he turned 40, he started worrying about his heart, becoming very aware of any sensation in his chest, often feeling what he called "pain" during waking hours, and waking up at night with the fear of having a heart attack. After having consulted with several excellent specialists, he was referred to me because all the tests, studies, and examinations had turned out negative: there was nothing wrong with his heart. Mr. P. had many erroneous ideas of psychoanalysis, and declared that he just wanted to get rid of his constant concern about his heart. After two entire sessions discussing his condition, he accepted that the experts had basically agreed that his thinking was causing his distress. I added that I agreed with him regarding stopping his obsession as soon as possible, but that I wanted his promise to stay with me after the symptom was gone in order to understand the origins of his misery and to immunize himself against the same or a similar symptom in the future.

It was evident that Mr. P.'s personality symptoms combined elements of his pathological somatizing with those of his obsessive-compulsiveness. When we started with New Hypnosis, I asked him to report, á la Tart (1970), based on the ten-point fantasy scale, where he would place himself on that scale when we were together in the session. He reported 5, saying that he was afraid of deceiving himself if he stopped worrying, confirming his obsessive-compulsiveness. He obtained a good level of relaxation and I suggested that, if the pain was not caused by any heart pathology, he would be able to manipulate it and change its location in the body, moving the pain from place to place in his body. Maintaining his relaxation, I suggested that the pain that was now on the left side could move to the right. After a very short period of time, Mr. P., smiling, stated that the pain was now on the right side of his body. Then I suggested that he could move the pain once more but this time away from his body. Where was the pain now with respect to his body? We did this a few more times and I recommended that he try to do this on his own until we met again in a few days.

From that first experience with hypnosis, Mr. P. devised his own therapeutic uses. Thus, when he started to feel his "pain" during the day, he would move the pain to another part of the body and then dismiss it. Slowly, he learned to perceive his pain as an intruder that had sneaked into his mind against his will. He started analysis after five or six visits. In his analysis we did many things that involved New Hypnosis. Although he began as a worrisome individual, he became more relaxed and learned to enjoy life with all its small pleasures, like eating slowly or walking for relaxation. He discovered that his cardiac concern was related to his mother, who had been a very effective caretaker but who had no sense of empathy toward her children, except for one of Mr. P.'s younger sisters, who had died of cardiac arrest when she was just a pre-teenager. His mother, in helpless pain, had become bitter and angry toward the whole world. Now, some of the changes he made in his life with the help of hypnoanalysis occurred in his relationships with people, especially close friends, with whom he started to be more open than before about his feelings and emotional needs, while showing sympathy and understanding toward their diverse emotional desires for validation, understanding, and support. The rule I follow is that the more somatic the complaint, the faster the patient should be guided into the psychosomatic connection by means of New Hypnosis.

## Summary

We have reviewed the principles of hypnotherapy, that is, the elements that will make it effective without weakening the psychoanalytic side of treatment and adding something valuable and efficient. I distinguished between *essence* principles and *practice* principles. Among the essence principles, I stressed *focusing*, often taken for granted in our culture, very much unlike the Buddhist philosophy that values focusing for meditation and mindfulness. In our culture we are lucky that our culture is starting to adopt these Buddhist practices in psychology, education, and medicine.

Throughout the chapter I emphasized New Hypnosis which, as we stated repeatedly, is patient-centered and naturalistic, avoiding all appearances of artificiality and obligatory behavior. Once the clinician who is new to hypnoanalysis recognizes the naturalness of the New Hypnosis and the value of Creative Imagination work, he will forget about "hypnosis" and concentrate on the activation of the patient's fantasy. The practice principles, in addition to the ethical need to learn, through training and supervision, how to use New Hypnosis in psychotherapy, emphasize the analyst's behaviors that are prerequisites to being effective as a hypnoanalyst. Finally, I presented the case of a patient who benefited greatly through hypnoanalysis. Thanks to New Hypnosis, he recovered his self-confidence and used his mind to control his body.

CHAPTER 9

# Mind Training/New Hypnosis as Experiential Learning

Experiential learning implies that the individual gets into the action even though she does not understand it, and finds in the experience itself new meaning and personal enrichment. That is the reason experiential learning is always eminently subjective and idiosyncratic. Many of the essential things we learn early in life come to us via experiential learning. Psychoanalysis in itself has much of experiential learning (think of transference) and, because it is a subjective experience, no one can ever predict with certainty what a person will reap from it. When it comes to hypnosis or, more exactly, successful hypnoanalysis, it is always supposed to be experiential learning.

Here I discuss the clinically practical aspects of hypnoanalysis as experiential learning. Simplifying a very complex process, we can state that the great majority of psychological problems people have are unconsciously self-made, what Buddhism describes as "we are what we are because of our thinking." The unique greatness of psychoanalysis is that it helps the patient make that discovery and start the process of reconstruction by working consciously with the strengths and positive resources that had been ignored or misused before starting psychoanalysis. Creative Imagination/New Hypnosis adds greater immediacy to the inner experience of the change from neurotic to healthy living. Thanks to the vivid experience of hypnosis in psychoanalysis, the patient is able, first, to recognize the new self she can become, and second, to accept what she must do in order to get there. Chapter 11 of this book, building on Maslow's (1968) *positive psychology*, which was actualized in the last two decades or so by Seligman (1995), concentrates on psychoanalysis as a "method" of self-enrichment and growth attained by means of the completed therapeutic work. This is the Buddhist aspect of psychoanalysis, which could well be called *positive psychoanalysis*. Once started, analysis never ends, because one of its benefits is the experiential learning of introspection. With New Hypnosis, introspection becomes an idiosyncratic method, and thus experiential learning. In what way does this happen? By accepting a new reality in one's mind, the patient often recognizes her own ineffective defenses, self-defeating deceptions, and excuses that she used before in order to have it both ways, namely, to believe that she is changing and to stay the same way she was before. In hypnosis the patient experiences herself differently, guided by the hypnoanalyst to employ the hidden inner resources for success, satisfaction, and enjoyment.

Not to get confused, it is wise to note that *emotional learning* is another expression used in contrast to *rational learning*. For the practical purposes of this book, we do not distinguish emotional from experiential learning. For example, by allowing ourselves to live in our mind (hypnosis) what we want to be, free from the symptoms that bother us, as well as to understand our inner dynamics, our emotions easily correspond to the positive events we are "living" in fantasy. Because nothing is introjected in a purely rational and conscious manner, our experiential learning is always packed full of emotion. This seems to be Wachtel's (1997) rationale for considering behavioral methods (homework, engaging in ego-dystonic activity that corresponds to superego functioning, etc.) also as methods of experiential learning. By getting actively involved in the mental action, the individual is having a new experience from which he learns something new, typically about himself.

> This was the case of Santi, a patient who said at the start of the first session that he was frustrated and upset because he had had a dream the night before that moved him deeply, and that he knew was important, but from the moment he woke up he could not remember a thing about the dream. He explained that he was still under the influence of the feeling elicited by the dream. The feeling was good and peaceful, and probably had something to do with his two brothers who had died, one the year before and the other four years earlier. In explaining why he thought the dream had to do with his two brothers, he said that he had been thinking of his alcoholic brother and how he wasted his life in his last seven years after he had been forced to retire against his will. Santi said that he was afraid of his own alcohol consumption, which had increased recently. The day

before he had bought a big bottle of his preferred liquor and paid good money for it, and had dismissed the thought about his brother while paying. He was told to check the thought he had dismissed and to let the entire thought develop as if he had not dismissed it.

Using the New Hypnosis approach of Creative Imagination, he was invited to imagine that he was dreaming now and to let himself go into the dream. In this hypnotic state he was instructed to let the dream develop. He spent no more than five intense minutes doing this. When he returned to his ordinary way of thinking, he said with emphasis that he felt very bad for his brother and angry at his neglect of his own health. He said, almost crying, that he did not want to follow in his brother's footsteps and was going to start taking his drinking seriously.

New Hypnosis, in this case, clarified Santi's dream and the message it had for him. It also made him face his resistance and self-deception, leading him to start in an AA program to regain control of his drinking and to stop using alcohol as a daily ritual. The hypnotic dream gave him an experiential understanding of where he was and where he had to go. He had experienced, hypnotically, his need to take his drinking seriously. Santi's powerful and real learning experience, which led him to change, became his cure and therapy.

It is also interesting to note that the entire dream work started with Santi's saying that he could not remember anything about this dream, though he knew it was important to him. Thanks to New Hypnosis techniques, he benefited from the forgotten dream. The dream that had been real but forgotten became the hypnotic dream that had a meaningful message for him.

## The Inner Experience as *Vivencia*

In psychoanalysis generally, we help patients have these vivid inner experiences. Elsewhere (Araoz & Goldin, 2004), I have used the Spanish noun *vivencia* to describe this powerful form of experiential learning. *Vivencia* is a vivid daydream or fantasy, thanks to which a person is emotionally and mentally fully experiencing the scene in great detail and using all of his senses (not only "the mind's eye" of Hamlet's exchange with Horatio). This is what happens when a patient, after having worked on a specific issue, comes to the point of true insight—which for Buddhism is enlightenment and for others is the moment of *eureka*, of complete awareness and certainty. In fact, psychological change is not possible unless there is *vivencia*. The person has to experience thoroughly in his own mind and body the possibility (and the reality) of change before it becomes his goal. Conversely, change becomes the goal of the individual only after he has had the *vivencia* of the clear realization of the change in his mind and body. Creative Imagination makes this realization vivid, spontaneous, easy, realistically possible, and natural. And, since the recent discoveries of neuroscience, we know that the *vivencia* activates the new neural circuit, making the change real. The following vignette may be helpful.

> Bill, 66 years old, was very unhappy in his marriage, which had lasted 36 years and produced a daughter, now 35, and two sons, 33 and 31, all of them already married. His fantasy about a good marriage, in contrast to his current one, was reasonable and realistic. His problem was how to approach his wife with his decision to end the marriage. Employing New Hypnosis, without mentioning the phrase, and stressing fantasy or imagination, I encouraged him to visualize the entire scene and to experience himself acting the way he wanted to act: "Be there in your mind, go through the whole scene now." I used hypnotic *vivencia* for Bill to feel comfortable (or not) with the change, going over details and strengthening or weakening his resolution to leave the marriage. However, in the midst of his vivid fantasy of the divorce process, Bill started smiling and showing great happiness. In his fantasy he was with one of his subordinates at work, a man in his forties, to whom he felt very attracted in a sexual way. The younger man had never been married, was intelligent, with many artistic and cultural interests, and had always shown friendly respect for the older co-worker. Bill's fantasy developed in his mind into a very explicit sexual encounter, during which he repeated that he did not want to admit to his homosexual preference, that he had been embarrassed, ashamed, and guilty for many years, during which he had experienced similar attraction to other men but kept repressing it on moral and religious grounds. He had never allowed himself to have the *vivencia* he just had in his hypnotic dream. New Hypnosis developed spontaneously into a vivid dream without any direction on my part.
>
> This led Bill into the unexpected direction of his true life-long sexual preference and forced him to face what he had been avoiding through repression all his life. Later, in the analytic, non-hypnotic section of our session, he revealed that he had been tormented by these fantasies since high school and especially in college. He suspected that this constant inner turmoil had made him a very good student, thus avoiding his sexual drive and obtaining high grades in all his undergraduate and graduate studies. He had married explicitly so that he would forget about the shameful and sinful attraction to males.

We may speculate that without his Creative Imagination in New Hypnosis, it would have taken much longer to come up with the truth, to face it and accept it, than with the use of it. In this case the patient discovered his self-deception with the marriage first, and now, knowing the reasons, he had to end it. A therapy session with his wife brought him great peace when she admitted that for many years she had been quite suspicious of Bill's sexual orientation, had read much about it, and had finally pushed the entire thing under the rug. She knew that her husband was functioning sexually with her "under duress" in order to please her but not because he wanted it. She loved him more like a brother or a good friend than like a husband, and was happy that they finally could bring this out into the open. She showed understanding and reassured him that she had nothing to forgive him for; that she felt guilty not having brought up this earlier for so many years.

New Hypnosis makes it possible to "live" the difficult future situation in one's mind before one has to face the reality that is so difficult to accept. This is experiential learning, as we have seen. But it also helps to go back to one's past mistakes and to learn from them and never do them again, as Bill realized when his unconscious made him face what his ego had been trying to keep hidden for so many years.

## Experiential Learning When Unconscious Material Is Reached

From infancy on, we learn from role models, as if we are saying to ourselves that "Mommy (or Daddy) is doing something and I like it, so I will try it myself when I can do so." In a true sense, even though formal thinking is not yet available, humans start very early "to think," as Piaget's (1952) studies have shown. If we could make an outline of the unconscious process, it would turn out that first we witness something that attracts our attention and interest. Second, we record it mentally, going over it in our fantasy. Third, after years of fantasy, once we have become familiar with it in our thoughts, we try it in our actions.

Later in life, most adults under the influence of societal objectivity and the uneasiness of subjectivity have become adept at avoiding this type of "thinking," although the exception seems to be much of the sexual material that often floods the adult mind before the individual attempts action. New Hypnosis, taking off from something the patient says or from some spontaneous gesture she makes, can use again the early type of model learning, which is a form of experiential learning, for a person's benefit.

Developmentally, the model we learn from is outside of ourselves but in this case the model is in one's mind, unconsciously introjected by unconscious identification. A simple example would be someone who knows he should be more assertive with his boss. He goes through the entire movie in his head of what he can do and say but he comes to a point where he convinces himself that he'll never act that way. In this case, he reinforces the negative outcome with his own negative self-hypnosis. The old neural pathways are too strong, and no halfhearted resolution to change will do, but only a determination to focus repeatedly on the opposite possibility, in this case, to visualize himself assertive in dealing with his boss.

In hypnoanalysis, taking advantage of a simple statement like "I can't do it," we can encourage the patient to have a *vivencia* of what he knows he can and should do. We can help him hold on to the role model in his mind. He identifies with his mental image of success, repeating the same mind exercise until it becomes possible and desirable. Obviously, he will show quite a bit of unconscious resistance, and this is where we get back to analyzing it: What deprives him of the benefit of doing what he wants? In insisting on the image of success, he is establishing the neural pathway that will make success possible and (almost) natural.

This form of experiential learning offers the advantage of using something that comes from the patient (for instance, "I can't do this") and contrasting it with what he wants. The use of personality parts or ego states, in this case, is a practical hypnotic way of making progress. The patient accepts that one part of him knows it is helpful to try a behavioral change and another part is afraid of it. Visualizing these two parts (or ego states), patients find it more acceptable to assume the responsibility for deciding what part of them will run their life.

## Other Uses of Hypnosis as Experiential Learning

This section briefly presents a specific situation that many therapists do not believe can be responsive to hypnotic intervention. My thinking

## 9. Mind Training/New Hypnosis as Experiential Learning

is that the case described below may help practitioners not familiar with New Hypnosis accept this as a valid approach to assisting patients in their efforts to change and improve.

Ellen and her husband, Corey, had been married for 22 years. After Ellen was diagnosed with multiple sclerosis (MS), in the last five years she had become an invalid, needing assistance for eating, turning in bed, going to the bathroom, having a bath, and any other activity. Her understanding and intelligence were not affected at all, but her speech was laborious and slow most of the time. She was in constant pain and the powerful medications prescribed for her upset her digestive system and made her feel even worse. Corey had become desperate, extremely anxious, and ineffective when Ellen's MS started to change his entire life, morning to bedtime. To continually see his wife in constant pain did not desensitize him to her suffering. It triggered in him depression, confusion, and negativism, in a generalized sense of being abandoned and punished. The agonizing confusion came from some well-meaning friends who advised him to hospitalize Ellen. He could not think of it, let alone plan it or do it. But Ellen had become more possessive than before her sickness, and demanded his constant presence and closeness. At this point he became my patient.

Because of the circumstances, Corey's therapy benefited Ellen directly when he was able to teach his wife to be more positive. I never saw Ellen, but Corey instructed Ellen on the hypnotic methods that he was learning and practicing. His wife's unusual participation in my patient's analysis went on for several weeks unknown to me, as it was revealed only later in the analytic work. This had two benefits. It was helping Corey feel more in control and do something positive for his sick wife, and it benefited Ellen with methods for reprogramming her mind with positive thoughts. Corey became less anxious and desperate, and was able to work more effectively on his analysis, while Ellen started very soon to benefit from the new way of thinking, which she was able to control naturally.

The mind exercises I proposed were hypnotic, taken directly from Buddhist teaching. The first practice consisted of a simple Zen-type meditation that Corey practiced with me before proposing it to his wife. Ellen was to concentrate on her breathing (fortunately not affected by the MS), counting 1 for inhaling and 2 for exhaling, stopping at 10. Then starting once more, counting the breaths from 1 to 10 as many times as necessary to unite her mind to her breathing. With this practice, Ellen started to become an "outsider" to her pain. She was observing her pain rather than just putting up with it helplessly. She started to master her mind and to change her brain physically by creating a new neural pathway. Now she was in control. She was not at the mercy of her pain as long as she continued to practice these hypnotic exercises. Corey reported to me that Ellen was doing this "all the time" and that she was feeling much better.

A few weeks later I proposed another hypnotic practice, also taken from Buddhist teaching and only slightly different from the first mind activity, which Corey, as before, tried first with me in the office before teaching it to his wife. This time, after becoming aware of her breath and relaxing, Ellen would concentrate on the way her body expands and contracts with breathing. Then she would pay attention to the nature and quality of her breathing: smooth, slow, rhythmic. Then she would think without effort of "impermanence" in all things, including her pain.

I never saw Ellen in person but, thanks to the techniques Corey had learned, she felt much better, less powerless, and much more detached from her pain, which now she was observing, not just helplessly suffering. Corey reported that he had joined his wife while she did the mind exercises. He felt free from his feelings of guilt, helplessness, and depression, and was able to analyze those feelings that had taken over his entire life just a few weeks before.

Calling this modality hypnoanalysis comes from the Creative Imagination activity that makes analysis possible in a more direct way. This is true if we agree that the center of psychoanalysis is the unconscious reality in the human soul (*Seele*), as Freud called what the English translation has as *psyche*. Hypnoanalysis is more direct because much of the unconscious activity is by means of fantasy, imagery, or imagination, the tools of New Hypnosis.

> The third mind practice, slightly different from the previous two, was for Corey to imagine himself happy, relaxed, and at peace, while enjoying every moment of living, knowing that the current malaise would soon end and give room to well-being. To activate this conviction, Corey elected to gently and inconspicuously rub his thumb and index finger the moment he realized that he was mentally moving into negative feelings about himself.

In this case, as the reader can see, rather arbitrary connections between inconspicuous physical activity and mood were made, later between breathing and more efficient immune system functioning, and in general between breathing and focusing of attention. Because of the adaptability of the limbic system (more exactly, the limbic-hypothalamic paths of sensory input) in the perception of sensory and fantasy stimuli, both unconscious and conscious (see Chapter 1), New Hypnosis can provide the patient fresh, positive experiences and contradict negative beliefs, fears, and attitudes. Thus, we find in this case once more that New Hypnosis facilitated the subjective perceptual change, as shown also in every one of the twelve hypnotic techniques described in Chapter 7 and in practically every clinical vignette discussed in this book. The experiential learning takes place because in the state of hypnosis the patient perceives the new mental stimuli as real, subjectively experienced by her as she experiences other ordinary stimuli. Some simple examples of experiential learning are those situations where a person learns by *doing* something, frequently found in Buddhism, where even the most menial activity, like carrying water or chopping wood, may be full of meaning and therefore precious. With New Hypnosis, Ellen was doing something naturally and with ease, which she was not able to do before she used New Hypnosis. The vast research conducted by Sheehan and McConkey (1995) validates the concept of experiential learning from the other end, that of the hypnotic subject's own report on hypnotic responsiveness, and of the meaning and value she gives this learning experience. Finally, applying the basic principles of neuroplasticity, we understand that repetition is essential to learning (or changing from not knowing to knowing) because it makes the new biological pattern possible; each time the neural pathway becomes more defined. In the case of chronic pain described earlier in this chapter, Ellen was able to alleviate her pain and make it more bearable. The regular psychoanalytic patient can also taste the attractiveness of non-neurotic living if hypnotic methods, often originating in Buddhism, enrich and transform his psychotherapy into hypnoanalysis.

> This was the case with Ed, another patient who had suffered anxiety with obsessive-compulsive disorder (OCD) for the last fifteen years or so. The OCD symptoms had started after having sex as a young teenager, when a friend told him that the girl who had been his partner probably had AIDS or some serious disease because she had been raped by three thugs shortly before Ed had met her. From that time on, sex had always been a source of great anxiety for Ed, who feared either getting a disease or giving the disease to his partner. This continued after he was married and faithful to his wife. After ascertaining that he had the necessary medical tests to make sure he was not infected, I reminded him that it was possible for him to experience the total opposite of anxiety. Because his mental condition was severe, and he refused even the thought of taking medication, I suggested "a mental method to experience non-anxiety," to have joy, happiness, and well-being as goals, even before we found out the inner dynamics that led him to all the years of misery. He questioned that possibility

but agreed to try. As expected, Ed rationalized his resistance to the new approach. Following Schwartz and Begley (2002), I helped him re-label his thoughts as beneficial and not beneficial. The latter he threw away in his fantasy, keeping the beneficial thoughts. Then he learned to re-focus on a subjectively beneficial thought. After a few attempts, Ed became very relaxed. I purposefully kept him in this enjoyable mental and physical state for a few minutes more than I normally would. He clearly took this event as a learning experience and used it as the means to reach the goal of absence of anxiety. As a matter of fact, whenever he became discouraged or negativistic in his analysis, in or out of the session, he went back on his own auto-hypnosis to "the good experience" and this motivated him to continue his hypnoanalysis.

# Summary

An important final comment on experiential learning is that New Hypnosis gives the analyst the flexibility to note minute differences each time the patient repeats the original mental image of his non-neurotic living, so that these differences can be analyzed. For instance, a new person appears in the patient's fantasy in the latest version, or the physical details of the place are different. In general, I have noticed that the patient becomes productively introspective sooner by using New Hypnosis than without it; the patient uses self-analysis sooner and better with auto-hypnosis than without it.

Because these New Hypnosis mind exercises are creating new neural circuits that produce pleasant effects, there is here an element of self-reinforcement, as the individual, unconsciously, tries the approach to the level of satisfaction again and again. Thus, I find that dreams increase in number and in meaning. Investigating this would be a productive topic for a doctoral dissertation. This experiential learning is what Freud attempts to provide the patient with free association: "turn off your logical thinking and let what is inside you come out." This is also what Zen Buddhism attempts by encouraging people to stop thinking of the self and to focus on the unity of the individual with the entire universe. Wilson Ross (1980) puts it this way: "Zen holds that the so-called rational mind is incapable of solving an individual's deepest problem: his meaning to himself and to life.... Final awareness, lasting freedom and true psychological equilibrium come only when the deepest intuitional faculties of the human being have been tapped.... [The goal is] to see life's wholeness and oneself in relation to it.... Since All-is-One, knowledge of one's own true nature predicates knowledge of all nature, or the universe itself" (p. 144). The language may be confusing but the idea is not too far from the goals of psychoanalysis and of any psychodynamic therapy: truth, true self-knowledge, and knowledge of the world in which we live.

CHAPTER 10

# Unconscious Resources Activated with Mind Training

The U.S. Army in the twentieth century used the motto, "Be all you can be in the Army," implying that joining the army would enrich the individual as a person. Consider also that the noun *education* and the verb *to educate*, from the Latin, literally mean "to bring forth" or "to draw out." This can be applied to the unconscious resources and qualities, talents, and opportunities that are hidden from the student, fostering the good ones and avoiding the others. In the words of Watkins and Barabasz (2008) "hypnoanalysis is a 'pulling out' ... in practice [it] involves the addition of the induction of hypnosis plus the use of special techniques that hypnosis makes possible" (pp. 15–16).

Because the hypnoanalysis we are dealing with uses New Hypnosis, it employs *indirect* suggestions that originate in the patient and that are so subtle, as suggestions go, that they barely deserve to be called suggestions. The use of hypnosis was understood differently by Freud (1888), who thought of hypnosis as a way to use direct suggestion. Simply put, *direct* suggestion is a command, telling the patient what to do (e.g., "The pain will be gone when I finish counting to ten," or "You will feel nauseous next time you smoke a cigarette," etc.) while *indirect* suggestion is an invitation, using fantasy to try in one's mind something new (e.g., "I wonder if you might imagine yourself getting up in the morning feeling happy to be alive," or "You may visualize yourself feeling self-confident and peaceful when talking with your boss.") These "weak," indirect suggestions, which we consider so important in identifying this hypnotic approach, are merely *utilization*, as Erickson (Rossi, 1980) called them. They refer to something concrete that is happening or will happen to the patient in the environment.

No contemporary hypnoanalyst uses direct suggestion because good psychoanalysis (and good therapy, in general) does not tell patients what to do. The combination of hypnosis with psychoanalysis exists only in order to facilitate the process of analysis, which is one of the powerful arguments Erika Fromm (1977) insisted on. With indirect suggestions and utilization, the patient has a greater chance of gradually lifting repressions, and of recognizing the beneficial power of his fantasies and thoughts, than if he were told how to act. We saw in Chapter 1 that Freud (1888), like most people in his cultural world, had a mistaken understanding of hypnosis, as if the subject or patient were under the control and at the mercy of the hypnotist. Here we focus on direct and indirect suggestion by which New Hypnosis "responds" to the patient's nonverbal communication through symptoms or spontaneous behavior, trying to find larger and deeper meaning in them. The benefit of doing so is that the metaphorical and symbolic language is answered in a metaphorical and symbolic manner. Contrary to direct suggestion that counters the symptom, in the thinking of Flemons (2008), among other Ericksonians, indirect suggestion uses the symptom as it encounters it, thus changing its nature from negative to positive. Therefore, indirect suggestions contribute to the changes in neural pathways, thanks to the neuroplasticity of the brain, establishing new (healthy!) pathways to improve the patient's life.

> An example is that of a patient who had a rich repertoire of facial expressions. Instead of asking him what a particular facial distortion meant, I asked him to make that face again or to make the opposite face to the one he had just made. Once he did, I wondered about the place and circumstances where he found himself in fantasy doing it and to describe it in detail. I also asked him to tell me about the people around him in his mind's eye, the ones he liked and felt comfortable with and the ones he did not. I may also have asked him about other fantasy details, like sounds or music, scents, and temperature. All these we can consider indirect "suggestions" to look deeper inside of himself, similar to the induced dreams discussed in Chapter 5. In both cases the suggestion leading to introspection generates effective insight leading to change.

It is easy to move from what we are talking about to the "unconscious resources" that can be activated with this approach. These resources may be grouped in the vast land of repression, and many of these consist of unused but genuine wealth for the individual. To cite merely one example, biographers tell us that Winston Churchill started painting when he was past 60, and he became quite proficient at it. There is no evidence one way or another but we may ask if he was repressing this talent without being aware of it, or perhaps he was deliberately keeping it in check in order to devote himself to the political matters he had to attend to. In psychoanalysis we very often see patients developing new talents that they had ignored or neglected earlier. These talents may be less concrete than artistic painting, but all psychoanalysts have had patients who did not know they could be more creative or athletic, assertive or organized, more self-confident, self-loving, or sensitive and generous toward others. Or, on the contrary, they discovered in psychoanalysis that they could be less self-effacing or condescending or less affected by others' behavior and opinion. These are just a few of the unconscious resources that psychoanalysis often helps patients discover, own, and put to work for their benefit.

I stated several times in previous chapters that frequently hypnoanalysis makes it possible to face these resources sooner and in less time than does regular psychoanalysis. It is true that Freud (1888) affirmed that behavior originating in hypnotic suggestions does not last, but he is not talking about the type of hypnosis we practice today and call "new." In the current modality of hypnosis, the clinician does not use direct suggestions, because they do not work and are not necessary. In sum, the difference between the two types of hypnosis is that, by activating the imagination with New Hypnosis, the patient can become very aware of what she wants or fears, of what possibilities or obstacles are realistic, and of the consequences to be expected from particular actions, whether positive or negative. Traditional hypnosis, as Freud (1905a) indicates repeatedly when commenting on the case of Anna O., relies mostly on direct suggestion, whereas New Hypnosis, as developed by Erickson, uses mostly *utilization* (see Rossi, 1980), which takes advantage of what is happening between the patient and the analyst, or with the environmental situation, and transforms it into indirect suggestions to help the patient enter the hypnotic state and work while in it. This is the outcome of "patient-centeredness" (Araoz, 1985b; Rogers, 1951), the imperative for the clinician to be intensely focused on the patient, which the next chapter will develop further. But this intensity is nothing artificial or forced. It is the outcome of the analyst's sincere interest in the patient. As indicated in Chapter 1, hypnoanalysis "utilizes" what the patient says or does in order to start the New Hypnosis work. This often includes the symptom itself, which the patient produces unconsciously. Unlike the purely cognitive-behavioral approach, which is essentially intellectual and rational (remember Albert Ellis's *Rational*-Emotive Behavior Therapy), we insist on experiential learning, and ask the patient to "be there, to see, to smell, to feel, to hear" in her fantasy and imagination.

When we, together with several of the hypnoanalysts mentioned in Chapter 3, refer to unconscious resources activated by the New Hypnosis, we have in mind the capability of the patient to change, to improve his life with true self-love, enjoyment, satisfaction, fulfillment, and the enrichment of those who deal with him, intimately or in passing. All these vague and abstract words translate into *changed behavior*, coming out of the freedom from unconscious dynamics that previously the patient thought were part of her nature and could not be altered. This is also the goal of Buddhism, with its emphasis on each person's connection with all things—"The Great Teaching of the Whole." It is the individual's responsibility to attain enlightenment by following the ancient teachings; by oneself evil is done and by oneself one is purified.

Once she "experiences" in New Hypnosis the empowered self in action, the transformation of the self occurs more smoothly than without hypnosis and becomes part of the patient's self-perception. The hypnotic experience is a preparation and condition for the psychic growth that Buddhism calls "enlightenment." It is a rehearsal of one's new reality. Again here we find the Virgilian assertion mentioned in Chapter 1: "You become what you imagine." Because the patient is aware of neurotic limitations and restrictions and has already learned to free herself from many of them, she often develops new interests that add satisfaction to her life.

## The Case of Del

> This clinical vignette exemplifies the contention of New Hypnosis clinicians. Del was in her mid-fifties when she started psychoanalysis three times a week, after having been in psychodynamic therapy on and off for over fifteen years with different therapists who used diverse methods, from groups to psychodrama, from systemic to existential. She worked in a large corporation, teaching management to business people and organizing programs that were presented all over

the country. The programs were quite introspective, and she helped the participants become aware of their own resistances and take the risk of looking at themselves honestly and truthfully. She now had the opportunity to retire early with excellent benefits, but wanted to assure herself that she would make the right decision. Because of her positive motivation and prior experience, I emphasized fantasy (hypnosis) from the very beginning, insisting on the *mind training* she would be engaged in. Del responded well and practiced on her own between sessions. After having "put together" and relived in her mind all the things that she had benefited from in the many years of therapy and of her own mental work, she imagined them as architectural foundations of a new beautiful and powerful building. To her it looked like a solid modern castle. From all the hypnotic practice and mind training, in sessions and alone, she saw the building as a symbol of what she would be after analysis. She focused on the specific details of what she wanted to be, thanks to her analysis. Many aspects of the building represented her and her desires: to have a solid character foundation, to be influential on others, to be useful, and so on. All these concepts were later analyzed while she stayed with this symbolic image of herself "enlightened," and she decided to go ahead with her retirement. Now she was wondering if she would continue part-time in the same or similar line of work, or if she would give that up completely. I want to focus here on how the hypnotic mind training helped Del. With it she found a fresh way of looking at herself, and the means to utilize her potential and activate her individual talents, to feel better about herself and to become more satisfied with her life. This kind of hypnosis helped Del to empower herself.

Another significant aspect is that of creativity through fantasy. Never before had Del imagined that the modern castle, symbolizing her "finished self," could be used as a fantasy that came spontaneously from her unconscious to reveal important dynamics and aspects of her personality. She had guided some of her corporate students to use fantasy in a creative manner, but for the first time now she had used the same exercise in an experiential learning mode. Patients may be invited to use their fantasy, especially when they, as in Del's case, identify a fantasy that includes them, or someone or something important to them.

## Psychoanalytic Speculation

From the psychoanalytic perspective, as well as from that of neuroplasticity, we can try to understand what happens to the person who is in this form of hypnosis. From the psychoanalytic perspective, Pine's (1990) general outline is useful for theory and practice. First, the *drive perspective* considers that unconscious resistance is always at work repressing memories, desires, fears, and many other feelings that are painful or too risky to show and share. In hypnosis the Oedipus complex is reactivated (Ferenczi, 1909) and the patient, young or old, becomes like the child wanting the total attention of the parent. Part of this transferential relationship is the patient's idealization of the hypnosis practitioner and the identification with him.

The *ego perspective* states that normally we work hard, though unconsciously, to protect ourselves, and use many defenses to maintain the egos we have adopted for ourselves and with whom we have identified. This hypnosis allows us to either confirm our choice regarding our egos or to change and modify our ego ideals so we can start moving in a new direction.

From an *object relations perspective*, we realize that there must be a positive transference allowing the patient to trust the hypnoanalyst, to the extent that the patient lets himself go, with the guidance of the analyst, in order to enter a different ego state. In a sense, he identifies with the analyst and projects a sense of love from her to him. In this hypnosis, the patient responds to the imaginary love of the analyst by cooperating in order to please her.

The *self psychological perspective* understands that once the individual has consciously agreed to use hypnosis (and we always mean New Hypnosis) the self shows its desire to benefit and grow from the experience. The individual becomes *actively passive*, as Buddhist language describes this mental attitude, and enters a different ego state than the one with which he is familiar. He remains actively open, receptive to any new experience, that is, passive. In other words, we can say that the ego takes over, allowing the patient to increase his self-esteem. Hypnosis becomes a positive experience for the patient, thanks to the many complicated transferential dynamics described by Kohut (1971, 1977).

We must remember what Pine (1990) emphasizes throughout his book, that the four perspectives (he calls them *psychologies*) work together and simultaneously. Ideally we should understand the event in question from each one of the four perspectives. New Hypnosis gives the person a new key to her true, genuine self, because active passivity demands confidence in one's integrity in controlling the experiment of being in hypnosis. I purposely use the verb *to control* as the function of the patient, very much contrary to the belief of Freud and many others, even in today's world, who are convinced that the patient in hypnosis is at the mercy of the "hypnotist." They forget, for instance, that the person who can undergo a surgical operation, without chemical anesthesia but merely with hypnosis as the sole desensitizer, can definitely give herself credit for having such control of her body and pain, rather than attribute the experience to the outside source of the hypnotist.

Regarding the explanation of neuroplasticity of this hypnotic mind training (Doidge, 2007; Kandel, 2006; Schwartz & Begley, 2002), according to Doidge (2007), Freud (1895) "proposed the 'synapse' ... (and) gave a description of how synapses, which he called 'contact barriers,' might be changed by what we learn" (p. 223). He also reminds us that Freud in 1888 developed "the first plastic concept ... that neurons that fire together wire together" (p. 223). This explains how patients like Del and many others have changed, and how all the changes happen in the adult brain, which formerly was believed to be a hard-wired organ. This discovery also justifies Freud's use of *free association*. How the therapeutic technique of free association is related to this concept of "association by simultaneity" is also elegantly explained by Doidge (2007): "Free association is based on the understanding that all our mental associations, even seemingly 'random' ones that appear to make no sense, are expressions of links formed in our memory networks" (pp. 223–224). When people are in hypnosis, the experience of free association is spontaneous and strong. The entire hypnoanalytic process leads to the uncovering of these old associations, *for the creation of new neural wiring and for the reinforcement of existing but dormant beneficial neural circuits.*

## More Applied Clinical Clarification

My hope is that the following brief case account of Ivan will serve to clearly explain the advantages in many cases of using this hypnotic method in psychoanalysis. Later I will comment on the criteria we have to determine which patients will most likely benefit from New Hypnosis or Creative Imagination, which patients make us doubtful and skeptical about the results of this clinical combination, and finally which patients should never be exposed to New Hypnosis.

## 10. Unconcious Resources Activated with Mind Training

Ivan was a very young-looking 47-year-old whose personality was easily stimulated in effusive ways, who took control of every social situation in such a smooth and charming manner that people wanted him with them and were grateful to him. He realized that those "performances," as he called them, came from his insecurity and fear of being ignored and rejected. He believed that this had become an "addiction" and that he "could not resist" his urge to be noticed. Together with this manifestation of his well-disguised insecurity, he also was oversensitive. He interpreted as insults negligible behaviors of others, like someone unintentionally pushing him in a crowd and not apologizing to him. He would pursue the person who had injured his "dignity" and get into a verbal or physical fight, demanding an apology from that individual.

Ivan, who when I met him was a popular community activist in a Spanish-speaking middle-class neighborhood in suburbia, knew that his behavior had to change. Several people had already complained of his exuberance, overactivity, and constant efforts to control situations in which he was not directly involved. As the responsible person that he was, Ivan decided to do whatever was in his power to slow down and to show respect for the people whom he had treated for many years as if they were inferior to him. However, he firmly believed that no change would be permanent and solid without medication. I was against this "short cut" in his therapy but, because of his high energy, rapid talk, and frequent change of attention from one topic to another, I suggested he consult a psychiatrist about taking medication. Diagnosed as bipolar, he was prescribed several medications in different doses without good results until 50 mgs. of Zoloft once a day started to make him feel much better. At this point "talk therapy" became possible and useful. Because of his vivid fantasies, which would come up in spurts, I realized that hypnosis was worth a try. He welcomed the opportunity to experience what he described as "something I've been interested in and curious about for many years." I guided him and he entered the hypnotic mode quickly but calmly. In hypnosis I asked him to imagine himself simultaneously in two different mental pictures, one talking slowly and concentrating well, as he had done in the recent past. The other mental fantasy was of him as he used to be. At my invitation to revert for a moment to his "self at high speed," as he had described himself in the past, he was able to engage in a fantasy conversation between the two manifestations of himself: a sharp focus of attention on moderation, reflection, prudence, and maturity on the one hand, and on the other hand wandering and superficial attention, impulsive spontaneity, irresponsible reactions and expressions, as well as imprudent behavior that might be damaging to himself and others. In this hypnotic technique of conversation between two ego parts, each ego part addresses the other until there is some resolution of the issue at hand, or at least some progress, even if this result is temporary and partial. In the case of Ivan, the two opposite images of the self were visualized in the same place together. First he visualized himself in his early twenties as the wild youngster he had been. He heard himself saying things like, "This is me, why would I want to change?" Then the current self took over and scolded the other part for still trying to run everybody's life, stating that he was in charge and he would tell the other part when to intervene.

Ivan understood that the change that had taken place in his late twenties, from wild to serious, had not been out of conviction. He had felt forced to stop being wild. This hypnotic experience opened up a vast area that needed to be analyzed, and that probably would have remained out of Ivan's reach for much longer without this approach. His almost four-year-long analysis could have lasted perhaps double that amount of time without hypnosis. The hypnotic work done in the office, plus his own practice at home, weakened Ivan's resistance and allowed much unconscious material to come to his assistance. Every time Ivan encountered his own resistance and negative self-hypnosis, he used the method described to allow the mature ego to rule his life. As a matter of fact, he found in New Hypnosis the concrete mental activity to engage in, as a reaction to his id tendencies that he, having read Weiner and Hefter's (1999) book, insisted on calling his "inner dummy." Ivan's original experience of hypnosis in treatment made it easy for him to react in favor of the new principles and values he had accepted in analysis. A comment he made was a helpful clinical hint pointing to the fact that earlier, when he found himself returning to his neurotic behavior, he would react intellectually, using reason and reasons to get back to the healthy, learned behavior of psychoanalysis, with questionable success. Now, with hypnosis, he was able to "relive" the healthy behavior in terms of inner pride and satisfaction, thus activating experiential learning that kept him in the non-neurotic path. He found himself using mostly the techniques of *mental rehearsal, ego states,* and anything connected with *self-love*. Without realizing it, Ivan was establishing and strengthening a new neural pathway that would eventually allow the old one to fade away. A serious study of this aspect of hypnoanalysis could provide more concrete ways of living one's analyzed life after termination of formal analysis. A good start in this direction is Chapter 11 here, on holistic hypnoanalysis, as well as the chapter on the therapeutic self in the book by Watkins and Barabasz (2008). Because these hypnotic methods are naturalistic rather than artificial, I call them *mind training*, and they are perceived by the patient as spontaneous and personal.

## Varied Hypnotic Susceptibility

Starting with indirect suggestions, toward which most people in our society are amenable, we have criteria to decide which patients will benefit from hypnosis, which are not ready for this approach, and which patients cannot use it. However, New Hypnosis, because it defines hypnosis in terms of one's capacity to fantasize, assumes that every normal person, with help from the clinician, is able to benefit from hypnosis. I should emphasize that these criteria have been developed in both the laboratory and clinical practice. There is a large collection of research studies organized in edited volumes. My choices consist of the following eight written or edited books: Frankel & Zamansky (1978); Erika Fromm & Shor (1979); Haley (1993); Hilgard (1978); Rhue, Lynn, & Kirsch (1993); Spanos & Chaves (1989); Watkins & Barabasz (2008); Zilbergeld, Edelstien & Araoz (1986). These books contain many articles that appeared previously in journals and represent good hypnosis and good hypnotherapy research.

When all is said and done, Josephine R. Hilgard (1970), summarizing the research results, shows us that the people who benefit most from hypnosis are those who are imaginative, enjoy fiction, and are more introverted than extraverted. These people are the ones that Ramonth (1985) found to be high in *absorption*, the ability to engage in imaginative activity with total attention. The second group of people who can use hypnosis but need some help to do it with positive results, according to Hilgard (1970) are people who believe in methods and programs for self-improvement, those who make a clear distinction between reality and imagination, and those who have a sense of adventure and like trying new experiences. Finally, the people who require special expert help when using hypnosis and should not be otherwise treated with hypnosis, are those for whom rationalization and intellectualization are their primary ego defenses, those who frequently confuse fantasy and reality, and those who easily enter a state of mind that is different from the reality shared by the majority of society. It is worth noting that no other research has radically challenged Hilgard's (1970) conclusions.

If we employ the traditional, more general classification of Emil Kraepelin (1913), we can say that neurotics will take to hypnosis and obtain good results with it. This applies both to symptom neurosis and to character neurosis. With psychotics and borderline patients, special cautions are required such that only a clinical hypnosis specialist can provide therapeutic hypnosis effectively, as Murray-Jobsis (1985, 1986) warned a long time ago.

These comments should be considered general guidelines that only strengthen the New Hypnosis basic principle mentioned earlier: *every person who uses fantasy can use hypnosis*. In other words, all normal humans are hypnotizable and the difference in degree is insignificant in clinical work. This is the reason New Hypnosis minimizes the importance of hypnotizability. Watkins and Barabasz (2008) also prefer rather vague guidelines and, interestingly enough, examine the unconscious reasons on the part of many patients that militate against their being in hypnosis. It should be added that in addition to ignorance or misinformation, clinicians also have unconscious reasons to reject hypnosis, most of them related to self-protection and fear of new concepts and ideas.

The last point is seldom mentioned. Because many psychoanalysts have accepted Freud's (1888) and Anna Freud's (1936) criticisms, they must recognize the difference between Freud's understanding and ours in both conceptualizing hypnosis and using it clinically. One of the main points in the difference refers to suggestion, of which we wrote earlier in this book. Only after reaching this awareness can we accept hypnosis as a therapeutic tool and use it. The comments presented by Watkins and Barabasz (2008) masterfully reveal what I like to call "the psychoanalytic sin," namely the avoidance of hypnosis because the Master disregarded it when, in truth, Freud was not speaking of the same hypnosis that we use today. The following words by Watkins and Barabasz (2008) give us a good summary:

> It is assumed that when one is hypnotized, the ego is laid aside, that it is not involved in the uncovering process, and that, accordingly, such material as does emerge cannot be absorbed and utilized by the patient for genuine change. The notion is that loss or reduction of symptoms must, thereby, be temporary because no change, or at best only a superficial one, has been made in the basic personality. Therefore the neurotic conflicts are assumed to reassert themselves, and the symptoms will then return as soon as the influence of the therapist is no longer present [p. 7].

The authors add that there is no evidence backing this notion. The clinician, in any modality of genuine psychoanalysis, is the most important variable in the healing process. As such, he or she must be convinced that hypnosis is a valid, reliable, and ethical method to be used as long as the analyst is adequately trained to apply hypnosis in psychoanalysis.

Consequently we can encourage patients with words and our own example to use this glorious ability of our nature and to activate our mind frequently for our own benefit, pleasure, and health.

CHAPTER 11

# Hypnoanalysis as Holistic Psychoanalysis

If we accept that *holism* means an integrated whole greater than the totality of its parts, we may refer to *holistic psychoanalysis* when we enrich it with hypnosis. But for many who do not know enough about the new way of hypnosis, the combination is seen as a weakening or watering down of psychoanalysis. To counteract this bias, Watkins and Barabasz (2008) consider hypnoanalysis "a form or variant of psychoanalysis in its broadest sense" (p. 1). Erika Fromm presents eleven points comprising "the psychological processes that are altered in hypnosis and ... increase the effectiveness of psychotherapy" (Fromm & Nash, 1997, p. 266). These points follow with my parentheses added:

1. Transferences are developed faster.
2. Transference resistances can more easily be avoided or circumvented.
3. Attention changes (becoming sharper).
4. Ego receptivity (i.e., acceptability and suggestibility) increases.
5. Awareness: heightened permeability between conscious and unconscious (psychic material).
6. Increased imagery or primary process (thinking).
7. Dissociation (is facilitated).
8. Fading of the general reality orientation (moving toward introspection).
9. Involuntarism ("letting oneself go" into non-deliberate activity, from arm levitation, for example, on one extreme, to exceptional relaxation on the other).
10. More affect becomes available (the subject is more in touch with feelings).

11. Regression in the service of the ego [Fromm & Nash, 1997, pp. 266–267].

We have considered these eleven points in describing patients, but the list offers a convenient summary. The abundance of clinical vignettes in this book confirms the applicability of hypnosis as an acceptable therapeutic method that fits into "ordinary" psychoanalysis. This narrative method is historically validated, theoretically and practically, by the psychoanalytic tradition, started by Freud himself, which studies human behavior and its dynamics by means of clinical cases. Even though none of the almost thirty cases presented in this book is exhaustive (not counting the Appendix, which goes into greater detail), each case highlights the possibility of adding hypnosis to make the analytic work more practically effective. All of them together cover Erika Fromm's eleven points.

Merely on the grounds that these points cover so many psychological processes, hypnoanalysis could be defined as holistic. But because psychodynamic therapy helps the patient change and improve according to her own values and life goals, the addition of hypnosis in the therapeutic process becomes a powerful means for keeping the gains made in therapy, by helping the patient correct her thinking in its many forms, be it in perceptions, in expectations, in decision making, in balancing work and play, in loving and relating to others and to the world, in order to enjoy life more fully. Psychoanalysis becomes truly holistic with the immediate experience of hypnosis. It reaches every single aspect of our lives, to the entire complex of physical, social, intellectual, and spiritual levels, as many of us believe it should do and as Buddhism encourages humans to do, so we can attain "a vivid awareness of the universe as an indissoluble unity, a totality of which man is an integral part — but not its arbitrary master!" (Wilson Ross, 1998, p. 143). In the experience of hypnoanalysts, the hypnotic experience in analysis facilitates the change of thinking about things, which changes the things we think about.

## Auto-hypnosis and Meditation

The hypnosis we are dealing with is closer to meditation than to traditional hypnosis, as the final chapter will explain in greater detail. Americans are familiar with the Tibetan branch of Buddhism because of the Dalai Lama, who has visited our country on several occasions. We also know about Buddhism thanks to several books joining Zen and Pooh, and motorcycle maintenance, and creative management, that became popular and well liked. Meditation, or zazen, is a practice that three major branches of Buddhism — Hinayana, Zen, and Tibetan — regard as essential to their way of life. As we would expect, others would consider different branches, like Mahayana Buddhism, more important than these three. In this respect, Buddhism is similar to many other movements or philosophies from Christianity to Existentialism. Many characteristics of the New Hypnosis are found in meditation. Buddhists, however, devote long hours to disciplined and ritualistic ways of meditating. Psychoanalysis and psychology generally have not ignored the ancient disciplines of the Orient. Jung participated in discussions with Buddhist teachers (Molino, 1998) and was very interested in Buddhism. Karen Horney was seriously attracted to the concepts common to psychoanalysis and Zen Buddhism (Molino, 1998). Daniel Goleman (2006), the researcher of "emotional intelligence," helped the Dalai Lama participate with his monks in an important scientific study of the mind and the brain, as the detailed description of Begley (2007) documents. But perhaps the analyst who was most captured by Buddhist thinking was Erich Fromm (Fromm, Suzuki, & De Martino, 1960) who wrote,

> Zen Buddhism helps man to find an answer to the question of his existence, an answer which is essentially the same as that given in the Judeo-Christian tradition, and yet which does not contradict the rationality achievements. Paradoxically, Eastern religious thought turns out to be more congenial to Western rational thought than does Western religious thought itself [p. 80].

That the only answer to the question of human existence is essentially the one of Judeo-Christian teachings is obviously incorrect. Buddhism emphasizes the existential need to be in contact with nature, the only true source of learning about our life, while Judeo-Christian dogma introduces God as a living being. Buddhism tolerated the mystery of not having the final answer to the question of existence, while in Judeo-Christian belief God is the answer. However, in spite of this big difference, the analysts mentioned, mostly of Judeo-Christian origin, show great interest in Buddhism and respect for its teachings.

Buddhism uses meditation to make sense of the mystery of existence and to accept that existence (ours and that of the cosmos) is beyond the seen and above the experience of daily living. In this way, Buddhist practice (Zen) goes to human life's center (or to "the midst"—*meditation*), to the core of one's being. New Hypnosis, being essentially psychodynamic or based in the unconscious, is also meditative, trying to reach to the human core, beyond the plain and superficial, to the inner self where much truth about oneself is hidden. The Middle Way of Buddhism leads to enlightenment, as for us psychoanalysis leads to greater true self-knowledge, with inner peace, well-being, compassion, respect for all other humans, and for all aspects of the universe, joy, satisfaction, and control of one's life. For psychoanalysis the ego takes the place of the id, and for Zen the individual is actualizing the *Buddha nature* of fully being what we are. After the Buddhist *Noble Eightfold Path*, as after the experience of the unique process of psychoanalysis, in essence similar in the two systems, the practitioner or subject reaches profound self-knowledge and enlightenment, together with freedom from dependency on external things (people, objects, places, negativisms, beliefs, illusions, shoulds, and the like). The eight Buddhist steps follow, and are compared to analytic practice:

- Right understanding, or awareness of our basic existential problem/Insight
- Right mindedness, or desire to change/Motivation
- Right talk/Free association and inner awareness in speech
- Right action/Honesty in analysis by living in consistency with it
- Right livelihood/Living according to one's nature and talents or abilities
- Right effort, with positive thinking/Habitual honest introspection
- Right attentiveness/Practical introspection and self-analysis
- Meditation/Auto-hypnosis and concentrated reflection

Just as Buddhism cannot help people change unless they follow the eight steps, psychoanalysis requires the work of the patient to change. What happens in the sessions with the use of hypnosis is repeated by the patient in private. And what happens is a new, empowering experience, a hopeful reaching out for a new reality, the reality of true human nature, in contrast to the unconscious self-defeating tendencies of the id that the patient had accepted as reality. Erich Fromm (Fromm, Suzuki, & DeMartino, 1960), discussing Jung's understanding of Buddhism, reminds us of the rich wisdom of psychoanalytic concepts:

> In Freud's view, the unconscious is essentially the seat of irrationality. In Jung's thinking, the meaning seems to be almost reversed; the unconscious is essentially the seat of the deepest sources of wisdom, while the conscious is the intellectual part of the personality. In this view of the conscious and the unconscious, the latter is perceived as being like the cellar of a house in which everything is piled up that has no place in the superstructure. Freud's cellar contains mainly man's vices; Jung's contains mainly man's wisdom [p. 96].

Both meditation and New Hypnosis delve into the unconscious, in which we find, according to Erich Fromm, our hidden vices as well as our potential and wisdom. Buddhism accomplishes much of the change process through meditation, which purifies the unconscious of "man's vices" and brings forth "man's wisdom," making the new reality that comes from the unconscious the possession of the meditation practitioner. New Hypnosis brings forth from the unconscious the patient's belief in change, the needed true motivation to change and to actually effect the change. The mental images of the "new self" become clearly possible and attractive so they become the new human reality of the individual.

In no way am I saying that meditation is the same as New Hypnosis or as psychoanalysis, or that he who uses meditation should bypass New Hypnosis, or vice versa. Because the hypnosis in hypnoanalysis is goal-oriented and functionally pragmatic, related to the presenting symptom, while Buddhist meditation is a goal in itself that produces the new self — the enlightened self — almost spontaneously, one does not substitute for the other. It can be said that Buddhism believes meditation in itself will produce the seven first steps of the Nobel Path, while psychoanalysis will "convince" the analysand of what she has to do to be truly honest and happy with herself.

Meditation is different from hypnoanalysis, although both resemble, reinforce, and enrich each other. The different emphasis is that Buddhist meditation aims at complete self-knowledge that in itself changes the individual totally, and hypnoanalysis aims at self-knowledge, but change occurs by new personal decisions that lead the individual to a fuller and more fulfilling life. Jung, struggling with these concepts, tried to integrate Buddhism and psychoanalysis into a new modality. From this perspective, we talk about holistic psychoanalysis; when New Hypnosis is combined with it, it becomes hypnoanalysis.

## Integration of Psychoanalytic Methods

Holistic psychoanalysis transcends the individual who benefits from it. Because of this, as Jung does, some wise psychoanalysts try to incorporate into it different psychotherapeutic approaches. Wachtel (1977) is one of the most prominent people who teach integration. His by-now classic volume on psychoanalysis and behavior therapy was followed twenty years later by a uniquely extended edition that includes in one volume the original book and a second part that entirely justifies its title, *Psychoanalysis, Behavior Therapy, and the Relational World* (1997), implying holism at its best. Many of the comments on holistic psychoanalysis in this chapter are based on Wachtel's work, who has become a role model of open-mindedness and respect toward those whom many of us have considered adversaries, learning from them and enriching our approach with their thinking and techniques. Hans Strupp (1977), in his preface to Wachtel's (1977) original book, reminded us that "[A] psychotherapeutic system ... is not a dogma but a set of provisional hypotheses in need of testing, refinement and further testing" (p. xvii, 1997 edition) and summed up the difference between psychoanalysis and behavior therapy in these words: "The greatest failing of psychoanalysis ... has been its scant regard for empirical data and the nitty-gritty of the patient-therapist interaction" (p. xvi), emphasizing the need to obtain factual data from events like transference and countertransference, from the interactional dynamic where the true information of psychotherapy is to be found in both psychodynamic and behavioral general systems. Thus, Wachtel, in Strupp's opinion, completes the concept of holism by implying that it does not have to limit itself to psychoanalysis, but that together with behavior therapy — the "integration" that Wachtel talks about, as we shall see later — amalgamates both into the unified discipline of psychotherapy.

Obviously, one of my interests in this book is to study the process and conditions by which New Hypnosis transforms psychoanalysis into hypnoanalysis. The proposed view is uncomplicated: if modalities like group therapy, behavior therapy, family therapy, and others can amalgamate with psychoanalysis, thus enriching both and making them more efficient, in Wachtel's (1977; Wachtel & Wachtel, 1986) explanation, hypnosis and psychoanalysis can also integrate and amalgamate smoothly into hypnoanalysis with beneficial effects for the patient and even for psychotherapy as a healing device. Starting with the patient at the center of our clinical interest, we assume a method that reasonably can be considered helpful to the client. However, rather than centering psychotherapy only on the patient, we revert to Sullivan (1953), Erich Fromm (1994), Winnicott (1953), Mitchell (2000), and other luminaries from the second half of the last century to recognize the real center of psychoanalysis in *the interacting dyad of patient and analyst*.

Fantasy, including dreams (see Chapter 5), is so natural to humans that the clinical use of dreams, roughly since the early nineteenth century, is for many evidence enough of their therapeutic efficacy. Consequently, integration of therapeutic methods and techniques results from our effort to apply them in effective combinations, after sufficient research to understand the new approach. It seems that even after all the labor of the Society for the Exploration of Psychotherapy Integration (SEPI) in the last two decades, many psychotherapists prefer to hold on to their old ways, refusing to investigate methods different from their own. In Wachtel's (2008) words,

> The fallacy in most arguments against integration is a failure to appreciate that a synthesis is a different entity than either of its constituents. It is a clinical and theoretical approach with its own structure. It can be selective in what aspects of each approach it incorporates, drawing on what seems potentially useful in constructing a new synergistic strategy, rather than upon what proponents of each as *separate* therapies regard as most important [p. 47].

We can without difficulty apply this thought to hypnoanalysis. Hypnosis in psychoanalysis is a different entity than hypnosis used for symptom removal, for personality enrichment, or for entertainment, as psychoanalysis with hypnosis is usually quite a different entity than mere traditional psychoanalysis or mere popular hypnosis. Integration is possible and useful because clinical hypnosis, having originated in therapy, shares with psychoanalysis the basic principle of unconscious dynamics. Because both have the same basic theory rooted in the unconscious, the integration comes about naturally if it is not obstructed. In fact, considering the historical start of psychoanalysis, it can be said that, to an important extent, hypnosis is the mother of psychoanalysis. And through the years, hypnosis has been refined by geniuses like Erickson into what we call *New Hypnosis*.

## Therapeutic Fantasy

Hypnoanalysis is constantly on the lookout for any patient manifestation that can be "translated" into fantasy. The theory behind this interest, discussed in Chapter 4, is that humans are actually using unconscious fantasy most of the time. Occupied in any activity, their thoughts may "go their own way" to past memories or future possibilities, and to those things that are impossible but real in one's mind. Here lies the junction of sexuality and fantasy (Araoz, 1986). In sexual matters, we are completely free in fantasy. We do what we want. No one stops us or criticizes us. For instance, a man driving a car may be involved in a very vivid sexual fantasy, to the point where he is physically aroused. By no means do I imply that fantasy is always or even most of the time sexual, but frequently it is. A woman, watching TV, follows in her mind the "movie" of the party she will be at tomorrow, where people she likes and others she dislikes will be present. While the man is driving, he is also with his lover in his imagination, and while the real TV program is playing the woman is already at tomorrow's party in her fantasy. The man, paying attention to the driving, is in a more superficial hypnotic experience than the woman ignoring the TV program. In the hypnosis modality of hypnoanalysis, the therapist does not encourage the patient to fight the fantasy but "to go with it" and find out in great detail where it is taking the patient, which is an entirely psychodynamic intervention. The agenda for the session, if there is any, is always secondary to the material that comes up spontaneously. Where is hypnosis in this case? Remember that New Hypnosis considers all fantasies hypnotic and any deep involvement in fantasy as hypnosis. In the two examples, both people were in hypnosis, according to the tenets of the "new" approach, although at different degrees of intensity or involvement.

When the analyst suggests that the patient "go back in his mind" to the scene he is describing, for example, of an argument with a fellow worker, she is using New Hypnosis without realizing it. The analyst intends the patient to experience his feelings vividly, and applies experiential learning, which very often is hypnosis, as Chapter 9 explained. As long as fantasy is directly related to the analysis, and part of it, and the analyst encourages the patient to get into the fantasy, we have hypnoanalysis. Often, when a fantasy develops, I invite the patient to notice everything that he visualizes, to pay attention to his sensations, to "listen" to sounds and noise, to be aware of any "scents," and to tell me about all this. How long this experience lasts depends in great part on the questions the analyst asks, such as, "Are you paying attention to any person (or persons) in particular?" or "What else are you aware of?" or "Does this remind you of any other similar experience you had?" Obviously, the number of questions is very large and it is impossible to cover all possibilities. The therapist must be calm and act calmly, without rush, trusting the unconscious of the patient and following what comes up in his mind. In cases like these, as we discussed in Chapter 5, we have induced dreams because the detailed attention of the patient's fantasy spontaneously evolves into a story, with many minutiae and mental connections, that often turns out to be a surprise to the patient. From this point of view, vivid dreams, the result of the patient's unconscious fantasy, are hypnotic, conversely, hypnosis often produces these intense dream-like experiences—the *vivencia* of Chapter 9.

I encourage patients to visualize and use therapeutically such mental products as memories, doubts, feelings, concepts, and opinions. For example, I might ask, "What comes to mind when you feel angry at your spouse?" But the intellectual report is not as important as the reliving of it when patients spontaneously bring up fantasy: "It's like fire inside of me," or "I feel it as if it were a hurricane," and the like. In other words, we must be quick in discouraging mere intellectual descriptions of events without comment on how they affected the patient. When the patient becomes introspective, we encourage her.

## Relational Hypnoanalysis

This concept, originating in Freud's theory of transference, was developed by Harry Stack Sullivan (1953) in the U.S., by W. R. D. Fairbairn (1958) in the U.K., and is now identified, among many brilliant theoreticians, with Stephen Mitchell (1986). I mention single names as representing a large group in each of the three categories just listed, the U.S., the U.K., and the last half-century, as well as in recent decades with Mitchell (2000), who created the term *relationality* shortly before his untimely death, after having devoted much of his professional career to the study of relational concepts in psychoanalysis. Among the early psychoanalysts, relational psychoanalysis concepts appeared in the work of

Ferenczi (1955), who influenced Balint (1949), who is considered to be the first to publish on the difference between one- and two-person thinking in building the relational theory. At the same time, Sullivan (1953), Erich Fromm (1994), and Horney (1939) practiced and explained what later came to be known as *relational analysis*. Finally, in the 1940s, the same concept was adopted by Carl Rogers (1951) as central to his new "counseling" method. Nowadays, relational psychoanalysis stands at a prominent place in the current developmental stage of psychoanalysis, as previous stages of emphasis were defined by the drive theory, ego psychology, object relations, self psychology, and other psychoanalytic trends, if we consider and include Jung, Adler, Spotnitz, Rogers, Lacan, and others who are often ignored or dismissed by many American psychoanalysts. The essence of relational psychoanalysis is to pay attention to the manner in which *subjective experience is intimately connected (including in analysis) with the events and persons that the individual is exposed to*. It studies the psychological reactions of the individual to the environment, all the surroundings, in order to utilize this in the analytic work. The psychological milieu in which the individual finds himself is used as central to understanding his personality. "The nature of human psychology ... is fundamentally responsive to context" in Wachtel's (2008, pp. 59–60) words, explaining relational theory and its application to psychotherapy.

But we must be clear about the meaning of "relational" and of practicing in a relational manner. Basically, more traditional psychoanalysis follows the one-person model, focusing on the patient, while the two-person model belongs to relational theory. The former places the patient as the observed; the latter considers the patient *and analyst* as interacting with and reacting to each other, each one with a set of feelings, fantasies, distortions, hopes, and expectations coming from the reactions to the other. *In therapy, as in other mutually respectful interactions, relational theory leads the two people to be open to each other and for each to step into the other's world.*

In more recent times, relational psychoanalysis restarted as a reaction against the rigid and stilted style that was taught in the 1940s, 1950s and even 1960s as "correct" psychoanalytic conduct, keeping oneself detached from the patient and dishonestly hiding one's reactions and feelings, because acting spontaneously and especially engaging in self-disclosure was taboo. This style (the analyst being a mystery to the patient) was taught with the rationale of protecting or not contaminating the patient's transference with the analyst's reactions. Analysts of that time were loyal to the one-person model, which was then considered the classical, orthodox, and only acceptable model. The principles that guided these behavioral injunctions given to analysts were really assumptions that had not been scientifically proven and that departed from what Freud himself actually did, as we know from former patients who had been analyzed by him and later wrote about their experience. Renik (2006) comments on the negative effects of this attitude (see Chapter 12).

In hypnoanalysis, relational theory explains and justifies New Hypnosis. The hypnoanalyst not only accepts the hypnotic fantasy experience of the patient but lets him- or herself go into it as much as possible. Let's imagine that the patient in a hypnotic dream is in a small maritime town in New England. In the dream, she is standing on the street in a beautiful spring day, looking up to a nearby elegant but modest house built on top of the short, gentle hill by the street. On the other side of the street is a busy marina with quite a few people by the ocean, where sailboats are docked. The patient is about to go up the few steps leading to the house entrance but, regardless of its general air of welcome, friendship, and hospitality, she feels anxiously hesitant and afraid to go up. She is saying to herself that the view of the harbor must be very pretty from up there but feels stuck where she is, without being able to go up to the house. The analyst, at this point, being focused on the patient, may say something like, "I am there too, noticing that you feel so hesitant." However, this could be an intrusive comment, not helping the patient's experience. In fact it inevitably changes the original experience she was having (Heisenberg's uncertainty principle).

The relational aspect of this fictional situation is the genuine *acceptance* by the analyst of the patient's fantasy/dream in hypnosis. This complete acceptance is often better *expressed by silence*, given the unique hypnotic experience the patient is having. Once the patient's hypnosis is concluded and the "regular" analysis continues, the validation of the patient's previous hypnotic dream will probably be verbal, although in an indirect manner. The analyst may talk about the hypnotic dream as if it were a reality as acceptable as anything else taking place in the interaction between him and the patient. This type of acceptance symbolizes respect for the patient, understanding, and empathy. Therefore "relational" does not mean necessarily "verbal" per se.

## Psychoanalytic Concepts in Hypnotherapy

To summarize what we have been discussing, we have the following interaction in hypnotherapy: *New Hypnosis ends in regression as the result of focused fantasy*. This activates a clear transference with suggestibility and dissociation from the "real" present moment. The entire experience lends itself well to relationality. To obtain the hypnotic state in psychoanalysis, the seven elements listed earlier are necessary, as we have already seen. In hypnosis we enter *fantasy* and leave behind or disregard our external reality. This maneuver is often a form of *regression* and, because the analyst is involved in the interplay, there is *transference*, a form of *dissociation* from the general reality orientation that establishes the *relational* interaction, which in turn activates *suggestibility*, bringing about *experiential learning*.

A more detailed explanation may be useful. The patient presents a situation or condition that seems strongly influenced by beliefs and values, conviction and faith that, as a whole, are unacceptable to the therapist. For example, a patient does not want to demand the twenty thousand dollars his brother owes him because "things happen for a reason and God knows what he is doing." The analyst cannot accept this. But the question here is: to what extent are the therapist's values normative for patients? In psychotherapy we must focus on general categories that may have different forms of expression. In the case above, supposing that the patient says that he does not want to give his money as a gift to his brother, we can be helpful by analyzing the contradiction between his words and his actions.*

In a case like this, New Hypnosis can be an effective way to help the patient change his belief and take the new corresponding action to enrich his life. Activating his hypnotic fantasy, he can imagine confronting the brother in a satisfactory manner. What I have called *regres-*

---

*For instance, it is a "scientific" fact that moderate exercise is beneficial for one's health. This is one of the general categories that psychotherapists must be in agreement with. Whether this will be fulfilled by playing tennis, jogging, or bicycle riding is up to the patient to decide, and the therapist cannot press racquetball over another sport because of her preference. The same is true of many other categories that we stand for, without giving advice on how to do it. These include self-respect and love of self, peace, respect for life, justice, truth, and fairness, mutual regard for others and their rights and property, verbal communication without violence, assistance to the truly needy, tolerance of differences, and so on, making a very long list.

*sion* is really a change of ego states with the color of a mental rehearsal for the future. In his fantasy he experiences himself differently than before.

In sum, relationality helps in the application of New Hypnosis, first, to live in the patient's mind what he was afraid to do in reality or what he was convinced he could not do. The second use of relational concepts in New Hypnosis appears as metaphorical. Any feeling in one's mind may be represented by images that surge spontaneously. This is unconscious material, very different from conscious images that the person may mention when asked what the feeling is like. The relational aspect consists of the fact that a large number of these spontaneous images refer to important people from the past or current life for both the patient and the analyst. The third way New Hypnosis becomes relational in analysis is by the change of ego states. Many patients make reference to an important figure in their life when they experience a different ego state. They also recognize that we are never "alone." Even when separated from others, we often engage in a dialogue between different parts of ourselves. In the experience of hypnosis this "being with another" when alone can become vivid and engrossing. This connects with the *retranscription* of memories, as Freud called the mental process of modification of memories in one of his letters to Wilhelm Fliess in 1896 (Masson, 1985).

The holistic quality of hypnoanalysis comes from engaging the physical self through fantasy more than many non-psychoanalytical approaches do. Regarding traditional psychoanalysis, there is the danger of lapsing into intellectual, rational, factual verbal interaction, moving away from the inner experience. This is what hypnoanalysis avoids easily and naturally, by insisting on the patient's fantasies about the experiences and events she is talking about.

CHAPTER 12

# Practical Hypnoanalysis

Renik's (2006) book on practical psychoanalysis offers usable wisdom in the practice of psychodynamic psychotherapy. He criticizes the rigidity of much traditional clinical psychoanalysis, with its blind adherence to outdated theories and techniques that were never proven to be scientifically relevant. In his own words,

> Practical psychoanalysis means remaining open-minded with regard to theory, holding nothing as axiomatic, and it means retaining an experimental approach to technique — that is, searching for whatever way of working together with a given patient seems to make progress toward the desired goals of treatment [p. 3].

Renik had probably been trained in the stiff dogmatism of four decades ago, to which all of us were then exposed. But fortunately, like many shining stars in our field (think of Erich Fromm, Bruno Bettelheim, Karen Horney, H. S. Sullivan, and a few others of high caliber) he held on to the essence of our work, always with the patient's benefit in mind in spite of the "official" narrow-mindedness of those days. Renik (2006) had previously stated the need of taking symptoms seriously, following Freud's early clinical practice with Breuer, which was very successful and brief with symptom removal.

> Therefore, unless insights are validated by correlation with symptom relief (an outcome criterion that is not theory-driven) a closed system is set up in which successful clinical analysis consists of *analyst and patient* discovering what the analyst assumed a priori to exist. Impractical psychoanalysis is also unscientific psychoanalysis [Renik, 2006, p. 2, my emphasis].

Hypnoanalysis, which Renik does not mention, is one of the interventions that fall under his category of *practical psychoanalysis* and *whatever may reasonably work for the benefit of the patient,* to paraphrase the quotes just cited. Especially today the use of New Hypnosis in psychotherapy, as expressed in the Introduction to this book, is scientifically proven, as long as it is sharply distinguished and separated from mechanical and superficial ways of doing hypnosis, as in entertainment and in other non-psychodynamic therapeutic methods that focus merely on the symptom. It is a proven "experimental approach to technique," as Renik (2006) put it above (see Rossi, 1986, 2006, Rossi & Cheek, 1988), that in the last two and a half decades has had neurological corroboration (Begley, 2007), and that is close to Buddhist mind exercises (Kornfield, 2008) like "mindfulness," only recently made popular in our culture. Kornfield (2008) describes the fascinating elements of CBT, already taught in Buddhism for millennia with its concern for the power of right thought. Similarly, there are many "virtues" honored by the ancient wisdom of Buddhism. Wisdom, yes, but not religion, as we must insist, as explained by eminent representatives like the Dalai Lama, because of the common ignorant belief that the Buddha is a god. Among these many Buddhist virtues, I select those that are close to hypnoanalysis in my view: to practice honesty in pursuing the truth about oneself, to identify one's true feelings, to be responsible for the inescapable effect of one's experiences, to recognize the damage of self-deception and illusion for oneself and for society, to experience the great importance of visualization and mental imagery (see Kornfield, 2008). These are just very few of the practical concepts that are also relevant in analysis and that can be effectively dealt with by means of New Hypnosis. Many of these mind techniques, like repeated visualization of desirable behaviors, have been proven effective for mental change by neuroscience, according to all the scientific sources cited in this volume.

## Convergent Forces to Improve Human Existence

This chapter tries to put together basic concepts of Renik's (2006) practical psychoanalysis in the modality of hypnoanalysis. Thanks to the neuroscientific endorsement of wise thinking using New Hypnosis, and to the wisdom of Buddhism, which validates and strengthens hypnotherapy, we can count on a powerful therapeutic tool in our professional work. Kornfield (2008) explains that Buddhist practice is not only close to hypnotic activity, but also offers a parallel to psychoanalysis as a process of liberation from limiting beliefs and habits, repetition compulsion, and addictiveness to hurtful behavior. Hypnoanalysis recognizes that the addition of Creative Imagination or New Hypnosis, with its emphasis on focused fantasy and visualization, can benefit the psychoanalysis commonly used without hypnosis. Renik's (2006) practical method of identifying the symptoms (what the patient wants to cure or improve), and defining the goals of treatment before engaging in the collaborative analysis and investigation in mutual partnership to help the patient, also applies to New Hypnosis. The patient has to understand clearly what the process is and how it releases creativity that comes from hidden unconscious ideas, inner resources, and experiences lived by the patient and applicable now to current conditions. The method of learning from our past experiences, a central part of the ancient program of Buddhism, embodied in the *Noble Eightfold Path*, described in the last chapter, is a program for living an honorable life comparable to psychoanalysis. Some Masters include in *right understanding* avoiding falsehood and illusions, living in reality with its limitation but also with all the good things, often small and taken for granted. *Right mindedness* includes being open to new experiences and events without preconceptions nor expectations, taking life as it happens, not as we want it to be. Because Buddhism is not rigid, some teachers find *right speech* in verbal and written communication, practicing and insisting on truth and honesty, clarity, and simplicity. In *right action* they stress respecting others, even in one's private actions, and acting not to hurt anybody, nor the nature we all share, and in *right occupation* they emphasize obtaining one's livelihood through work that is meaningful or fulfilling and considers others. *Right effort* means being positive and optimistic with oneself, with others, and with the world in general, and *right attentiveness* has to do with introspection and self-analysis, realizing that many of people's actions can be explained without attributing them to malice and malevolence. Finally, *right concentration* signifies using one's imagination in order to find the goodness of things and people (use of auto-hypnosis to be productive and happy). Out of this last "step" in the *Eightfold Path* comes the value of meditation and the effort to make this practice an essential part of one's life. Like psychoanalysis, Buddhism also takes the unconscious very seriously (see Kornfield, 2008), from which Jung developed the *collective unconscious,* which, as in Buddhism, is a shared reservoir of collective memories, images, concepts, and desires.

Hypnosis is an effective method to obtain focus and concentration, absolutely essential to Buddhist meditation, as Erich Fromm remarked half a century ago (Fromm, Suzuki & De Martino, 1960). The addition of New Hypnosis, in Buddhist language, is very close to *mindfulness*, a process that teaches us to focus undistractedly on what we want to attain within the *Eightfold Path of Awakening*, as it is also called. Hypnotic mindfulness as a process is taught with the acronym RAIN (which, incidentally, is interpreted in many different ways by different Masters), standing for *Recognition* of the natural and spontaneous inability of the human mind to focus, *Acceptance* of this fact and resolution to teach oneself how to do it (mind training), *Investigation* of one's mood, motivation, desire, disposition to learn and practice mindfulness, and finally, *Non-identification*, which has to do with finding one's true ability to learn mindfulness, not mimicking a teacher or anyone else in one's effort to learn and practice mindfulness. It emphasizes the uniqueness of each individual and demands respect for that uniqueness, as well as for the uniqueness of the universe. In addition, we refuse to identify with our negative tendencies. Buddhism is a rich form of CBT, with the added constant introspection regarding the psychodynamic unconscious. Once we recognize our negative tendencies, similar to the Freudian *id*, we accept their presence in our lives. Then we investigate or introspect and find our own unique way to do it (Freud's *ego*) without identifying with what we recognize as our negativism nor with any "model person."

Erich Fromm (1960) insists on *presence of well-being* as opposed to *absence of illness* and explains that well-being is "being in accord with the nature of man" (p. 86), which is the basis of Buddhism: to grasp what we are and how we can be fully ourselves by learning from nature. He also proposes a constant interest in living that is taught in Buddhism and applies to psychoanalysis as well. Here is one of his poetically deep examples:

> Birth is not one act; it is a process. The aim of life is to be fully born, though its tragedy is that most of us die before we are thus born. To live is to be born every minute. Death occurs when birth stops. Physiologically our cellular system is in a process of continual birth; psychologically, however, most of us cease to be born at a certain point. Some are completely stillborn; they go on living physiologically, when mentally their longing is to return to the womb, to earth, darkness, death [p. 88].

As Buddhism motivates us to be "fully born," hypnoanalysis is constantly helping us to visualize ourselves as we can be and as we shall be if we go through the voyage of true self-discovery — our rebirth. In this way analysis becomes the Buddhism of the West.

## Scientifically Correct

For many people, including well-educated professionals, hypnosis is closer to witchcraft or magic than to science. This ignorance can be corrected. First we must differentiate between entertainment or stage hypnosis and clinical or therapeutic hypnosis. What most people are familiar with is stage hypnosis, but the method of New Hypnosis, in itself, is worth understanding from a scientific perspective, especially after the discoveries of neuroscience since the mid–1980s. We have mentioned many times in the previous chapters the validity that neuroscience gives hypnosis. Those who started hypnoanalysis, without realizing what they were doing, among them Ferenczi, Jung, Erich Fromm, Wolberg, Watkins, Erika Fromm, and a few others, were applying scientifically proven methods of change at the cognitive and behavioral levels of human functioning without having the benefit of scientific evidence for what they were doing. I believe, much like Renik (2006), that the scientific evidence in psychoanalysis, in all its variations, consists *in the improvement that the individual patient experiences during the process and because of it*. This *is* scientific evidence. Those who want to be "more scientific" about the evidence for the validity of our method may recall that working with human subjectivity requires acceptance of unexpected change in all the variables involved from clinical cases in the research. When the patient gets better and is free to enjoy life more than before, when this continues for several months and in various difficult circumstances, we have *scientific evidence* that the method worked. Science, we hope, is the method by which to find the true nature and results of things.

Thus, the addition of New Hypnosis (not stage hypnosis!) to psychoanalysis, creating hypnoanalysis, has produced a long list of patients who have benefitted by it. The authors mentioned above have provided examples of clinical success over half a century, but only in the clinical situation. Those extremely concerned with objective evidence are not satisfied. However, it may be unfair to demand more evidence. Rather, it makes questionable sense to demand of a subjective, interactive process the same type of evidence that is expected in, let's say, the interaction of medication in the human organism. For many, religion is the simple way to know everything, with the same degree of conviction. This kind of explanation forgets that science itself is constantly changing, as we have the privilege to witness thanks to the highly sophisticated instruments that make us understand in different ways what we were taught a few decades ago about so many aspects of our existence, from the universe to the individual self. Our scientific understanding today is very different than that of eminent scientists from a few decades ago. Religions are mostly *semper idem*, like God, always the same. Science always changes (*semper mutans*) with new evidence, which, like it or not, is appearing practically every day, forcing us to respect the new evidence of many changes that surprise us constantly (see Doidge, 2007).

# Clinical Applications

As a practitioner and a psychology member of the National Academies of Practice, my main interest is in adapting the hypnoanalysis method to our clinical work. Hypnoanalysis, by integrating psychoanalysis, New Hypnosis, Buddhism, and neuroscience, is a different reality than traditional psychoanalysis. This chapter respects Renik's (2006) view on psychoanalysis, which can also apply very well to *hypnoanalysis*. If we could consider every possible and legitimate psychodynamic theory as mixing colors in a painter's palette, we could accept the possibility of altering, improving, modifying, and adapting the work of psychoanalysis and what it produces. The freer we are in using the palette and mixing colors (responsibly!), the more helpful we can become to the patient. The palette represents the possibilities of finding other theories and approaches beneficial to the patient. If they work well *for the specific individual*, the analyst integrates them with the basic psychoanalytic concepts and, as in the case of New Hypnosis, facilitates the analytic process. For instance, when a patient comes to treatment stressed out because of difficulties in driving to the office, or because of recent crises with a child, a spouse, a friend, or a boss, I may suggest a moment of relaxation through Buddhist mindfulness, with calm abdominal breathing and relaxation. In about five minutes the patient finds herself focused on her therapy and does not have to waste the first half of the session dealing with her "tension." Another example might come from difficulties a patient has remembering a recent meaningful dream. I remind him that he does not have to remember it as it was but right now *he can produce a hypnotic dream* based on the forgotten dream that we can analyze on the spot, as it were. Finally, a patient may say something like, "I find myself hating what I do [smoking, yelling at my child, etc.] but liking doing it." I ask myself, *Where does this come from?* I respond by inviting her to relax, and to gently allow her unconscious to bring this up without having to think logically or to intellectualize about it. I ask her to let me know what comes up on her mental screen. Psychoanalysis transformed into hypnoanalysis has more possibilities and "tools" to help the patient recognize and understand her true self.

In hypnoanalysis, it is easier and more "natural" than in traditional analysis to avoid logical thinking and intellectualizations and to convert the analytic session into a *vivencia* (Chapter 9), which becomes a meaningful and healing experience for the patient. The emphasis is *to trust the unconscious*, the part in us that keeps us alive and works for our full living (cf. the birth process mentioned by Fromm, quoted earlier). Thus the patient can allow the unconscious to bring up new "things" that may sound irrelevant, absurd, or ridiculous, so that then the two people involved in the analysis will accept and understand, with all the implications for change that that understanding may carry. Again, "the unconscious in the obvious," as Saretzky (2007) puts it, which means that what looks nonsensical is often the real "stuff" of the unconscious that psychoanalysis is all about. When a patient has been engaging in "irrelevant" talk, I may ask why she is talking about this. Whatever the answer, I suggest that she relax and listen to her unconscious and pay attention to any images that may spontaneously emerge. With a patient who may find it difficult to connect with the unconscious, I mention a big movie screen that is still dark and soon will start to show mental images. I insist on her taking time to feel the relaxation, and that the screen will light up when she is relaxed. The analyst must be in no hurry waiting for the mental images to appear spontaneously. Doing this, I am frequently surprised at the wealth of unconscious material that comes up and that lends itself to examination, speculation, and discovery.

The respectful use of fantasy with the help of New Hypnosis allows patients to taste the deep sense of inner peace and unique self-identity that Buddhist monks experience in their meditation practice, as described by many, such as Begley (2007), in discussing the neuroscientific conferences organized by the Dalai Lama, or by Kornfield (2008), commenting on his own experiences and research, or by Goleman (2006), reporting on the cooperative research on the effects of meditation on the entire personality and physical body of the practitioners. I consider, agreeing with Erich Fromm (1960), that when this special experience of fulfillment as a unique human individual becomes habitual, the ultimate goal of psychoanalysis has been reached. This goal is well-being, which Erich Fromm (1960) described at length, explaining his basic definition: "Well-being is the state of having arrived at the full development of reason" (p. 91). Coincidentally, in April of 2010, as national Health Care Reform was being enacted, the National Academies of Practice (NAP) proposed the idea that "national well-being should be the primary goal of health policy, not just crisis intervention," explaining it as "Health is an individual's state of well-being based on integration of biological, psychological and social functioning within the context of social, cultural, family and other environmental conditions" (Rodgers, 2010, p. 9).

Hypnoanalysis is a natural form of mental rehearsal, thanks to which the patient learns experientially, with little effort and in relatively short time, how to overcome his negativism, self-limitations, illusions, illogical thinking, self-deception, close- mindedness, fears, lack of confidence, of trust, of healthy ambition, of enjoyment, and of self-empowerment, adopting instead a new positive attitude, contrary to all the above, in all aspects of his existence. The clinical application of hypnoanalysis goes through steps, similar to those of Buddhism (described earlier). Here are my eight progressive steps in hypnoanalysis.

- First, dissatisfaction with something in her life; she is not happy with the way things are going for her.
- Second, attempts to resolve the problem by herself, often following the advice of friends and relatives.
- Third, the often reluctant recognition that she cannot do it by herself and that she needs outside help.
- Fourth, searching for a "Master" or therapist. This can take months or even years.
- Fifth, contacting the analyst and making an appointment. All

## 12. Practical Hypnoanalysis

through Steps 4 and 5 there are questions, hesitation, at times even cancellation of the appointment made.
- Sixth, the first session, mostly for getting her impression of the practitioner.
- Seventh, questions and doubts, ending in "I'll give it a real try."
- Eight, psychotherapy starts and the true psychodynamic work begins.

Hypnotic "stuff" is accepted as part of the therapeutic process (as long as the analyst is trained in hypnoanalysis). Each session strengthens the motivation to continue until the goal of well-being is reached. This usually takes a fairly long period of time, due to the many connections of the individual with parts and pieces of his history, of his current functioning, of his different feelings for each connection, real or imagined. A good analysis always takes time, but hypnoanalysis facilitates progress and encourages the patient to work on his own between sessions, thus becoming somewhat briefer.

The issue of professional training is worth considering, because it is difficult to find instructors, given the few psychoanalysts who practice with hypnosis. With the new knowledge from neuroscience and the validation this research gives hypnosis at this point, training in hypnoanalysis has to contain the scientific aspects of it and the instructor must be well trained in psychoanalysis. Moreover, this training has to consider hypnosis as *a method of activating one's mind to make practical use of one's brain in order to change one's world.* The training cannot consist of a ritual that must be followed rigidly. Hypnosis must be regarded as a useful, natural, and practical technique to make the unconscious effectively and more quickly available for analysis. There should not be emphasis on the constructs I rejected from the beginning in this volume, like hypnotizability, depth of hypnosis, hypnotic amnesia, etc., which have very little to do with psychotherapy. To satisfy those who perceive real — substantial — distinctions between the two, *hypnoanalysis* training could be limited to psychoanalysts, whereas *hypnotherapy* training could be targeted to professionals trained in psychodynamic psychotherapy, including psychoanalysts. This training should have an historical/scientific theoretical part, a second practical/clinical part, and finally a supervised part of at least fifty patient sessions conducted by the trainee.

## Summary

Our intent and goal as mental health professionals is always to assist those who seek us out to help them solve their psychological problems. Symptom relief is our immediate goal. Our less clearly defined goal, however, is larger: to experientially teach patients to avoid similar situations in the future on the basis of what they learn with us. This becomes possible through psychoanalytic intervention. After the symptom is handled and controlled, we start the investigation of its cause, function, origins, and much more. The symptom is not the whole story (Araoz, 2006), but it *is* a part and has to be taken care of first in most cases. How do we do this? By means of any and all therapeutic methods that are reasonable, acceptable and ethical, proven effective, not harmful to the individual, and easily available. New Hypnosis within hypnoanalysis fits the bill perfectly. This entire volume discusses the use of hypnosis (New Hypnosis) in psychoanalysis so that there is therapeutic benefit, measured by the weakening or complete control of the original symptom.

Training in how to apply hypnotic methods in psychoanalysis is necessary, as we said before. Once the clinician is trained, the benefits of advertising oneself as a specialist in hypnosis, as a hypnotherapist or hypnoanalyst, are very significant because most people, even not knowing anything about therapeutic hypnosis, are more receptive to hypnosis than to "therapy." However, the risk one takes is that, for many, the mere remote smell of hypnosis of any kind means "miracle," and "one session will do it." Once we are face to face with the "candidate" we explain how the patient himself can learn to cure his symptoms by changing his thinking and practicing on his own. What the analyst does is all geared to empower the patient, teaching him to change by using his thinking—the old "thinking makes it so" of Shakespeare's *Hamlet*. Doing this, we correct the impression (at least we hope so) of many possible patients, who mistakenly will not consider entering psychoanalysis (for whatever reasons) but will consider hypnosis. Approaching psychoanalysis from the hypnoanalytic perspective, the patient finds new motivation to take care of her whole life. Hypnoanalysis is therapeutically beneficial for the patient and practically favorable for the analyst. At this moment in history we have, for the first time, the convergent circumstances of practice, history, and science to strengthen New Hypnosis.

# Conclusions and Recommendations

To conclude this book, I would steal (if I could) either Yalom's (2002) *The Gift of Therapy*, or another of my favorite books on psychoanalytic psychotherapy, Renik's (2006) *Practical Psychoanalysis for Patients and Therapists*, and would insert it here. (If you wonder why I would do this, please read both short books and you'll find out.) There are many more such volumes, written by Erich Fromm, Karen Horney, Bruno Bettelheim, Harry Stack Sullivan, and a long list of others. My preference for these authors is that they follow the spirit of psychoanalysis rather than the letter of it — the essence rather than the rules. And in so doing they become individually creative and original, often independent of the mainstream. (Obviously, I do not think of actually stealing any of those works.)

However, none of these authors emphasizes fantasy and imagination as much as I do, understanding and respecting Buddhism's principles, applying them by means of hypnosis (the mind training technique that is so mislabeled), and presenting its validation and scientific proof from neuroscience. Adams (2004) and others come closer to my focus on visualization and mental pictures in therapy. My book stresses imagery, though I do not say that not to do it as much as I do it is incorrect. I merely present the Jungian fantasy principle, discussed below, as a choice and option for making psychotherapy effective and successful. I insist upon the value in our work of using imagination, which is the manner of thinking that humans use most frequently. The importance of this cognitive mechanism is shown by the psychoanalytic use of the Latin word *imago* to refer to important mental productions.

This emphasis also makes clear the value of mind training in the creative process that all healthy humans possess, but which is not especially fostered or developed in our culture. We teach that an idle mind is to be avoided — it is the "devil's playground" — even though current evidence shows the value of expanding imagery in patient and therapist. However, it is most difficult to challenge our own convictions and, because they are so deeply rooted in our entire mental structure, we do not even want to try to make the effort of allowing ourselves to think differently. Intelligent, highly educated people have responded to my invitation to try the basic steps of Buddhist meditation and visualization with a condescending smile and the trying-to-be-polite comment of "That's not for me," which hides the less polite expression of a profound conviction, "That's a lot of pure nonsense." Strong believers in God, for instance, do not even allow themselves to *consider the possibility* that God is the imaginary companion of many adults and the simplistic explanation for all the mysteries in the universe and in our lives. As someone said, a closed mind indicates the refusal to think.

My hope is that this book may help people feel more comfortable with imagination in general, and with their own imagination in particular, and that they may see the tremendous value that it has in our life. Here is a point to consider: all things made by humans were in the imaginations of the persons who did them before they became reality. Think of magnificent sculptures, buildings, castles, bridges, and breath-taking mountain roads, of technological marvels like airplanes, submarines, computers, long-distance communication devices, from radio to television, to mention just a handful of things that humans first thought about, *imagined*, before they became real. Think of the adventurers and the physicists who imagined new lands and new planets and solar systems before they discovered them for the rest of the world. History tells us that often many of their contemporaries considered the inventors and discoverers of these new devices and physical objects crazy, dangerous, diabolical, and sometimes even tried to kill them. Perhaps our emphasis on rationality and objectivity has to be less rigid than our educational philosophy makes it. Notice that when budgets are reduced in school districts, some of the first things to go are art, music, and sports. What's the message? Clearly, they seem to tell us that art, music, and sports, the non-intellectual disciplines, are really unnecessary for a good education. You will be well educated even without them. America wants facts, not mental images.

In our field, we have the danger of joining this over-rationalistic attitude. Freud's well-known description of the ego taking the place of the id, quoted in practically every book on psychoanalysis, can be used to avoid "crazy thoughts and impractical imaginings." But new thoughts, imagination thoughts, are not necessarily demented and impossible. Freud's statement, to me, means that ultimately everything should be rational: the crazy thought of humans flying was made rational because it was not dismissed based on the literal and simplistic interpretation of it. Already Scholastic Philosophy had claimed, five centuries before Freud, that the function of the intellect is to control and rule all and every action of humans. In practice, this means that every thought, no matter how insane it looks at first sight, can — and should — be considered. Consequently, encouraging our patients, as well as our children, to use their imagination may open up new horizons of creativity and self-enrichment, of human growth and enhancement. Those who insist on not bothering with "this nonsense" would do well to honestly analyze this.

## Imagination in Psychotherapy

Hypnosis is a mental activity mostly of the imagination, as we have mentioned many times in the previous chapters. The Jungian *fantasy principle*, with a faint resonance of the sad separation between Jung and Freud, who talked about the *reality principle*, comprises three aspects: that fantasy, logically, precedes reality, as happens with inventions; that fantasy creates most of reality, shaping it and giving it sense with mental images and pictures; and that fantasy in our thinking represents reality, so that we sometimes confuse fantasy with reality and vice versa. This brings us to psychotherapy and its goals.

What do people want to get from psychoanalytic therapy? Ultimately it is a better sense of self — either a more complete sense of self, or a more positive one, or both. I like the metaphor of *reengineering oneself* because the etymology of the word is far from mechanical, but rather humanly uplifting. It has the same root as ingenious (Latin, *ingenium*, natural ability), and is connected with the Latin *genus*, which is behind *generate, gene, generation, general*, and other similar words. Therefore, I say that patients want — at least unconsciously — to reengineer themselves in psychotherapy, because I perceive them as working hard, with my help, *to be all they can be,* as the U.S. Army proclaimed to young people as an incentive to join toward the end of the last century. The process is quite typical: an individual has unwanted symptoms (for instance, he often makes wrong decisions that hurt his career or his family life) that he wants to correct, and also understand. He wants to change. He wants to reengineer himself, to make the responsible effort of becoming the person he suspects he can be. If his therapy is mind training or hypnoanalysis, he will start from the first visit to change his way of thinking about himself and will take home precious mental tools to assist him in continuing the (auto-) therapy every day until the next session. Practically everything that he brings up with the analyst will be used as a subject of imagination activity — what he did that he regrets and what he could do differently, the events he remembers that could be related to the problem, and so on. The long-standing psychoanalytic interactions, counting on transference and repression, recognizing resistances, self-deceptions, and repetition compulsions, exploring the unconscious and analyzing its material, suggesting awareness of unconscious manifestations in dreams, daily mistakes or forgetfulness, expecting distortions and falsehood in the patient's narrative, and the like, are definitely essential parts of the work. The facilitating comments or questions are still the same as in regular psychoanalysis, but always with much stress on the patient's imagery. The general rule of hypnoanalysis is "always use Creative Imagination in working with patients."

## Recommendations

With the help of Yalom (2002), I am summarizing ten recommendations for the purpose of hypnoanalysis, always emphasizing the use of imagination whenever possible:

1. Make sure that the patient believes he or she can change and grow.
2. Be convinced that the patient will use her relationships as resources to grow.
3. Using Creative Imagination, tune in so that you provide a special therapy for each patient.
4. Keep getting feedback from the patient: what is helping, what is not.

## Conclusions and Recommendations

5. Your feelings in the session are clear data on the patient.
6. During sessions, do not repress your fantasies. Encourage patients to do the same.
7. Never disclose without first having the patient's expressed fantasies about you.
8. Use your imagination to see yourself changing and growing. The patient will too.
9. Ask the patient to imagine meaning, freedom, values, etc., before discussing them.
10. Always encourage cartoon-like imagination when nothing comes to mind.

I shall comment briefly on each recommendation. It may take some sessions before you can say to yourself that the patient is ready for the adventure of serious therapy or auto-reengineering. In these first sessions you have to let the patient know that you truly care about her, that you understand her feelings of distress, and that you are not labeling or judging her. In these beginning sessions you can use imagination: what she imagined the psychotherapist to be, what I am thinking of her between sessions, and so on.

The second guideline is there to remind us that therapy can be an affective rehearsal for life. You pay attention to her interactive style, effective and counterproductive traits. You also get information on her relationships: with parents and family, with friends and colleagues, with strangers. All this information will be useful when it becomes necessary to boost her spirit in the future.

By "special therapy for each patient" I mean Erich Fromm's concept of having a real conversation of one human to another in the therapeutic exchange. But I add the sharing of fantasies and images that come to mind during this genuine "conversation," making sure that I am extremely cautious about what I disclose. If I am in doubt about something I am considering saying, the best rule to follow is simply "Wait!"

The fourth recommendation is based on the fact that the patient's imagination is constantly working. "What mental images come to mind when you hear this or that from me?" is the type of question that can be helpful.

The way you feel about the patient in each session is a reflection of his current behavior. You may say at the right moment, "I'd like to look into the way I'm reacting to you today," and start analyzing your restlessness, your boredom, your shortness of temper, or whatever feeling that was triggered by the patient. How do you know that this feeling is connected with the patient? I agree with Yalom (2002), who says that your own psychoanalysis should have given you a clear understanding of your inner self and a realistic awareness of your many blind spots. If that is not the case, the therapist may forget the fifth recommendation and return to his own psychotherapy.

The sixth point is also related to one's own psychotherapy. Fantasies will regularly come to our minds during sessions. They may be a warning from the unconscious, or a connection, or a confirmation, and so on. They are not to be repressed and, depending on the circumstances, some of them can be shared with the client. Encourage him to get into the habit of paying attention to his fantasies. Number seven is related to this, because self-disclosure requires much caution, but can become your reward to the patient for sharing with you his fantasies about you.

The eighth point requires humility on your part. For you, the practice of therapy is not merely a way to make a living; it should be a glorious source of self-growth and enrichment. Especially after each session, take a moment to recognize this. If you do it as an experiment, soon you will discover that the patient is also recognizing her personal growth and enrichment.

Point nine refers to the fact that imagination strengthens our convictions and keeps them strong. Abstract concepts become real due to images, in this case our own. The entire advertising industry is based on this. By using imagination in this way, you help the patient deepen her convictions.

Finally, what can be called the Rule of Imagination is that thoughts do not have to be realistically correct. If the patient is silent and insists that nothing comes to mind, suggest that she imagine herself (or the two of you) in a different place: what sort of place, where, doing what, what is surrounding you, during what time of day or night, what weather, etc. The cartoon-like aspect comes from the fact that anything that comes to mind will have some meaning: flying like an eagle, deep in the depth of the ocean, seeing oneself as a worm or as a dinosaur, etc. The purpose of this mind exercise is to recognize unconscious material that comes up as distortions and diverse images.

The final recommendation is to remember that all the fuss of *empir-*

*ically validated therapy*, taught nowadays at many (most?) universities even at the doctoral level, is misdirected and useless. It may come from the health insurance companies (for profit!) that constantly look for reasons to limit the amount of payment to reimburse. But what is taught does not apply to psychoanalytic therapy.

It is a mistaken trend because psychodynamic therapy is unscripted, being as it is an honest interaction of the patient with the therapist. This means that new things come up: events that were forgotten, feelings of all kinds, new awareness of old things, and old connections with the new things being transacted. All this cannot be strictly measured to decide if this therapy is valid or not. The type of research conducted on behavioral therapies cannot be used with the analytic approach. It is like trying to measure liquid with a ruler. In behavioral research there is a clear, single symptom complaint; the subject follows specific steps (exercises from a specific guide) that a person with minimal experience can administer; the results of those exercises are measured frequently; unconscious material is completely ignored; and feelings are dismissed as distractions (deviations?) from the main task of behavior change.

The empirical validation for psychoanalytic therapy is coming steadily and strongly from neuroscience, with its technology to investigate the psychoanalytic tenets, such as the tripartite structure of the mind or psyche, or *die Seele*, as Freud called it. The powerful fMRI (functional magnetic resonance imaging) has shown the complexity of many operations of the mind. Consequently, it is very worthwhile to take a look at Doidge's (2007) Chapter Nine, in which he explains clearly the way changes due to psychoanalytic therapy are possible because of brain plasticity.

The book started with integration in its title. It ends with the practical benefits of integration for patients and mental health practitioners alike. However, there can be no integration with a closed mind. Learning means to stretch the frontiers of knowledge, to have the courage to look into something new, to try what previously was considered undoable or even unthinkable. What I intend with this book is to give the reader the possibility of the impossible in the field of psychoanalytic and psychodynamic therapy which, in our culture, is the version of spiritual growth, much as in other cultures are, for example, Zen Buddhism and Taoism, or diverse methods of spiritual growth, some imbued in religion, or "the love of wisdom," that Socrates developed as a way of making the individual truly human, quite different from what philosophy is today for most people. I use the phrase *spiritual growth* to encompass all aspects of being part of the universe, in Taoist thinking. The familiar *personal growth* can be interpreted, unfortunately, in limited and very self-centered ways

In sum, I hope that many readers will have the courage to mix New Hypnosis with psychoanalytic work, as described in the book, which will enrich the work we do. My wish is that this book will be a contribution that helps bring psychotherapy to its original luster, thus replacing the superficiality preferred today by so many who claim to be psychotherapists.

# Appendix: A Case of Gender Confusion

Address presented on September 21, 2009, by Daniel Araoz in honor of Eva Hymer, M.A., director of the Long Island Chapter of the New York Center for Psychoanalytic Training, at the center, Port Washington, New York.

Her name (fictitious) was Maxie. She was referred to me by a community agency that had me on the list of sexuality specialists. Maxie had had the intake interview at the agency, where she was diagnosed as bipolar with depressive personality. Age: 30; occupation: waitress; education: high school, and college starting at 20 years. Living on her own after 19 years of living in her mother's house. Father deceased. Siblings: three older brothers (40, 38, 36), all in good, stable careers: CEO of a medium-sized corporation, lawyer, and M.D.

Maxie's motivation to start analysis now: to truly become herself. She was seen for therapy initially three times a week. After nine months we reduced the number of sessions to twice a week. This regimen lasted for over two and a half years, and then once a week for over a year. After "official" termination, Maxie was seen once a month for another year and a half. The total number of sessions was over 500 in a period of just over five years.

My psychoanalytic approach (Araoz, 2006) with New Hypnosis is a form of *hypnoanalysis* (Fromm & Nash, 1997, Watkins & Barabasz, 2008; Wolberg, 1945). It has also a close relationship to the *relational model* as developed by Mitchell (2000), and to the Buddhist practice of *mindfulness*. The relational model that I find solid and effective is the one that considers the important contributions of H. S. Sullivan (1953). The way I integrate these concepts shares the practical philosophy of Renik (2006).

# Appendix

## First Session

She was punctual for her appointment, well dressed, wearing styled makeup, and smiling with a warm and seemingly genuine smile. She was absolutely beautiful, a perfect body, naturally sculpted face, with the right height and weight of a model. She greeted me in a very pleasant, educated, and relaxed voice and manner.

Maxie did not look depressed at all, but she told me that she had just turned thirty and was in "an existential crisis," wanting to be her truly unique self; she was unhappy with her lifestyle and needed help to find herself. She added that she had read a lot about psychoanalysis and thought that she would benefit from it, knowing that it was tough, but believing that she had to go through this "surgical operation of the mind" in order to be whole as a real person. I asked questions taken from her intake interview. She believed herself to be different (meaning "better"?) from her brothers but added that she was unhappy and ashamed of herself compared to them. This is why she had little contact with them, and only saw them once a year for a big New Year's party that her parents had held every January 1st for all their friends. Even at this party, the brothers did not speak to her, nor did her seven nephews and nieces know who she was. She did not want to tell me why she felt ashamed of being her brothers' sister, other than her lack of higher education. Later I realized that she was deathly afraid of being rejected by me, as she had been rejected by her father and, as a consequence, by her brothers and extended family.

Before ending the first session, I asked her to tell me what came to her mind when she thought of her "new self," an expression she had used several times. I led her into a comfortable relaxation through concentration on her breathing and diminution of muscle tensions. Once she relaxed I asked again how she imagined herself to be in a couple of years, after having gone through analysis. She became agitated, abandoned the hypnotic ego state, and refused to go *experientially*. Then Maxie became very rational, arguing that she could not speak about it until she had actually been in analysis. I had asked her about her understanding of analysis and she realized that it would be intense and demanding on her. So I suggested sessions three times a week to begin with. Maxie agreed to sessions on Mondays, Wednesdays, and Fridays.

After this first session I called a colleague and friend who was my clinical consultant, also a psychoanalyst and originally from Argentina, like me, obviously familiar with my cultural background. I was upset because I saw Maxie as most attractive sexually and I was afraid I could not work with her because my countertransference was all about her as a sexual partner. I had never experienced such a strong attraction to a patient and I felt from the start that I could be so distracted with her that it would be impossible to deal with her as a patient. My friend simply said, "This is your chance to understand *in vivo* what is countertransference." He further explained that my id wanted her as a sexual partner, but that my ego knew this had to be redirected.

## Second Session

With my friend's wisdom, I met Maxie for her second session, again on time. Once more she was friendly, willing to work, and sexy, distractedly seductive, crossing her legs so that I could notice their beauty, touching her arms and legs in a soft, sensual way, looking at me with what my countertransference perceived as an inviting smile. She started telling me details of her childhood and her poor interaction with her brothers who, she remembered, had never been friendly to her. In fact, she described a situation where she was sexually abused by her second brother, the one who is now a lawyer. When I inquired about details she was not very clear. I wanted to know if there had been intercourse and she said, "No, only mutual masturbation and oral sex." She added that she liked it and because of it, the sexual interaction took place for about an entire year. She was then about 13 or 14 years of age. I wanted to know why this special relationship stopped. She simply said that her brother started dating seriously and did not want to continue his sexual play with her. Asked how she felt when her brother told her this was the end of their sexual games, Maxie said simply, "I was mostly relieved and felt good about it. But another side of me was very sad about losing the only brother who paid attention to me." Because of this ending I asked her about her early sexual experiences. She told me how her mother wanted very badly to have a girl and she was very happy to be that girl. She remembered her mother playing with her as if she were a doll, dressing her in special clothes, bathing her, and calling her many endearing names that made her very happy. She also said that her mother came to her bed to tuck her in and spent time playing with her genitals and kissing her on the mouth, with her tongue deep in Maxie's mouth. She liked this very much and once, when her mother was sick, Maxie felt hurt and rejected because the mother did not come to wish her goodnight.

Again this second time, I tried hypnotically to help Maxie experience herself in the future, when her problem would have been resolved to her satisfaction. But she resisted once more, saying that she was not yet ready to look into the future. This "resistance" was very conscious. However, she was able to become very relaxed mentally and also physically. Before she left, she looked and acted more real and less seductive. Her last words were, "I think I'll be ready next time." I purposely did not ask her what she meant. Did she mean ready to use hypnosis or ready to tell me something important (what Jung called "the confession")? I had the feeling that something very unexpected would be revealed, but I refused to speculate and guess its nature.

## Third Session

At her next session, three days later, she looked nervous and eager to talk. I invited her to relax, as she had done in our previous session. She closed her eyes and took a few deep breaths before saying very slowly, "I think I am ready." Then she added that in the first two sessions she had been "testing" me, trying to find out if I really cared about her, if I was tolerant of "other people," and whether she could trust me. I waited through a long silence, after which she smiled and said, "You'll be very surprised.... I have a big surprise for you." Waiting for the surprise, my countertransference was sexual. Would she ask me to have sex with her, as other patients had done on two occasions many years earlier? But my behavior did not change. I just waited. Then she blurted, "I'm not a woman." I tried to maintain my external composure, even though my true reaction was far from calm. She kept looking at me with a faint smile, waiting for my response. I was getting more and more nervous, and angry; I felt she was teasing me. Trying to control my true feelings I said, "Maxie, you just said something that, I believe, needs explanation. I'm confused. Tell me more." Then, for the rest of the session, Maxie told me the whole story. His mother, after three boys, desperately wanted a girl and tried to treat him as such from the very beginning of his life. She denied the maleness of her youngest son. Maxie had pictures that I later saw of him dressed like a girl at different ages, with long hair and painted nails. The father, who slept in a different room than his wife, seemed to be completely oblivious to what was happening to his youngest son in his own house. The brothers were commanded to treat him like a girl: this was their sister, whom they had to protect and care for. Maxie insisted that his mother tried to persuade the other three boys that even though their "sister" looked like them, there had been "a mistake of nature" because she was really a girl. When time came to go to school, the mother enrolled Maxie as a girl. She taught her child how to go to the bathroom so that nobody would find out she was a he.

Maxie believed that he had forgotten many details but he remembered well incidents when his mother engaged him in sexual activities with her. These were real perversions, like her playing with his penis, touching and kissing it with the normal reaction of erection on his part and then complaining that this was "a mistake of nature," that the penis did not belong in his body but that he would be able to use it as a toy all his life. Then she would force him to penetrate her, saying that she wanted to hide (in the mother's vagina) this mistake of nature. The child was also moved to the mother's bed many nights, where she engaged in erotic play with him until she reached orgasm. Alone, Maxie became a frequent masturbator, hoping to eliminate his erections as something that would please his mother. By the age of 16 he was masturbating from three to five times a day.

He found out later that his mother had arranged with physicians to enlarge his breasts without Maxie's knowing it. At 17 years he had well-developed breasts and a good feminine figure. His mother caressed, kissed, and fondled his breasts with passion and even reached orgasm doing this. But then Maxie believed that his life took a big turn for his benefit after his 17th birthday. A female friend who discovered that he was not a girl and who was very interested in transsexualism introduced him to a group of people who were transsexuals and transvestites. He found himself at home in what turned out to be a rather large community in New York City. He celebrated his 18th birthday at a party/orgy that included about thirty people, most of them "trannies."

After this event, Maxie became convinced that he was a special type of "man-woman" because he could please sexually both sexes. He joined the tranny community and got a job as a waitress at a famous tranny restaurant in Manhattan. Although he still lived at home with his mother (the father had died when Maxie was 16) he had access to an apartment that belonged to two of his friends in one of the neighborhoods of Queens in New York City. Maxie moved into the apartment and felt happy. Surprisingly, his mother was very receptive to the changes in Maxie's life. He stayed in the tranny community, working as a waitress at the restaurant and socializing within the same community. Later, when he was already 23 years old, at the suggestion of another male transvestite friend, Maxie started welcoming "selected gentlemen" who wanted sexual excitement with a beautiful girl with a penis. This friend lived in the same building with his lover. Both of them were big, black men, strong and very manly. They offered to act as his bodyguards when a "client" came to see him; they would screen the costumers and run to Maxie's protection if he needed any help. Subsequently Maxie found out that the two friends had secretly developed and installed a sophisticated TV system by which they could watch him when he was "entertaining" one of his costumers. He accepted that lack of honesty as partial payment for his security.

The third session had been like turning on the lights in a dark room. I knew now whom I was dealing with. After giving me all the detailed information just outlined, he repeated his initial plea about being confused and feeling like a living lie. I asked Maxie to get in touch with his current feelings, using again the hypnotic method (slow breathing, relaxation, and imagination). His response, since it was toward the end of the session, did not allow us to work on his feelings but, thanks to his power of introspection and his great sensitivity, he did a lot of work on his own on his feelings, practicing auto-analysis until the next session two days later.

## Fourth Session

Maxie started the session reporting on his auto-analysis. He said he was excited and sad, afraid of my true reaction to his transvestism and of what would happen to him in the future, angry at his mother but depending on her and excusing her at the same time. This was an important point in his analysis, because he brought up my feelings and fantasies about him as a woman in the first two sessions, explaining he was trying to seduce me.

In this session, still appearing as the very beautiful woman I had first met, Maxie tried to convince me to examine him. To my refusal, he responded with comments on my not accepting him, on feeling rejected by me. I took a firm stance, recognizing his manipulative maneuver, telling him that he was wasting time and that we had much to do to help him. Reverting to a seductive approach, he asked what if he was lying. I kept my stern and firm demeanor, responding that if he was lying he was an idiot. That brought about a sincere apology and we were able to start the true psychoanalytic work. Maxie came in dressed like a woman for more than a year.

And still, after that, he asked me directly if I had been sexually excited by his appearance and conduct, which I perceived as a risk he took, a test of my genuine positive regard for him and basically as a sign of confidence on his part. Recognizing that I had to be a role model of honesty for him, I admitted my initial reactions and we talked about my self-deception and wishful thinking from my id. We also touched on his indirect manipulation of other people's feelings that gave him a sense of power, his fear of the unknown future, his sadness on losing friends because of his decision to change and stop being a transvestite, and his need to resolve so many problems about his identity and his future. He became very apologetic for what he had done to me. This led us to a hypnotic practice on his unconscious ego states, the part of him that felt guilty and the other part that felt proud for having succeeded in forcing a strange man, like me in the first sessions, to react erotically to "her." In the state of hypnosis, he considered the sense of power that being a woman gave him. He also contrasted it with the wonderful sensation of being true to himself and to others. He role-played both parts in a emotionally verbal dispute to win the domain of Maxie's life. He resisted it by expressing fear of multiple personalities, but he finally handled his ambivalence by identifying completely with the "true self," as he spontaneously called it.

Later on we made frequent reference to the fourth session, which was the point at which he definitely decided to move on to the goal of being a normal, healthy, and happy man, no matter how hard this would be and how long this would take. As in any analytic process, analyzing the ups and downs of his feelings was slowly making him stronger and more convinced of his therapeutic goal.

APPENDIX

# Analytic Progress

The ten points that follow are a summary of clinical information, useful and convenient to understand the patient as well as the progress of the clinical case. They are

1. Dynamic assessment
2. Ego strengths and weaknesses
3. Id, ego, and superego
4. Defenses and resistances
5. Character structure
6. Transference and countertransference
7. Fantasies and dreams
8. Anxiety level
9. Personal growth
10. Initial and changing diagnosis.

*Dynamic Assessment*

The family and Maxie's relationship with his mother were, evidently, powerful dynamics in his life. When he started with me, he was confused and chronically depressed, angry at his mother but guilty for that feeling, perceiving himself a freak, and without any sexual desire but faking great sexuality. He reacted with repugnance to his sexual activities with men, with the experience of being a weird "specimen" used as an object, and insisted that he wanted more interaction as a man with women, having had only two such experiences, not counting his mother. He also was very disturbed by his mixed feelings about his mother, still missing the sexual activities with her as a symbolic sign of a deep and special love, while at the same time loathing them and her. His identity had been confused and he felt like a monstrosity, genderwise. We engaged in fantasy (hypnotic) work. He saw himself at 50 years of age, slowly progressing to 90 by mentally rehearsing the different decades. This forced him to focus on himself, not on what his mother would have liked. I helped him to stress *his* intentions and desires, leaving aside his mother's.

He also resented the "loss" of his three brothers, and blamed his mother for it. He hoped to be accepted as a male by them, though he was very afraid of their rejection, fearing their blame for what happened.

He often referred to the three brothers as a unit. What one thought or did the other two would do or think also, which may have come from the fact that he was isolated from his brothers as if he were different and better for being special, according to his mother's prolonged brainwashing.

All his feelings toward his father were very negative, describing him in the worst pejorative terms and lamenting that his lung cancer, from which he died, did not last longer so he could suffer as he deserved. "I feel only hatred toward him," he repeated several times. "He betrayed me." This was his initial attitude, which slowly changed to compassion and sadness as he recognized his father's behavior as a result of "weak character, lack of spine, and having accepted my mother's craziness as normal."

In terms of the neurology of cerebral plasticity (Doidge, 2007), Maxie's crisis can be explained by the fact that the neural pathways established firmly for so many years remained active, insisting that he was a special feminine–masculine person, the way his mother had convinced him. Maxie had terribly difficult periods with suicidal ideation and psychotic features. The apprehension of abandoning this neural pathway created acute confusion, fear, and paralyzing insecurity. The hypnoanalytic treatment progressively and very slowly established a new neural pathway through repeated visualization of his life as a man, increasingly accepting positive feelings about it. My hope, which was fulfilled, was that once the new neural pathway or circuit was established and strengthened, the old ones (his being a unique human specimen and his father being guilty of Maxie's unique upbringing) would weaken and disappear through lack of use.

## *Ego Strengths and Weaknesses*

Some of Maxie's ego strengths were: the fact that he was seeking psychotherapy; the current introspection of his psychosexual development as twisted and corrupt, which had started several years earlier; his desire to recover his true gender. He was a good person, compassionate, generous, and helpful. His efforts to attribute his "years of slavery," as he called them, to a very serious mental disorder of his mother, part of which was her ability to hide all this from the world, was another strength, gradually avoiding self-blame and maternal accusation. His understanding did not weaken his anger and disgust, but slowly it had become objective and mature. Finally, an important ego strength was his vision of a good future to enjoy his manhood and to make up for the first part of his life, with all the abuse he had suffered. This, incidentally, shows the powerful influence of fantasy in human endeavors and in psychotherapy. We engaged in mental rehearsal (see Chapter Seven) many times. This strengthened his motivation to keep "trying" to be his true self and to move away from his past.

His ego weaknesses were rather circumstantial. He was afraid and insecure, having lost most of his friends in the tranny community, which had been like his extended family and very helpful to him, emotionally and even financially. He wanted to date women and fantasized about it using hypnosis but the reduction of his breasts was not an overnight event and his self-confidence in this area was very weak. The use of fantasy, a form of auto-hypnosis, as we have repeatedly seen throughout the book, saved him from despair. Several times in analysis he reverted to what Kohut (1971) called *narcissistic rage*. However, he recovered quickly from it and resumed his positive attitude. New Hypnosis helped him to be hopefully optimistic.

## *Id, Ego, and Superego*

There was massive confusion among the three component parts of the self. At the id level, with the encouragement of his psychotic mother, Maxie had learned early in life to react sexually to many situations. But he realized that his sexual reactions were erroneous and perverse, becoming aroused by children of both sexes and by men, in addition to his normal reaction to attractive women. He kept saying that he did not react as a normal man. Early in Maxie's recovery process I wondered to myself if he was bisexual, but realized that he had to be much better before we could be sure of his sexual orientation. But the way his recovery developed proved clearly that it was heterosexual.

His reality at the ego level included orgasms that were confusing, always biologically pleasurable but rejected psychologically as unnatural when the sexual object was not an attractive woman. In hypnosis we worked repeatedly to change this so that his female sexual stimuli increased in strength, as he, rationally, wanted. In his symbiotic merger with his mother, Maxie was not sure of the morality of his sexual activity, but did not feel good about it and had to work intensively to judge himself fairly.

In the past his superego had become inverted, transforming his constant sexual experiences with his mother into good, and perceiving himself as bad because he was uncomfortable with them. At another level of exaggerated narcissism, he believed those experiences to be good for him because he was special, so he cherished them and was proud of them. But the secrecy, not being able to share his thoughts and questions with anybody for many years, created anxiety, anger, insecurity, and fear of discovery. This helped the creation of more hypnotic situations that were "normal" for him and that he could, theoretically, discuss with people. Until he joined the tranny community, Maxie had believed that the relationship with his mother was special, unique, and healthy, but misunderstood by ordinary people. People were bad, he was good, an example of the Kleinian (1975/1984) splitting reaction. He was privileged and extraordinary. His distorted superego considered him "bad" not to please his mother even when he did not feel like it. We worked hypnotically to reverse that. After the preparatory focus on breathing and relaxation, which now he did very easily, Maxie "saw" himself mentally as the adult he was now, talking with the eight-year-old boy he once was. He was understanding and caring, telling his young self that his mother was sick and crazy, that he was a real boy, not a mistake of nature, that he would be very happy accepting the truth of his nature. The younger Maxie interrupted several times, claiming that "Mommy said...." The older self repeated patiently what he had said before about his mother. All through this, Maxie was "living" the two roles. It was a true experience, not just intellectual thinking.

Maxie had been suffering not merely from gender confusion but from identity disturbance, with serious transferential distortions reaching the *alter ego transference*, in Kohut's (1971) language. He also felt very lonely and had a great need to have friends, which became a strong motivation to "get well soon" and become a normal man. His vision for the future had become sharp and clear. He was becoming his own healer, as the Buddhist tradition teaches.

## Defenses and Resistances

These are some of the severely neurotic ego defenses used by Maxie: denial of anything wrong; rationalization of his limited world from childhood to 17; distorted love for his mother leading to self-deception regarding his gender and sexuality; social self-limitation, also in order to please the mother; passivity and lack of judgment regarding his mother's distortions of reality. He had great confusion because of the projection and internalization the mother, in her psychotic relationship with her son, had not allowed to develop normally (Klein, 1975/1984). We might benefit in understanding this patient if we distinguish his early defenses as coping mechanisms in order not to lose his mind, and his more current ones, during analysis, used to define his true self, having become narcissistic in Kohut's (1971) sense, but at the level of "therapeutic transformation."

## Character Structure

His mother negatively influenced Maxie's character from very early in his life. Thus Maxie had a central character disorder, manifested in his passivity toward his mother and his pathological identification with her, in his willingness to please her, and in his inability to recognize reality outside of the belief instilled in him by her regarding his "superiority." Though hard to pinpoint in this case, Maxie could be said to have a character disorder that derived from reaction formation. Maxie's character traits and the outcome of his serious intrapsychic conflict, however, were clear. The task of analysis was to replace reactive character traits with sublimatory ones. Because of this, transferential dynamics were of high importance in Maxie's analysis, leading to character correction through new identifications. Again, we find the neuroplasticity process of strengthening one set of beliefs and the resulting behavior in order to develop a healthy neural pathway, as Schwartz (Schwartz & Begley, 2002) explains.

What was Maxie's character structure? We must go back to his inner strengths in Number Two, above. One way of putting it is to say that he had the qualities of being a normal, decent, valuable person in society. He was born, however, with the curse of not being allowed to be what he was, and this made it very hard for him to be his true self. Fortunately, he chose psychoanalysis to find himself and become a normal person, in spite of his tremendous handicap since the moment of his birth.

## Transference and Countertransference

Initially he was very careful not to say anything bad about his mother: she loved him, she protected him from his brothers who did not like him from the moment he was born, she did for him what his father was not willing (or able) to do in order to give him security in a household where he was not welcome. He mentioned several times in the first stages of the analysis that he was not sure about me: Would I be like his father or his brothers? Later in the analysis he said repeatedly that I was like his mother, having purified her psychopathology in order to keep her acceptance and love of him as an individual. Further into the analysis, when he recognized factually the mother's mental pathology, he expressed the fear that I might "reveal her behavior to the authorities," that I might dismiss him in disgust, or, on the contrary, that I was the good father he never had, caring for him in a mature way, accepting what he was, and believing in his becoming a successful, worthwhile, and happy man.

My countertransference in the beginning of treatment was the distraction of having to deal with a beautiful woman, who spoke about her overloaded sexuality. Later in the psychotherapeutic process, I did feel like a father, and had to restrain myself from showing my affection in order to remain professionally caring. As Maxie progressed I felt proud of him and had to be careful not to react *socially*, to use again Kohut's (1971) term.

## Fantasies and Dreams

As I will explain later, my work with Maxie, as with most patients, relied on the material that emerged from the unconscious, especially fantasy material. I take advantage of hypnosis, following Erika Fromm (Brown & Fromm, 1986) and Watkins and Barabasz (2008), in order to elicit more fantasy material than would come up without hypnosis. So the old question, "What comes to mind now?," is repeated often in order to encourage the patient to stay with his fantasies to slowly become more conscious of his inner self.

The difference between psychoanalysis and hypnoanalysis, which may accelerate therapeutic progress, lies in the greater use of anything imaginative: what the mind fantasizes is used hypnotically and becomes experiential learning. Thus, the first year of analysis Maxie went through many situations of unrealistic expectations about his "normal life," which slowly changed into constructive fantasies.

As a passing observation, many of the good results that Maxie obtained with this type of mind work seem to come from the special force that images have in creating new positive neural circuits. This is a good research topic for a doctoral dissertation, and can be kept in mind in clinical work. Instead of merely substituting ideas and thoughts ( à la CBT) the analyst can insist on images, fantasy scenes, and other works of the patient's imagination.

### Anxiety Level

Maxie could be labeled as suffering from anxiety neurosis, in Fenichel's (1945) terms. Maxie was abnormally tense in the beginning, afraid of me but trying to please me, unable to relax and sleep well, several times talking about suicide and feeling in desperate need of help. But he slowly started to see me and my approach as the ultimate hope for his recovery and health. One method that helped him was to identify what parts of his body were affected by the anxiety. Then he visualized that particular physical area and the form and force of the anxiety. All this was done very slowly. The next step was to mentally visit the interior of his brain. He imagined himself regulating the flow of anxiety by using imaginary buttons or keys to do so, while checking all the time the effect these "alterations" had on the organ previously identified.

His anxiety was intimately related to what Mahler (Mahler, Pine & Bergman, 1975) explains regarding *individuation*. Normally, the starting point of one's personality (*psychological birth*) is the connectedness (*symbiosis*) with the mother, which produces in the child a feeling of fusion, with images of oneness with the mother. After this (at the latest by the third year) the child begins the process of separation and individuation, or differentiation. Maxie had become fixated on the symbiosis and had no opportunity to be psychically separated from the mother. This abnormality ("I am not myself"), caused by his mother's psychosis, generated chronic anxiety in him. As he got psychologically stronger, growing as an individual, the anxiety became weaker and more manageable. The patient was getting closer to his true nature, in which, according to Buddhism, one experiences union with the entire universe.

### Personal Growth

As we shall see, Maxie made gigantic decisions to grow out of the hectic world his insane mother had created to enslave him, and to be himself, finally to attain a regular level of happiness in his new life as an adult male with a new career and a woman with whom to share his successes. The five years of analysis were a process of slow personal growth, in spite of the many ups and downs. Below I list Maxie's reaction to different techniques.

### Free Association

Many images of being alone, close to another (mother) but being hurt, beaten, rejected with anger and violence. For instance, being trapped as if in jail, being in a public market naked, people offering money to him, seeing himself as a whole woman but with a penis that could disappear completely (confusion about sex and gender). Flying free like a beautiful gigantic bird, but being a woman. Because of my interest in hypnoanalysis, often I would ask him to visualize himself and be imaginatively in the situations that his free association brought to his mind, discouraging intellectual interpretations on his part. My theory is that free association teaches us to be free from reasoning and intellectualism, as the best way of truly learning in depth what we have been exposed to in school and society. We enrich our contact with the rest of reality with this experiential way of learning, following the advice of Buddhism: "Look within; thou art the Buddha," which agrees with Suzuki's (1960) explanation that "seeing into one's nature," being loyal to one's nature, is considered the highest level of enlightenment.

### Dreams

The repeated dream in the first half of analysis was of being alone, walking in a large, deserted place. Very tired, ready to give up. In a cave, trying to get out but stuck inside. A fight with a woman who is very big. Somehow he has a knife and tries to hurt (kill?) her. Wakes up screaming and sweating.

After the first part of his analysis, all dreams represented sunny and beautiful places. Friends in relaxed parties, talking about interesting things, and he relaxing with no fears or apprehensions. Much soft and classical music as a constant background making him feel safe, secure, and happy. Frequent laughter on his part, feeling completely comfortable with the people around him. These dreams consistently made Maxie feel energetic and ready to face life in spite of work, effort, and even failures or disappointments.

## Fantasy in Hypnosis and Hypnotic Dreams

Maxie found it helpful to see himself as a happy man, giving him insights and strength to be proactive. He enjoyed using mental rehearsal and practiced it repeatedly at home. However, he used to regress easily, feeling sad that Mommy is gone. He is all alone and no one loves him, but the mental image of a light of hope in the sky brings him a sense of inner peace. There was a progressive increase of positive feelings and images in the last three years of analysis. Later, of course, while being in contact with Mechy, his new girlfriend, the fantasy and hypnotic dreams became consistently nurturing, self-enhancing, and positive. His imagination activity gave Maxie the ability to transcend discomfort, pain, tiredness, irrational pain, and other mental difficulties. He started to believe that he used his reason more effectively after having spent some time in fantasy.

## *Initial and Changing Diagnosis*

Following the *Psychodynamic Diagnostic Manual* (*PDM*, 2006) I saw in Maxie traits of mixed personality disorders of depression, anxiety, and dependency. Later in treatment, I used the diagnosis of "Major Constrictions and Alterations in Mental Functioning" and finally, as Maxie was progressing into health, I settled for "Gender Confusion." Ultimately, after four years of psychoanalytic work, the last diagnosis was "Cured of his symptoms with reasonable hope of a full and successful life."

The *symptom* that Maxie wanted to overcome was his fear and reluctance to be what he biologically was. The symptom involved the guilt regarding his mother, who had convinced him that he was a mistake of nature. The *goal* of analysis, then, was to succeed in being who he knew he was— not a woman. The other side of the goal was to accept his mother's mental illness, of which he finally was absolutely convinced. Maxie showed definite progress that forced me to modify the diagnosis, as just described. The two sides of this progress were, first, to accept his real gender and to strive to become realistically a happy and successful adult male. The second side of Maxie's goal was to perceive his mother as a psychiatric patient who refused to be treated as she needed. In the first level he included finding a meaningful and stable relationship; in the second, not to feel responsible about his mother's health, happiness, and treatment.

## Highlights in Treatment

Maxie approached me with trepidation, hoping that I would be able to help him. When he was satisfied that I could, he presented the very complicated symbiotic self that his psychotic mother had created. One interesting aspect of this case is that Maxie made practically no demands for himself on his mother. He acted as if he were possessed by the mother, overly identified with her to the point where he had practically no sense of self. It was as if even Maxie's unconscious was dead. Until he joined the tranny community, he was one with his mother. The mother, in her insanity, probably thought that Maxie had fully accepted the artificial femininity when he showed interest in the transvestites. In reality, the tranny community was Maxie's salvation. He saw firsthand the goodness and suffering of these people: forceful self-deception, depressive atmosphere, social and employment limitations, superficial attempts to be happy and have fun, and the constant wish to be accepted by society at large that never comes. Trannies show unique courage and strength but see themselves as outcasts. They deserve support and encouragement to accept wholly who they are, or to change their lifestyle if they want to do that. Maxie realized that he did not want that life for himself. However, there was a *hidden observer,* as Hilgard (1977) called it, namely his unconscious, which was, as it were, recording all the horrors and rejecting the forced situation he was not able to change when he joined the tranny community.

Because all patients start with the idea of change in mind, I concentrated on Maxie's fantasy (including dreams, both nocturnal and day reveries), sexuality and hypnosis, what I call the *psychoanalytic kaleidoscope.* Fantasy, among many other things, includes both nocturnal dreams and reveries. When he was talking about his mother, I would suggest that he go into a hypnotic state and concentrate on the mental presence of the mother, as well as his reactions and feelings toward her, in great detail: the look on her face and the feelings it revealed, as well as his own reactions to that scene. Initially he was annoyed at my interrupting the trend of his talk but soon he found it helpful and did it on his own. I try to elicit the fantasy of what the person is talking about, because it usually comes from the unconscious and thus the hypnotic fantasy brings us to his true inner reality. When he said on several occasions that he could not see himself doing this or that, like leaving the tranny community or starting to appear publicly as a man, I would guide him into an hypnotic dream of doing what he found difficult to do, by suggesting that he test it by allowing himself to enter into a dream where he would be doing exactly that. In similar cases, I always added that he should expect to have a night dream that might follow this experience or that might correct the hypnotic dream — a sequence I have discovered in many years of using this hypnoanalytic approach.

Mahler's stages (Mahler, Pine & Bergman, 1975) leading to healthy self-identity require success in *separation and individuation*. Maxie needed the feeling and experience that he was different from his mother. We used diverse fantasies, like hypnotically experiencing himself moving away from his mother, becoming the man his mother had not allowed to exist, being fully his own masculine creation regardless of what his mother wanted and, as a bag to put everything in together, his mother not being able any longer to decide who he should be. Only then would he be able to have the feeling of *who he was*. Because the patient had no intrapsychic autonomy, to discover and accept the characteristics of being his own individual, much effort in analysis was centered on his true identity formation, comprising a clearly defined self. For instance, we used hypnotic techniques like visualizing himself as he wanted to be. Here is where New Hypnosis served him well. I helped the patient develop in his mind a clear image of his new self. I used the metaphor of sickness (his being a woman) and health (his returning to his natural gender). He was encouraged to practice auto-hypnosis on his own between sessions to reinforce the reality of his new self. I insisted on his thinking about it twice a day for at least fifteen minutes each time.

On one occasion, Maxie became very upset talking about changing his lifestyle and appearance in order to look like a man. Again using New Hypnosis, I invited him to imagine himself as frightened and insecure but, next to this picture of himself, he could imagine his new self, confident, sure of himself, and determined to act differently. He was going to recognize these two aspects of the self: what he had been forced to be, and what he was physically in his biology. If the "experiment" in my office was successful, I would recommend that he try it again at home on his own. If it did not succeed, I would gently propose that he could try to do this alone to see what would happen. Patients seem to discover the value of fantasy for their benefit, and then report practical gains.

The patient soon learned that night dreams are not to be dismissed.

Maxie brought in many dreams, often complaining that he could not remember them. I always encouraged him to tell me whatever he remembered, even if it was a very short picture, just a segment of the dream. If there was no meaning to be drawn, I reflected that we should remember the small dream piece to find out if it would fit with another future dream. Thus Maxie had a dream, still looking and acting like a woman, after deciding that he would appear as a man, but the only part he remembered was standing in a piazza in Rome laughing very hard. He knew he (a woman) was in men's clothing and without any friends in the piazza. Of the few people who were around, nobody paid attention to her as a him. The next session he recounted another dream where he was changing his clothes in what looked like a gym with a lot of men around but nobody paying attention to him. I asked him what this could possibly mean and if it had any connection with the previous dream. He said something along the lines that he was ready to change and the world was also ready for his change. It was at the next session that he appeared dressed like a man. This was the first time he was dressed like a man, at 31 years of age. It was winter and he had on a loose overcoat that disguised his breasts. At the same session he told me that he had made an appointment to start the treatment to reduce the size of his breasts.

Though the activity had made fairly good money for him, Maxie was bothered by the memories of his sexual involvement with men who enjoyed the curious uniqueness of a beautiful girl with a penis. Again in this instance I helped him use his fantasy for his own good. He could have "memories of the future." In the session, I directed him to think of himself sexually involved with a woman and enjoying it greatly. He repeated the mind practice three or four times and I reminded him to do it at home as an important daily assignment until the next session, following the current neuropsychological teaching that thinking vividly and repeatedly will make the reality more effective and easier (Schwartz & Begley, 2002). When we met again, he was enthusiastic about his success. In fact he had started to pay attention to women and to mentally select the ones he would like to have as sexual partners.

During this stage of his analysis he brought in rich dreams. He was remembering his dreams much more and more completely than in the past. I have selected only two of his many dreams. He saw himself (as a man) talking to a cute girl, around twelve years of age, about the fact that it was beautiful for her to be a girl. She was happy and relaxed with him but asked what was so special about that; she was a girl and happy. Then, appearing more adult than before, she talked about being happy about one's gender. He felt very good and proud of being a man. He reported that he woke up in the middle of the night with a healthy erection and pleasured himself "like a man." Remember, under the influence of his mother, he masturbated to make the erection go away, because his penis was a mistake of nature. Not any more. He went back to sleep and had the following dream. It was dark and he was standing by the sea, looking into the black night and feeling cold. The only sound was that of the sea. Unexpectedly he heard the cries of a woman who was drowning someplace nearby, although he could not see her. The sound of the waves did not allow him to identify the exact direction from which the woman's cries came. But then he saw himself jumping for joy, dancing and laughing while he was saying, "I'm happy she is dead. I'm free. I'm me." Then, all of a sudden, the sun was shining bright and strong, the sea was calm, and a woman's voice, strong and tender, stated firmly, "I am gone but you are yourself." He was singing very loud, "I'm happy, she is gone, never to come back." Later he woke up feeling full of energy and vigor. He again had a strong erection. Contrary to what was the case in the past, erections were now something positive and natural for a man.

The interpretation was rather obvious in terms of Mahler's *individuation* stage. He was getting rid of the feminine aspect of his life that he had lived for so many years. Because he had identified with being a woman, he felt comfortable with women in his dreams advising him, teaching him, and supporting him. In his unconscious, he was eliminating the woman he once was and preparing himself to deal with women as a man. Thus, a dichotomy appears in these dreams and he is comfortable with it: the men in the gym not paying attention to him were thus paradoxically showing their acceptance of him. The same occurred in the piazza, where people went about their business without stopping to pay attention to him.

It is illuminating to note that all these dreams are related and consistent, a good indication that Maxie's unconscious was now "pushing" for his true identity. Other dreams showed him paying attention to women and being interested in them, always normalizing his identity as a male.

# Conclusion

Maxie came to analysis for what he called an existential problem, his gender confusion. He had made great progress and stayed in analysis till he felt in his mind and heart truly separated from his psychotic mother and his past. As in all successful analyses, he had learned introspection. New Hypnosis helped him to fantasize the reality he wanted as a man in spite of the apprehensions he had. Because he was using his fantasy power, he moved more quickly than if he had not. He got into the habit of using auto-hypnosis for anything of which he was afraid or uncertain. In hypnosis he was able to do genuine and in-depth introspection. The patient had finished analysis in over four years but he wanted a few "follow-up" sessions a year.

Toward the end of the year after his analysis, while he had started to build his true identity, he began to date. Having spent close to nine months dating, he felt that he loved a woman for the first time in his life (he was by now almost 35). His girlfriend, Mechy, had been a lesbian for a few years when she was in her early twenties and then had entered therapy and stayed in it for almost ten years. She also had a turbulent and very neurotic family of origin. This experience helped Mechy understand and support Maxie. One important thing happened: Mechy helped him change his name from the legal Max to Soren. He felt very good with this masculine name. In one of the follow-up sessions after the name change, he explained that now he felt totally like a man, that Maxie was the girl and woman of the past, that he was now truly free. Mechy and Soren had postponed marriage but had moved together into a comfortable apartment. She was financially well off so that he did not have much worry about making a living. He was working in a large bookstore, where he became very knowledgeable about authors and writers.

Other changes related to his psychoanalysis with hypnosis were that Soren wanted to confront his mother. After discussing it in his sessions, and not expecting big results, he visited his mother and presented her with his verbal picture of her. She was somewhat receptive, mostly because she was feeling worse and worse without him in the absurd role she had placed him. Her other sons had cut off all communication with her, recognizing her insanity and disagreeing with her refusal to seek help.

Another change was that he decided to start a career. He decided on psychotherapy, and enrolled in a Master's program for licensed professionals trained to provide psychotherapy. He also started to write memories from his experience in order to publish them some day in the future. He wanted to help people with their family relations, suspecting that many parents needed guidance in the psychological raising of their children. Having gone through his long and painful experience, he hoped to assist patients with similar problems.

Now that Soren was firm in his gender, he started a second analysis with another analyst, not motivated by any crisis or anxiety. He is very interested in knowing more about his true self and has two sessions a week. Once in a while he contacts me reporting his progress.

# References

Adams, M. V. (2000). Compensation in the service of individuation: Phenomenological essentialism and Jungian dream interpretation. *Psychoanalytic Dialogues, 10,* 127–142.

Akhtar, S. (1989). Narcissist personality disorder: Descriptive features and differential diagnosis. *Psychiatric Clinics of North America, 12,* 505–529.

Alexander, F. (1943). Fundamental concepts of psychosomatic research: psychogenesis, conversion, specificity. *Psychosomatic Medicine, 5,* 205–210.

Alliance of Psychoanalytic Organizations: PDM Taskforce (2006). *Psychodynamic Diagnostic Manual: PDM* (1st ed.). Silver Spring, MD: Alliance of Psychoanalytic Organizations.

Al Rubaie, T. (2003). The use of hypnotic dreaming in psychotherapy. *European Journal of Clinical Hypnosis, 5*(3) 2–8.

Amen, D. G. (1998). *Change your brain, change your life.* New York: Three Rivers Press.

American Psychiatric Association (2000). *Diagnostic and Statistical Manual of Mental Disorders, IV-TR.* Washington, DC: American Psychiatric Association.

American Psychological Association. (1979). *Journal of Abnormal Psychology,* Hypnosis and Psychopathology: Special issue, 88, 5. Arlington, VA: American Psychological Association.

Araoz, D. L. (1981). Negative self-hypnosis. *Journal of Contemporary Psychotherapy, 12,* 45–51.

Araoz, D. L. (1982). *Hypnosis and sex therapy.* New York: Brunner/Mazel.

Araoz, D. L. (1985a). *The new hypnosis.* New York: Brunner/Mazel.

Araoz, D. L. (1985b). The new hypnosis: The quintessence of client-centeredness. In J. Zeig (Ed.), *Ericksonian Psychotherapy. Vol. I: Structures* (pp. 256–265). New York: Brunner/Mazel.

Araoz, D. L. (1986). Human sexuality, hypnosis and therapy. In J. K. Zeig and S. R. Lankton (Eds.), *Developing Ericksonian therapy* (pp. 438–445). New York: Brunner/Mazel.

Araoz, D. L. (1992). *The new hypnosis in sex therapy: Cognitive-behavioral methods for clinicians.* Northvale, NJ: Jason Aronson.

Araoz, D. L. (2005–2006). Defining hypnosis. *American Journal of Clinical Hypnosis, 48,* 123–126.

Araoz, D. L. (2006a). *The symptom is not the whole story: Psychoanalysis for nonpsychoanalysts.* New York: Other Press.

Araoz, D. L. (2006b). Psychoanalysis and hypnosis. *Analytic Insights, 4,* 62–73.

# References

Araoz, D. L., and E. Goldin, (2004). The importance of *vivencia* in the hypnotic treatment of sexual dysfunction. *Australian Journal of Clinical Hypnotherapy and Hypnosis, 25,* 68–76.

Arlow, J. A. (1969). Unconscious fantasy and disturbance of conscious experience. *Psychoanalytic Quarterly, 38,* 1–27.

Arlow, J. A. (1983). Unconscious fantasy. In B. E. Moore and B. D. Fine (Eds.), *Psychoanalysis: The major concepts* (pp. 155–162). New Haven: Yale University Press.

Bach-y-Rita, P. (1972). *Brain mechanisms and sensory substitution.* New York: Academic Press.

Bach-y-Rita, P. (1980). Brain plasticity as a basis for therapeutic procedures. In P. Bach-y-Rita (Ed.), *Recovery of function: Theoretical considerations for brain injury rehabilitation.* Bern: Hans Huber Publishers.

Baker, E. L. (1981). An hypnotherapeutic approach to enhance object relatedness in psychotic patients. *International Journal of Clinical and Experimental Hypnosis, 124,* 136–147.

Balint, M. (1949). Sandor Ferenczi. In *Problems of human pleasure and behavior* (pp. 243–250). London: Maresfield Library.

Barber, T. X. (1976). *Pitfalls in human research: Ten pivotal points* (1st ed.). New York: Pergamon Press.

Barber, T. X. (1979). Suggested ("hypnotic") behavior: The trance paradigm vs. an alternative paradigm. In E. Fromm and R. Shor (Eds.), *Hypnosis development in research and new perspectives* (pp. 217–272). New York: Aldine Publishing.

Begley, S. (2007). *Train your mind, change your brain.* New York: Ballantine.

Beres, D. (1958). Vicissitudes of superego functions and superego precursors in childhood. *Psychoanalytic Study of the Child, 13,* 324–351.

Berliner, B. (1958). The role of object relations in moral masochism. *Psychoanalytic Quarterly, 27,* 38–56.

Bernheim, H. (1884). *De la Suggestion dans l'État Hypnotique et dans l'État de Veille.* Paris: Octave Doin.

Bettelheim, B. (1977). *The uses of enchantment.* New York: Vintage Press.

Blechner, M. J. (2001). *The dream frontier.* Hillsdale, NJ: Analytic Press.

Bokay, A., D. Giampieri-Deutsch and P. L. Rudnytsky, (1996). *Ferenczi's turn in psychoanalysis.* New York: New York University Press.

Borges, J. L. (1952). The meeting in a dream. In J. L. Borges and R. L. C. Simms (Trans.) *Other inquisitions (1937–1952)* (pp. 97–105). Austin, TX: University of Texas Press.

Boss, M. (1977). *I dreamt last night.* New York: Wiley.

Bowen, M. (1978). *Family therapy in clinical practice.* New York: Jason Aronson.

Breger, L. (2009). *A dream of undying fame: How Freud betrayed his mentor and invented psychoanalysis.* New York: Basic Books.

Breuer, J., and S. Freud (1893/2000). Studies on hysteria. *Standard Edition, 11:* 183–306.

Brown, D. P., and E. Fromm, (1986). *Hypnotherapy and hypnoanalysis.* Hillsdale, NJ: Lawrence Erlbaum.

Cooper, A. M. (1988). The narcissistic-masochistic character. In R. A. Glick and D. I. Meyers (Eds.), *Masochism: Current psychoanalytic perspectives* (pp. 117–138). Hillsdale, NJ: Analytic Press.

Dalai Lama (2005). *The universe in a single atom.* New York: Morgan Road Books.

Desoille, R. (1971). *Marie Clotilde. Une psychothérapie par le rêve éveillé dirigé.* Paris: Peyot.

# References

Diamond, M. J. (1987). The interactional basis of hypnotic experience: On the relational dimensions of hypnosis. *International Journal of Clinical and Experimental Hypnosis, 35*, 95–115.

Diamond, M. J. (2007). *My father before me.* New York: Norton.

Doidge, N. (2007). *The brain that changes itself.* New York: Penguin.

Dor, J. (1998). *The clinical Lacan.* New York: Other Press.

Eisen, M. R. (1993). Psychoanalytic and psychodynamic models of hypnoanalysis. In J. W. Rhue, S. J. Lynn, and I. Kirsch (Eds.), *Handbook of clinical hypnosis* (pp. 123–149). Washington, DC: American Psychological Association.

Epstein, G. (1981). *Waking dream therapy: Dream process as imagination.* New York: Human Sciences Press.

Erickson, M. H., and E. L. Rossi (1989). *The February man: Evolving consciousness and identity in hypnotherapy.* New York: Brunner/Mazel.

Fairbairn, W. R. D. (1958). The nature and aim of psychoanalytic treatment. *International Journal of Psycho-analysis, 39*, 374–385.

Federn, P. (1952). *Ego psychology and the psychoses.* New York: Basic Books.

Fenichel, O. (1945). *The psychoanalytic theory of neurosis.* New York: Norton.

Ferenczi, S. (1909). Letter from Sándor Ferenczi to Sigmund Freud, Budapest, March 21,1909. In *The correspondence of Sigmund Freud and Sándor Ferenczi, Vol. 1, 1908–1914* (pp. 50–51). Hillsdale, NJ: Analytic Press.

Ferenczi, S. (1955). *Final contribution to the problems and methods of psychoanalysis.* New York: Brunner/Mazel.

Fink, B. (2007). *Fundamentals of psychoanalytic technique: A Lacanian approach for practitioners.* New York: Norton.

Flemons, D. (2008). Hypnosis, indifferentiation, and therapeutic change. *Family Therapy, 7*(4), 14–23.

Frankel, F. H., and H. S. Zamansky (Eds.) (1978). *Hypnosis at its bicentennial: Selected papers.* New York: Plenum Press.

Freud, A. (1936). *Collected writings.* New York: International Universities Press.

Freud, S. (1888). Preface to translation of Bernheim's *Suggestion. Standard Edition, 1*: 75–85.

Freud, S. (1895). A project for a scientific psychology. *Standard Edition, 1*: 281–391.

Freud, S. (1897). Abstracts of the scientific work of Dr. Sigmund Freud, 1877–1897. *Standard Edition, 3: 223–257.*

Freud, S. (1900). *The interpretation of dreams* (J. Strachey, Ed. and Trans.). New York: Wiley.

Freud, S. (1905a). Fragment of an analysis of a case of hysteria. *Standard Edition, 7*: 1–122.

Freud, S. (1905b). *Three essays on the theory of sexuality* (J. Strachey, Trans.). New York: Basic Books. (English edition, 1962).

Freud, S. (1908). Creative writers and day-dreaming. *Standard Edition, 9*: 141–154.

Freud, S. (1911). Two principles of mental functioning. *Standard Edition, 12*: 213–226.

Freud, S. (1915). Instincts and their vicissitudes. *Standard Edition, 14*: 117–140.

Freud, S. (1916). Introductory lectures on psycho-analysis. *Standard Edition, 15*: 1–240.

Freud, S. (1923). The ego and the id. *Standard Edition, 19*: 1–66.

Freud, S. (1933). New introductory lectures on psycho-analysis. *Standard Edition, 22*: 1–182.

Freud, S. (1940). Outline of psychoanalysis. *Standard Edition, 23*: 139–195.

Fromm, Erich (1951). *The forgotten language: An introduction to the understanding of dreams, fairy tales and myths.* Oxford: Rinehart.
Fromm, Erich (1960). Psychoanalysis and Zen Buddhism. In D. T. Suzuki, E. Fromm, and R. De Martino (Eds.), *Zen Buddhism and psychoanalysis* (pp. 77–141). New York: Harper & Row.
Fromm, Erich (1973). *The anatomy of human destructiveness.* New York: Henry Holt.
Fromm, Erich (1994). *The art of listening.* New York: Continuum.
Fromm, Erich, D. T. Suzuki and R. De Martino (1960). *Zen Buddhism and psychoanalysis.* New York: Harper & Row.
Fromm, Erika (1972). Ego activity and ego passivity in hypnosis. *International Journal of Clinical and Experimental Hypnosis, 20,* 238–251.
Fromm, Erika (1973). Personal communication.
Fromm, Erika (1977). An ego psychological theory of altered states of consciousness. *International Journal of Clinical and Experimental Hypnosis, 4,* 115–128.
Fromm, Erika (1992). An ego psychological theory of hypnosis. In E. Fromm and M. R. Nash, (Eds.), *Contemporary hypnosis research* (pp. 131–148). New York: Guilford Press.
Fromm, Erika, and M. R. Nash (1997). *Psychoanalysis and hypnosis.* Madison, CT: International Universities Press.
Fromm, Erika, and R. S. Shor, Eds. (1979). *Hypnosis: Developments in research and new perspectives.* Edison, NJ: Aldine Transaction.
Gabbard, G. O. (1989). Two subtypes of narcissistic personality disorder. *Bulletin of the Menninger Clinic, 53,* 527–532.
Gieser, L., and M. I. Stein (1999). *Evocative images: The Thematic Appercetion Test and the art of projection.* Washington, DC: American Psychological Association.
Goleman, D. (2006). *Social intelligence: The new science of human relationships.* New York: Bantam Books.
Gottlieb, R. M. (2003). Psychosomatic medicine: The divergent legacies of Freud and Janet. *Journal of American Psychoanalytic Association, 51,* 857–881.
Gourguechon, P. (2007). The canary in the coal mine: Psychoanalysis and health. *Psychologist-Psychoanalyst, 27*(3), 19–22.
Grandin, T. (1995). *Thinking in pictures: And other reports of my life with autism.* New York: Doubleday.
Gravitz, M. A., and M. I. Gerton (1981). Freud and hypnosis: Report on postrejection use. *Journal of the History of the Behavioral Science, 17,* 68–74.
Groddeck, G. (1923). *The book of the it.* New York: International Universities Press.
Haley, J. (1993). *J. Haley on Milton H. Erickson.* New York: Brunner/Mazel.
Havens, R. A. (1996). *The wisdom of Milton H. Erickson: Hypnosis and hypnotherapy.* New York: Irvington Publishers.
Hilgard, E. R. (1977). Controversies over consciousness and the rise of cognitive psychology. *Australian Psychologist, 12,* 7–26.
Hilgard, E. R. (1978). Covert pain in hypnotic analgesia: Its reality as tested by the real-simulator design. *Journal of Abnormal Psychology, 87,* 655–663.
Hilgard, E. R. (1992). Dissociation and theories of hypnosis. In Erika Fromm and N. Nash (Eds.), *Contemporary hypnosis research* (pp. 69–101). New York: Guilford Press.
Hilgard, J. R. (1970). *Personality and hypnosis: A study of imaginative involvement.* Chicago: University of Chicago Press.

Hobson, J. A. (1989). *The dreaming brain*. Washington, DC: American Psychological Association.
Hobson, J. A. (2011). *Dream life*. Boston: MIT Press.
Horney, K. (1939). *New ways in psychoanalysis*. New York: Norton.
Horney, K. (1950). *Neurosis and human growth*. New York: Norton.
Janet, P. (1889). *L'automatisme psychologique: Essai de psychologie experimentale sur les formes inferieures de l'activite humaine [Psychological automatism: An essay of experimental psychology on the inferior forms of human activity]*. Paris: Felix Alcan.
*Journal of Abnormal Psychology*. 1979. Special issue: Hypnosis and Psychopathology. 88, 5:459–603.
Jung, C. G. (1934). A study of the process of individuation. *Collected works of C. G. Jung, Vol. 8*. Princeton, NJ: Princeton University Press.
Jung, C. G. (1963). *Memories, dreams, reflections*. New York: Vintage.
Jung, C. G. (1973). *Letters, Volumes I and II*. G. Adler, A. Jaffe, and R. F. S. Hull (Eds.). Princeton: Princeton University Press.
Jung, C. G. (1977). Mysterium coniunctionis. *Collected works of C. G. Jung, Vol. 14*. Princeton: Princeton University Press.
Kandel, E. R. (2006). *In search of memory: The emergence of a new science of mind*. New York: Norton.
Karlen, A. (2008). Erotic transference and countertransference. *National Association for the Advancement of Psychoanalysis News*, 31(1), 20–21.
Kernberg, O. F. (1984). The couch at sea: Psychoanalytic studies of group and organizational leadership. *International Journal of Group Psychotherapy*, 34, 5–23.
Klein, M. (1975/1984). Notes on some schizoid mechanisms. In *Envy and gratitude* (pp. 1–24). New York: Delta Books.
Knafo, D., and K. Feiner (2006). *Unconscious fantasies and the relational world*. Hillsdale, NJ: Analytic Press.
Kohut, H. (1971). *The analysis of the self*. New York: International Universities Press.
Kohut, H. (1977). *The restoration of the self*. New York: International Universities Press.
Kornfield, J. (2008). *The wise heart*. New York: Bantam Books.
Kraepelin, E. (1913). *General paresis. (Monographic Series, No. 14)*. New York: Nervous and Mental Disease Publications Company.
Kris, E. (1952). *Psychoanalytic explorations in art*. New York: International Universities Press.
Lacan, J. (1977). *Ecrits. A selection*. New York: Norton.
Lewes, K. (1998). A special oedipal mechanism in the development of male homosexuality. *Psychoanalytic Psychology*, 15, 341–359.
Liebeault, A. A. (1866). *Le sommeil provoqué et les états analogues*. Paris: Octave Doin.
Linley, P. A., and S. Joseph (2004). *Positive psychology in practice*. Hoboken, NJ: Wiley.
Lippmann, P. (2000). *Nocturnes: On listening to dreams*. New York: Routledge.
Lips, H. (1997). *Sex and gender*. Mountain View, CA: Mayfield.
Loewald, H. W. (1974). Psychoanalysis and the fantasy character of the analytic situation. In *Papers on psychoanalysis* (pp. 352–371). New Haven: Yale University Press (1980).
Mahler, M. S., F. Pine and A. Bergman (1975). *The psychological birth of the human infant*. New York: Basic Books.

Maslow, A. (1968). *Toward a psychology of being.* Princeton: Van Nostrand Reinhold.
Masson, J. M. (1985). *The complete letters of Sigmund Freud to Wilhelm Fliess, 1887–1904.* Cambridge, MA: Harvard University Press.
McWilliams, N. (1994). *Psychoanalytic diagnosis: Understanding personality structure in the clinical process.* New York: Guilford Press.
Meissner, W. W. (1978). Theoretical assumptions of concepts of the borderline personality. *Journal of the American Psychoanalytic Association, 26,* 559–598.
Mitchell, S. A. (1986). The wings of icons: Illusion and the problem of narcissism. *Contemporary Psychoanalysis, 22,* 107–132.
Mitchell, S. A. (2000). *Relationality; From attachment to intersubjectivity.* Relational perspectives book series, vol. 20. Mahwah, NJ: Analytic Press.
Molino, A. (1998). *The couch and the tree: Dialogues in psychoanalysis and Buddhism.* New York: North Point Press.
Murray-Jobsis, J. (1985). Exploring the schizophrenic experience with the use of hypnosis. *American Journal of Clinical Hypnosis, 28,* 34–42.
Murray-Jobsis, J. (1986). Hypnosis with the borderline patient. In E. T. Dowd and J. M. Healy (Eds.), *Case studies in hypnotherapy* (pp. 254–273). New York: Guilford Press.
New York Academy of Sciences (1977). *Conceptual and investigative approaches to hypnosis and hypnotic phenomena.* Annals, Vol. 296. New York: New York Academy of Sciences.
PDM Taskforce (2006). *Psychodynamic diagnostic manual.* Silver Spring, MD: Alliance of Psychoanalytic Organizations.
Pert, C. (1987). The emotions and bodymind. *Noetic Science Review, 2,* 13–18.
Pfeffer, B. (2006). Events in the news, events in the office: Countertransference and sexual diversity. *Analytic Insights, 4,* 14–27.
Piaget, J. (1952). *The origins of intelligence in children.* New York: International Universities Press.
Pine, F. (1990). *Drive, ego, object, and self: A synthesis for clinical work.* New York: Basic Books.
Psychoanalytic Consortium (2006). *Psychodynamic diagnostic manual.* Silver Spring, MD: Alliance of Psychoanalytic Organizations.
Raison, C. (2010). *CALM.* Atlanta: Emory University.
Ramachandran, V. S., and S. Blakeslee (1998). *Phantoms in the brain: Probing the mysteries of the human mind.* New York: Morrow.
Ramonth, S. M. (1985). Dissociation and self-awareness in directed daydreaming. *Scandinavian Journal of Psychology, 26,* 259–276.
Rapaport, D. (1953). On the psycho-analytic theory of affects. *International Journal of Psycho-Analysis, 34,* 177–198.
Reich, W. (1933). *Massenpsychologie des Faschismus. Zur Sexualoekonomie der politischen Reaktion und zur proletarischen Sexualpolitik./Collective psychology of fascism. On the sexual economy of the political reaction and of the proletarian sexual politics.* Washington, DC: Unknown.
Reik, T. (1948). *Listening with the third ear; The inner experience of a psychoanalyst.* Oxford, England: Farrar, Strauss.
Renik, O. (2006). *Practical psychoanalysis for patients and therapists.* New York: Other Press.
Rhue, J. W., S. J. Lynn and I. Kirsch (Eds.) (1993). *Handbook of clinical hypnosis.* Washington, DC: American Psychological Association.

Rodgers, D. (2010). Health redefined by National Academies of Practice. *National Psychologist, 19*(4), 9.
Rogers, C. (1951). *Client-centered therapy: Its current practice, implications and theory.* Boston: Houghton Mifflin.
Rossi, E. L. (1980). *The collected papers of Milton H. Erickson on hypnosis.* New York: Irvington Publishers.
Rossi, E. L. (1986). *The psychobiology of mind-body healing: New concepts of therapeutic hypnosis.* New York: Norton.
Rossi, E. L. (2002). *The psychobiology of gene expression: Neuroscience and neurogenesis in hypnosis and the healing arts.* New York: Norton.
Rossi, E. L., and D. B. Cheek (1988). *Mind-body therapy.* New York: Norton.
Rychlak, J. A. (1968). *A philosophy of science for personality theory.* Boston: Houghton Mifflin.
Sacerdote, P. (1967a). Therapeutic use of induced dreams. *American Journal of Clinical Hypnosis, 10,* 1–9.
Sacerdote, P. (1967b). *Induced dreams.* New York: Vantage Press.
Safran, J. (2003). *Psychoanalysis and Buddhism; An unfolding dialogue.* Boston: Wisdom Publications.
Sandler, J. (1975). Sexual fantasies and sexual theories in childhood. In *Studies in child psychoanalysis: Pure and applied. The scientific proceedings of the 20th anniversary celebrations of the Hampstead Child-Therapy Course & Clinic.* Oxford, England: Yale University Press.
Saretsky, T. (2007). Personal communication.
Schilder, P. (1923). *Medical psychology.* New York: International Universities Press.
Schilder, P. and O. Kauders (1926). Lehr-bucher hypnosis (A textbook of hypnosis). In P. Schilder (Ed.) and G. Corvin (Trans.) *The nature of hypnosis* (pp. 45–184). New York: International Universities Press.
Schwartz, J. M., and S. Begley (2002). *The mind and the brain: Neuroplasticity and the power of mental force.* New York: Harper Perennial.
Segal, H. (1991). *Dream, phantasy, and art.* New Library of Psychoanalysis. New York: Tavistock/Routledge.
Seligman, M. (1995). *The optimistic child: How learned optimism protects children from depression.* New York: Houghton Mifflin.
Seligman, M., and M. Csikszentmihalyi (2000). Positive psychology: An introduction. *American Psychologist, 55,* 5–14.
Shedler, J. (2010). The efficacy of psychodynamic psychotherapy. *American Psychologist, 65,* 98–109.
Sheehan, P. W., and K. M. McConkey (1995). *Hypnosis and experience.* New York: Routledge.
Shore, A. N. (2002). Dysregulation of the right brain: A fundamental mechanism of traumatic attachment and the psychopathogenesis of posttraumatic stress disorder. *Australian and New Zealand Journal of Psychiatry, 36,* 9–30.
Simpkins, C. A. and A. M. Simpkins (2010). *The dao of neuroscience: Combining eastern and western principles for optimal therapeutic change.* New York: Norton.
Simonton, C. O., and S. Simonton (1978). *Getting well again: A step-by-step, self-help guide to overcoming cancer for patients and their families.* Toronto: Bantam Books.
Spanos, N. P., and J. F. Chaves (Eds.) (1989). *Hypnosis: The cognitive-behavioral perspective.* Buffalo, NY: Prometheus Books.

Stevens, M. (2000). Introduction. In S. Freud, *Three essays on the theory of sexuality*, (pp. xxxi–lii). New York: Basic Books.
Strupp, H. (1977). Foreword. In P. L. Wachtel, *Psychoanalysis and behavior therapy* (pp. xvi–xviii). New York; Basic Books.
Sullivan, H. S. (1953). *The interpersonal theory of psychiatry*. New York: Norton.
Sullivan, H. S. (1973). *Clinical studies in psychiatry*. Oxford, England: Norton.
Suzuki, D. T. (1960). Lectures in Zen Buddhism. In *Zen Buddhism and Psychoanalysis*, E. Fromm, D. T. Suzuki and R De Martino; pp. 1–76. New York: Harper & Row.
Tart, C. T. (1964). A comparison of suggested dreams occurring in hypnosis and sleep. *International Journal of Clinical and Experimental Hypnosis, 12*: 263–289.
Tart, C. T. (1965). The hypnotic dream: Methodological problems and review of the literature. *Psychological Bulletin, 63*:87–99.
Tart, C. T. (1970). Self-report scales of hypnotic depth. *International Journal of Clinical and Experimental Hypnosis, 18*, 105–125.
Virgil (1989). *Eneida*. Translation to Spanish by Victor José Herrero. Madrid: Colección Gredos Bilingüe.
Wachtel, E. F., and P. L. Wachtel (1986). *Family dynamics in individual psychotherapy*. New York: Guilford.
Wachtel, P. L. (1977). *Psychoanalysis and behavior therapy*. New York: Basic Books.
Wachtel, P. L. (1997). *Psychoanalysis, behavior therapy, and the relational world*. Washington, DC: American Psychological Association.
Wachtel, P. L. (2008). *Relational theory and the practice of psychoanalysis*. New York: Guilford Press.
Watkins, H. H. (1978). Ego-state therapy. In J. G. Watkins, *The therapeutic self* (pp. 93–138). New York: Human Sciences Press.
Watkins, J. G. (1954). Trance and transference. *Journal of Clinical and Experimental Hypnosis, 2*, 284–290.
Watkins, J. G. (1978). *The therapeutic self.* New York: Human Sciences Press..
Watkins, J. G., and A. Barabasz (2008). *Advanced hypnotherapy: Hypnodynamic techniques*. New York: Routledge Taylor & Francis Group.
Watkins, J. G., and H. H. Watkins (1979–1980). Ego states and hidden observers. *Journal of Altered States of Consciousness, 5*, 3–18.
Watkins, J. G., and H. H. Watkins (1992). A comparison of hidden observers, ego states and multiple personalities. *Hypnos, 19*, 215–221.
Waxman, D. (1989). *Hartland's medical and dental hypnosis*. London: Bailliere Tindall.
Weiner, D. L., and G. M. Hefter (1999). *Battling the inner dummy: The craziness of apparently normal people*. Amherst, NY: Prometheus Books.
Weitzenhoffer, A. M. (2000). *The practice of hypnotism* (2nd ed.). New York: Wiley.
Wilson Ross, N. (1980). *Buddhism, a way of life and thought*. New York: Vintage Books.
Winnicott, D. W. (1953). Transitional objects and transitional phenomena: A study of the first not-me possession. *International Journal of Psycho-Analysis, 34*, 89–97.
Wolberg, L. R. (1945). *Hypnoanalysis*. Oxford: Grune & Stratton.
Yalom, I. D. (1980). *Existential psychotherapy*. New York: Basic Books.
Yalom, I. D. (2002). *The gift of therapy*. London: Piatkus.
Yapko, M. D. (1996). *Trancework: An introduction to the practice of clinical hypnosis* (2nd ed.). Philadelphia: Brunner/Mazel.
Zilbergeld, B., M. G. Edelstien and D. L. Araoz (Eds.) (1986). *Hypnosis questions and answers*. New York: Norton.

# Index

Adams, M. 171
Adler, A. 157
Akhtar, S. 94
Al Rubaie, T. 62, 63, 67
Amen, D. 39, 104
anxious personality 105
Araoz, D.L. 8, 9, 11, 12, 17, 19, 23, 27, 28, 32, 36, 37, 73, 127, 138, 145, 155, 179
Arlow, J. 23, 25
auto-analysis 16
auto-hypnosis 3, 5, 44, 45, 57, 75, 131, 134, 136

Bach-y-Riga, P. 90, 96
Baker, E. 43
Barabasz, A. 8, 11, 12, 136, 145, 179, 191
Barber, T.X. 23, 28, 48
Begley, S. 6, 7, 8, 24, 27, 100, 108, 115, 142, 168, 190, 197
Bergman, A. 192, 196
Berliner, B. 96
Bernheim 18, 20, 31
Bettelheim, B. 113, 161, 171
birth as process 164
Blechner, M. 62, 65, 66, 69
Borges, J.L. 24, 48
Boss, M. 63
Breuer, J. 36, 191
Brown, D. 11, 37, 191
Buddhism 3, 6, 12, 23, 35, 96, 134, 139, 149, 152, 164

Charcot, E. 18, 36, 38, 83
Chaves, J. 145
Cheek, D. 28, 29, 49, 162
Chevreul pendulum 30
clinical cases 13, 52, 57, 58, 64, 67, 76, 80, 82, 88, 90, 93, 95, 97, 99, 101, 102, 104, 106, 109, 110, 122, 126, 128, 131, 133, 139, 143

clinical hypnosis 3, 11–16, 17–35; training 170
cognitive behavior therapy (CBT) 9, 86, 192
compensation theory 69
concentration 8, 25, 29, 115, 123; *see also* focusing
Cooper, A. 96, 116
Creative Imagination 3, 6, 8, 11, 12, 17, 18, 94, 98, 102, 110, 115, 116, 119, 121, 124, 125, 128, 132, 163
Csikszentmihalyi, M. 28

Dalai Lama 6, 149, 150, 168
DeMartino, R. 115, 150
dependent personality 101; *see also* inner wisdom
depressive personality 98; *see also* inner friends
Descartes, Rene 63
Dessoille, R. 63
Dhammapada 6
*Diagnostic and Statistical Manual (DSM)* 19, 84, 94, 109
Diamond, M. 42–43
dissociation 18, 26–27
dissociative personality 111; *see also* independence
Doidge, N. 7, 8, 27, 90, 142, 166
Dor, J. 51
dreams 62–74, 118, 126–127, 195; awaken 63; clinical use 70–72; dynamics 69–70; and fantasy 65–66; induced 63–72, 128; and new hypnosis 68

Edelstien, M. 145
ego receptivity 19
ego states 40, 78, 130, 143–144; *see also* personality parts
Eightfold Path of Buddhism 151, 163

Eisen, M.R. 36
Ellis, A. 139
Erickson, M.H. 4, 22, 27, 41, 45, 73, 154
experiential learning 4, 125, 128–129, 130, 134, 139, 155

Fairbairn, W. 156
fantasy 4, 12, 13, 14, 22–25, 31, 48–61, 155
Faria, A. 20
Feiner, K. 23, 113
Fenichel, O. 39, 192
Ferenzi, S. 36, 38, 141, 157, 165
filling the void 94
Fink, B. 15, 61, 62, 72
Flemons, D. 112, 115, 137
focusing 25, 115, 123
Frankel, F. 145
Freud, Anna 146
Freud, Sigmund 11, 12, 20, 23, 36, 38, 48, 49, 50, 51, 52, 53, 55, 56, 62, 66, 113, 137, 138, 142, 146
Fromm, Erich 62, 72, 85, 115, 150, 152, 154, 157, 161, 164, 165, 166, 171
Fromm, Erika 8, 11, 12, 19, 23, 38, 41–42, 64, 77, 79, 112, 137, 146, 165, 179, 191

Gabbard, G. 94
general reality orientation (GRO) 41
Gerton, M.I. 11, 36
Gieser, L. 113
Goldin, E. 23, 32, 127
Goldman, D. 150, 168
Gottlieb, R. 49
Grandin, T. 81
Gravitz, M. 11, 36

Haley, J. 63
Hamlet 16
Havens, R. 91
Hefter, G. 75
hidden observer 26, 28, 40
Hilgard, E. 18, 27, 28, 38, 40, 145, 195
Hobson, J. 74
Holism 148–160
Horney, K. 108, 157, 161, 171
hypnoanalysis 3, 11–35, 142–144, 161–170; principles 114–124
hypnosis 17, 37
hypnotic reversal 89
hypnotizability 30
hysterical personality 109; see also self-love

ideal self 79–81
imagination 3–8, 14, 29, 115, 118, 173

independence 111
induction of hypnosis 25, 29–35
inner friends 98–99
inner healer 103–104
inner wisdom 101–102
insight 127, 151
introspection 126, 134, 151, 156, 164

Janet, J. 18
Joseph, S. 23, 28
Jung, C. 43–45, 47, 62, 69, 115, 165

Kandel, E. 7, 27, 142
Karlem, A. 52
Kauders, O. 38
Keinians 23, 189
Kernberg, O. 94
Knafo, D. 23, 113
Kohut, H. 141, 189, 190
Kornfield, J. 162, 168
Kraepelin, E. 145
Kris, E. 41, 76

Lacan 51, 65
learning: experiential vs. intellectual 125; using creative imagination 130; and *vivencia* 127
Linley, P. 23
Lippman, P. 24, 68, 69
Lips, H. 53
Loewald, H. 24

Mahler, M. 192, 196
Maslow, A. 23, 125
masochistic personality 96; see also mental cleaning
Masson, J. 51
McWilliams, N. 86, 90, 93
meditation 5, 7, 115 149, 152
mental cleaning 96, 98
mental health 168
mental rehearsal 86, 88
mind training 8, 67, 118, 125, 140, 144
mindfulness 23, 27–29, 115, 127–129
Mitchell, S. 38, 154, 156, 179
Molino, A. 115, 150
multiple personality 111; see also independence

narcissistic personality 94; see also filling the void
Nash, M. 11, 23, 38, 41, 42, 77, 79, 148, 179
National Academies of Practice 168
negative self-hypnosis (NSH) 3, 28, 75, 111

210

# Index

neuropathway 7, 18
neuroplasticity 8, 16
neuroscience 2, 6, 28
New Hypnosis 3, 4, 5, 7, 12, 15, 21, 23, 33, 34, 37, 46, 61, 85, 96, 111, 116, 119, 133, 138
New York Academy of Sciences 27

obsessive-compulsive personality 107; *see also* ten-point scale

paranoid personality 89; *see also* hypnotic reversal
passive activity 4, 41
patient-centeredness 12–16, 73, 136
Perls, F. 45
personality parts 40, 78, 130, 143–144; *see also* ego states
Pfeffer, B. 60, 61
phobic personality 103; *see also* inner healer
Piaget, J. 129
Pine, F. 141, 192, 196
point of entry 32
process thinking, primary and secondary 81–82
psychoanalytical speculations 142
*Psychodynamic Diagnostic Manual* (*PDM*) 19, 79, 84–85, 92, 102, 109, 111, 194
psychodynamic therapy (PDT) 1, 2, 84
psychopathic (antisocial) personality 92; *see also* superego attunement

Ramachandran, V.S. 100, 115
Ramonth, S. 145
Rapaport, D. 41
regression 75–84
Reich, W. 94, 107
Reik, T. 39, 47, 62
relationality 156–160
Renik, O. 6, 89, 114, 161, 162, 165, 171, 179
research 2, 15, 27–29, 84–86, 153–154
Reychlak, J. 62
Rogers, C. 73, 138, 157
Rossi, E. 7, 8, 11, 18, 22, 27, 28, 29, 49 54, 115, 138, 162

Sacerdote, P. 64, 66
Safran, J. 22, 23, 24
Sander, J. 48
Saretzky, T. 49, 167
Schilder, P. 38, 39
schizoid personality 86; *see also* mental rehearsal

Schwartz, J. 7, 8, 24, 27, 108, 190, 197
Segal, H. 50, 59
self-love 109–111
Seligman, M. 23, 28, 73, 125
sexual myths 51–55
sexuality 5, 48–61
Shedler, J. 2
Shor, A. 21, 145
Simonton, C. 49
Society for the Exploration of Psychotherapy Integration (SEPI) 154
somatic feelings 100
somatizing personality 100
somnambulism 18
Spanos, N. 145
Spotnitz, H. 157
Stein, H. 113
Stevens, M. 53
Strupp, H. 153
suggestibility 18, 58
suggestion 19–22, 58–60, 146; indirect 22, 136–138
Sullivan, H.S. 62, 154, 156, 161, 171, 179
superego attunement 92
Suzuki, D. 115, 150

Tart, C. 63, 122
"TEAM" 42
ten-point scale 107–109
therapeutic fantasy 155
transference 20, 21, 22, 52, 190

utilization 29, 138

Virgil 24
*vivencia* 32, 127–135, 156, 167

Wachtel, P.L. 86, 126, 153, 157
Watkins, J.-G. 8, 11, 40, 136, 145, 146, 165, 179, 191
Waxman, D. 63
Weiner, D. 75
Weitzenhoffer, A. 17, 19, 22
well-being 168, 172–173
Wilson Ross, N. 134, 149
Winnicott, D. 99, 154
Wolberg, L. 8, 11, 39, 41, 165, 179

Yalom, I. 69, 70, 171, 174
Yapko, M. 18

Zamansky, H. 145
zen 4, 6, 134, 150–151, 177

www.ingramcontent.com/pod-product-compliance
Ingram Content Group UK Ltd.
Pitfield, Milton Keynes, MK11 3LW, UK
UKHW041959140426
5217IPUK00015B/887